D0984688

The religion of
the machine age

Design for a communist mass festival (i.e. rally) dedicated to 'the visible god', the machine. (Drawing by M. Dobnyinski, from *Geist und Gesicht des Bolschewismus*, René Fülöp-Miller, Amalthea Verlag, Zurich, Leipzig, Vienna, 1926.)

THE RELIGION OF
THE MACHINE AGE

Dora Russell

Routledge & Kegan Paul
London, Melbourne and Henley

First published in 1983
by Routledge & Kegan Paul plc
39 Store Street, London WC1E 7DD,
296 Beaconsfield Parade, Middle Park,
Melbourne, 3206 Australia, and
Broadway House, Newtown Road,
Henley-on-Thames, Oxon RG9 1EN
Set in Century, 10 on 12pt, by
Input Typesetting Ltd, London
and printed in Great Britain by
T. J. Press (Padstow) Ltd
Padstow, Cornwall

British Library Cataloguing in Publication Data

Russell, Dora

The religion of the machine age.
1 Industrialization   2 Industry–
Social aspects   3 Industry–Political
aspects
303.4'83   HD82

ISBN 0–7100–9547–3

To
my son Roderick Barry
and my friend Robin Ball
but for both of whom
this book would never have been written

Contents

Preface: The Soul of Russia and the Body of
      America (1920–1921)   ix

Preface: 1982   xvi

Epigraph   xviii

1 Human beings   1
2 The old gods   11
3 Those intellectual Greeks   38
4 Gods versus kings or power: temporal and spiritual   58
5 Christendom in Europe   83
6 Consciousness expands   114
7 Alone in the face of the universe   133
8 You cannot stop progress!   158
9 Machine power   175
10 Full speed ahead   187
11 The machine: God visible and manifest   197
12 The machine makes war   206
13 Humanity: eclipse or deliverance?   218
14 Liberty and love   231

Epilogue   254

Select bibliography   256

Index   259

Preface: The Soul of Russia and the Body of America

by Dora Russell (then aged 26)
Text exactly as written in 1920–1921

It is not difficult to define what is meant by the body of America. As one writes the words, the imagination conjures up visions of sky-scrapers with swift elevators; vast factories where materials can be seen travelling fantastically on moving platforms to emerge at the exit as finished products; huge freight cars thundering their way from one busy town to another, immense liners ploughing the Atlantic; wide fields of cotton, great expanses of ripening corn. America stands, in fact, for the most complete example of the mechanism of industrial production on which the whole economic life of the West is based. It is an impressive mechanism, so impressive that quite three-quarters of those involved in, or in contact with, it forget that it is but a mechanism and nothing more. They come to imagine that this organisation of economic life, this speed, this comfort, are in themselves civilisation and the goal of human endeavour, that all the best creative energy of man should be turned to developing resources producing goods, inventing processes to speed up production.

They endow this machine with a soul and a message which is to be carried to the uttermost parts of the earth, to be taught if need be, by bullying, or at the point of the sword. To those who, despite every effort to the contrary, cannot bring themselves to accept such a primitive notion of civilisation, this machine worship is as horrible and superstitious as the adoration of the savage for his painted block of wood or stone. There have been, in the past, many of these dissenters. And one sees them now, in America, enquiring distressfully what is the matter with their country, feeling dimly that the trouble lies in her barrenness of ideals and emptiness of soul, and, looking round from one party to another, and one class to another, seeking a possible source of regeneration.

In Europe, too, idealists are trying to find some motive for building prosperity anew, and the disgust and despair in which the war has left them are but heightened when they look across and see in America the image of what they may become, of what America is capable of making of the whole world. They see this excellent body, this shell of a state, and the soul of man walking mournfully through it, as through a wilderness, seeking an oasis where it may perchance rest for a moment, not hoping to find a home.

It is not from America that regeneration can come. There is every sign that her people, like the industrial peoples of Europe, will first seek relief from the intolerable mechanical burden of their lives in the worn-out pastime of imperial conquest. Yet all that America could give to a subservient world would be her body, her industrial efficiency, a valuable gift in days gone by, and still needed in the present and the future, but not enough. America can give us no new ideals, and it is for new ideals that the whole world, from the east Atlantic to the west Pacific, is hungry. Thinking Europe has become conscious at last that it cannot live with the industrial machine unless new ideals can be found to control and govern it. In China, also, the question on the lips of all intelligent people is: 'Since it seems we must follow in the path of the industrial nations, how shall we do so without becoming as horrible and degraded as they?'

One nation in the world has set out to answer that question in practice, and that is Russia. For this reason the most cynical have turned to her in joyful surprise; even her bitterest and blindest opponents are conscious that she has found something new which she is trying to expound to the world and, while they do their utmost to destroy her in the act of realisation of her ideals, they yet have a sneaking hope that they may not succeed. So desperate has the need for hope become in our blackened and ruined world.

It is not easy to give a clear picture of the soul of present-day Russia. Not only has it been so much misrepresented by friends and enemies alike, but those who should express it, the Bolshevik leaders themselves, do not convey their meaning to us, because they speak through old Western formulae, which no longer fit Russia's thought. Then too, many of the leaders are not alive to the miracle that is happening, they are still thinking in old categories; such are those who have returned from America and are dominated by admiration for the industrial machine in itself and out of touch with the peculiar genius of their people.

The prestige of that America, which was to Russia the Land of Liberty, plays a great part in influencing their outlook. To these men – as perhaps to Americans in general – the epithet of Wellsian Martians recently hurled at the Bolsheviks in general may justly be applied. If they become dominant, Russia may develop on American lines. But their point of view is neutralised by that of the Russian people, the rank and file, still confused and stammering and unable to express clearly the ideas by which they are moved. And Lenin, in his policy for Russia, though not in his polemics, seems to be the most coherent expression of Russia's beliefs. When the Russians, through Lenin and their propagandists, profess themselves orthodox disciples of Marx and denounce the West as heretical, one cannot but smile at their perversity.

To me every fibre of the Russian's being is opposed to the Marxian determinist outlook. If only they would recognise this, they would make it their glory and their pride that they are splendid heretics to Marx, and thereby do the whole world a magnificent service. Not only are they heretics to Marx, but to the entire Western outlook. Western visitors to Russia (such orthodox Marxians) exclaim at the 'breakdown of civilisation' by which they mean the terrible material suffering and disorder that prevail. Yet Russia today is perhaps the most civilised country in the world. Where does civilisation lie if not in the designs and purposes, the ideals of men? And where, except in Russia, is an ideal that fits modern life to be found? Russia's communism is not 'the guardian of Western civilisation', it is a new ideal of civilisation, which, if we could but be induced to listen to it, could re-civilise our own barbarous and hateful lives.

This is to me the supreme fact about Russia, that she is a country just emerging from the medieval ages of faith into the valorous adolescence of the Renaissance. Her thought is burning and her courage high. Honour and glory, faith, are for her words still charged with meaning, scepticism has not yet dimmed her ardour, nor materialism blurred her soul. Russia's instinctive belief is in a heroic figure of man, demi-god, Promethean, grappling with and subjugating a hostile universe, or triumphing over it, even in material defeat, by the indomitable courage of his spirit. She still breathes the air of Shakespeare and has not known the caustic age of Voltaire.

A nation that approaches the latest developments of sophisticated political science in this mood is apt to be puzzling. Scientific thinkers denounce her as romantic, romantic thinkers hail her short-cuts to communism as the quintessence of science. Both agree that the term 'scientific' is the highest that could be bestowed. But to me the very merit of Russian communists is that, with some exceptions, they are quite unscientific, if we take scientific in its popular sense, that of dispassionateness, materialism, indifference to human values. Russia, by dint of having escaped a process of complete capitalist development of industry, which has taken place in England, Germany and America, has escaped the background of thought associated with it – and which Marx claims to arise directly out of it.

But she has not escaped all contact. She has skimmed the cream of advanced thought and, blending with this her own heroic and artistic outlook, has produced communism, the ideal which could animate our Western industrial system, that is still enslaved to a worn-out philosophy. Just because she had not a tradition of developed industry, her thoughts and hopes have been free to soar. Now she maintains that she will develop her industry, ideally, in the service of man, giving him not only comfort, but leisure, art and science. The West points to her disorganised railways, her ignorant, unskilled people, her mere handful of intelligent workers, and urges that the spirit of communism is useless without the industrial body, that first the body must be created, then the soul. Russia assents – she wants the body, but her counterthrust is unanswerable: 'You have the body, but where is the soul?'

This question comes as a challenge to the determinism of the West. For two centuries we have first tacitly assumed, then openly declared, that we are, down to the minutest action of our lives, the creatures of habit, moulded by economic circumstances, or scientific laws over which we have no control. We have visualised our development, not only as physical, but as a moral evolution. We have therefore been content to wait and allow economics to mould us. We have risked no 'rough hewing' of our ends, confident of their shaping by some methodical deity – or force of science. The only result is that we are today bankrupt of living thought, puerile in action, the puppets of the huge material forces that we have allowed to grow at random, and that now, so far from contributing to our moral and intellectual advancement, threaten to engulf us in hideous destruction. It seems as though this cannot continue; we must stop short and re-awaken the slumbering human spirit to assume control and re-assert the dignity of man and his sovereignty over the earth.

The Russians believe themselves to be against capitalism only, but the study of Russian writers before the Revolution shows that it is the whole fabric of our life that they despise. I think they are right to condemn it, but in error when they imagine, as their present leaders do, that the fabric of our life is the creation of capitalism only. Life in any period of history appears to me as a fabric of economic forces and ideas inseparably woven together, of ideas engendered by economic forces and economic forces that owe their origin to, or are directed by, ideas and scientific thought of the past. The journey from cause to effect in political life is not so easy as the economic interpretation of history would have us believe. The fabric of life changes, but I doubt if it changes more because of the movement of matter than because of the movement of ideas.

All that can be safely said is that new ideas are present beside new economic factors, without risking the establishment of a casual relation either way between the two factors. The whole texture of and shape of a human body and face can change under the influence of a change of character or outlook; it can change also by material habits or occupations. What we see is neither the expression of the thought and emotion produced by some material circumstances, nor the effect of thought and emotion on the body. The two things are the same, the matter in movement is the idea, the idea is the matter in movement. Both are aspects of a change or event.

Often while in Russia and since returning, I have wondered whether we are right or they. We, who have conceived of communism as budding and blossoming like a flower on the sturdy plant of competent and organised industry, or they, who see it as a whirling heart of fire that must consume ancient evils and then, cooling, transmute itself into the crust of material expression, creating industrialism anew, a thing, it may be, of undreamed of power and beauty. To us, tutored in determinism, economic circumstance is the decisive factor in politics. We think of the industrial machine as having an irresistible momentum, we imagine Russia in its grip, changing ideals and character, assimilating rapidly to the industrial nations of the West. But when we do so, we forget how far the industrial system, as *we* conceive it, is the product of the thought of our past, how it perpetuates old prejudices, how it bears like every thought or institution in the world, the unmistakable stamp of its origin and date.

Two visions came repeatedly before my eyes. In the one the machine in America grew increasingly rapacious and cruel, while in Russia it triumphed over human forces, and Europe and Asia were sucked into its maw. There were long hours of mechanical slavery, black and ugly factories, fatuous towns and futile luxuries. Thought and art were dead; the populations petulant and trivial.

In the other the spirit of communism in Russia had leapt like a great wave to meet the West, and Western science and skill – its twin brother – had reared its head and sprung to the meeting with an exultant roar. So they met at last, soul and body, and went springing skywards in a clear, green pyramid of joy. The filth of factories and the grime of poverty were washed away and everywhere there emerged a new and smiling world. Human life was restored to harmony; men were no longer cramped and twisted to serve as wheels and cogs; they found that leisure to savour the whole life of man is better than empty luxury that cogs cannot enjoy. The power of the machine was broken forever; it served instead of commanding, and everywhere the bright roofs of lovely hamlets, the spacious factories, the grassy tree-girt spaces where children and students met to chatter and play, and workers to dance and sing after their easy labours; the quiet arbours where the artist would seek loneliness to brood, or the men of science peace for arduous discussion or complicated thought – all these testified to what life might be, not for the few, but for all, if the spirit of man in justice and humanity would but conquer and yoke the mechanical monster to his will.

Our Western industrial body can give birth to this vision, but can it unfold the spirit that could achieve its realisation? But I am confident that communism, cutting out from the industrial system the motives of profit and exploitation, and administering it in terms of humanity and justice, could so transform industrialism as to make of it a thing of beauty, not of terror.

Preface: 1982

The idea for this book arose out of my first experience of the United States in 1917, when I accompanied my father Sir Frederick Black on a war-time mission; followed by my visit to the Soviet Union in 1920.

In both countries it seemed to me that the power and influence of machine civilisation on political and economic life was of far greater importance than the conflict between capitalism and socialism or communism. On this Russell and I had frequent arguments during our stay in Peking. The up-shot was our book *The Prospects of Industrial Civilisation* (1923). As explained in the present book, no other studies of industrialism *in itself* were published until 1962 and 1965.

In 1922 I had begun writing my book on the *Religion of the Machine Age*, the first chapter of which was to illustrate the contrast between the USA and the USSR as they were at that time. It was entitled 'The Soul of Russia and the Body of America'. And, in March 1923, I signed a contract with Routledge & Kegan Paul for that very book.

But, among my political and intellectual friends, I found no one who encouraged me or understood what I was trying to say. The claims of my family and the political campaign for birth control intervened, preventing the concentration that such a book required.

I abandoned the book, but wrote instead the *Right to be Happy*, to emphasise the importance of biological rather than intellectual values, as a basis for social structure.

Having seen, as I believe, some of my prophesies come true;

and the growth of understanding of the biological thesis, and ecology, I decided to write the original book.

However, in a wider perspective than that of the 1920s, I asked myself when and why did we invent the machine at all?

As a result of my research and reflections, I now offer my book.

It would seem appropriate to include as an introduction that first chapter, exactly as written by me in 1922, illustrating what were the reactions of a young person of 26 to the inspired mood of the Russians of that date.

What is more, it may be regarded as a tribute to Routledge & Kegan Paul, who then, as now, are my book's publisher.

Dora Russell
November 1982

Epigraph

I must be God, because when I talk to God
I find that I am talking to myself.

The Young Peer in Peter Barnes, 1969
The Ruling Class

Besides, Heyst, in his fine detachment, had lost the habit of
asserting himself. I don't mean the courage of self-assertion
either moral or physical, but the mere way of it, the trick
of the thing, the readiness of mind and the turn of the hand
that come without reflection and lead the man to excellence
in life, in art, in crime, in virtue, and, for a matter of that,
in love.

Thinking is the great enemy of perfection. The habit of
profound reflection, I am compelled to say, is the most
pernicious of all the habits formed by the civilised man.

Author's note to Joseph Conrad's novel *Victory* 1920

CHAPTER 1

Human beings

Since Darwin wrote *The Origin of Species*, people, in what are called advanced civilised societies, have come to believe that the animal species and plant life on our planet gradually evolved, and that we ourselves, in similar fashion, evolved from ape-like origins. Scientific research and excavations, together with painstaking study of the objects found, bones, skulls, primitive stone tools and so on, have tended to confirm this belief.

Very recent inventions, such as television cameras, rapid wide-ranging transport and many others, have ministered to the enthusiasm of intrepid explorers in their adventurous researches into the natural world. To all of these the armchair explorer owes a debt of gratitude, more especially to David Attenborough, who has been able to bring to the screen the story of biological life, from its infinitesimal beginnings, right up to the emergence of man. Here is revealed the vast conglomeration of creatures that have crawled, crept, walked, run, swum or flown over the face of our earth; their almost incredible shapes, methods of reproduction and ways of living. As we watch them, the overwhelming impression must be of how competently they do all these things, eating the appropriate foods, finding mates as needed, multiplying their kind. On second thoughts we take note that, while some species grow in size and numbers, others fade out with the disappearance of the foods and environment on which they depend.

What is it like to be one of these creatures? Are they aware of what they are doing to survive? The tiniest organism has the impulse to grow, expanding by absorbing from the environment; larger creatures perform necessary functions, eating, sleeping, mating, hunting. Is there not some conscious element in the brain of the animal that hides from danger, or lies in wait for its prey; in the sideways slant of the small head of the bird as it wonders if this is the safe moment to swoop down on that coveted crumb or worm? What goes on behind the eyes of our domestic dogs and cats, as they watch in hope of food or signs of goodwill from their masters and mistresses? Animals, we say, act from instinct.

This simple explanation of the behaviour of the multitudes of live creatures with whom we share this planet did not satisfy the more inquisitive of human investigators. Of recent years there has been much painstaking study of animal behaviour, in search of signs of action following on evidence of conscious thought. Apes were observed thinking out the problem of how to obtain an apparently inaccessible banana. More than this, Jane Goodall's remarkable observations from living close to apes, her latest films, with her husband, of other animals in the wild, as well as the books of Konrad Lorenz, have revealed a great deal about family and social customs of animals which have a pattern and even formality of gesture that mean something more than the sudden spontaneous prompting of instinct. Yet these customs do relate to the preservation and protection of each particular species and may be held to be ultimately by instinct determined. They do not come near to what we mean when we speak of consciousness in human beings.

Human consciousness has been ascribed to the expansion of the size of the human brain in the course of evolution. Humans have, too, the longest period of infancy, a considerable time for learning; the human baby is less competent at birth than the newborn of what we call the lower species of mammals. The storage of information in the larger brain may afford more possibility of conscious thought. It may seem elementary to attempt to define the difference between conscious and instinctive behaviour; none the less, it can be useful.

A human body acts on its own, without need of guidance, in all internal functions such as digestion, elimination and so forth. No attention is given to these activities, they are not even styled instinctive. But eating, sexual intercourse, perhaps also running or hiding from danger, may be called instinctive. On the other hand, to stand your ground and fight has an element of a conscious decision. In fact, it is when human beings become aware of sensations and impulses, that they become conscious of – and henceforth able to foresee and direct them. Pleasure experienced from certain foods eaten, as from sex, will suggest more of similar, but now-conscious, activity in that direction; pain may give warning that internal processes need attention. Progress in conscious control may be observed in the development of babies and young children. A human infant has no control even over the movement of its arms and legs; but its mouth finds the breast. A few months later one may notice a baby in its cot deliberately moving its legs and solemnly concentrating on bending one finger after another in the pleasure of acquiring conscious control. As they grow, children acquire increasing mastery over body and mind and move on to the control of their immediate surroundings. It is interesting, however, that the acquisition of skills both in work and play rests upon the deliberate conscious learning of the essential movements, followed by their habitual use, which is all the better for becoming *instinctive*. Any athlete, dancer, actor, singer, or even poet or writer, will know well the experience of how a performance may be marred by the critical over-concentrated intervention of the conscious mind.

The story of the development of human consciousness, together with its relation to the life of instinct, is, in the last analysis, the true history of mankind. It represents something over and above what Darwin's genius revealed in biological evolution; it is humanity's attempt, in a bewildering and dangerous world, to control its own destiny. In the light of present-day knowledge such may be the conclusion reached by a philosophic mind, though it is unlikely to receive general acceptance. After all, it is only a hundred years since the theory of evolution itself was first propounded; to this day there are millions of human beings in the world who have never heard of it, as well as others who still refuse to accept that it may be true.

In several parts of the world today peoples are living at what we now regard as various stages of human development. Not so very long ago, a plane in flight discovered in a valley a totally unknown tribe of primitive men and women; other

tribes still exist in the rain forests of South America; there
are peoples who live as nomads herding cattle, others depend
entirely on agriculture. Among these peoples there is an
immense variety of – often very complicated – systems of
taboos, customs and beliefs based on what, at successive stages
in their history, they have come to learn and imagine about
that part of the planet in which they happened to find themselves. One can picture these very first men and women in
small groups, in their limited explored space, experiencing day
and night, sunshine and rain, intense heat or cold, the changing seasons. They had to learn by experiment what, in their
environment, was good to eat, or, later, animals they might
hunt.

There was nothing to tell them how they got there or why,
or the meaning of all that they saw about them. Instinct moved
them, as it did other animals, to satisfy hunger by eating;
instinct must also have taught them that they were attracted
to a fellow human being, man or woman, differing from themselves, and of whom, because different, they will have also
been half afraid. But sex brought them together; children were
born, yet birth, life, and presently death, remained a terrifying
mystery. In a certain sense, one might say that their experience is repeated each time a baby is born, for the baby also
enters a new, strange and frightening world, in which everything has to be learned from the experience of the five senses.

It is very difficult to guess what went on in the brains of
prehistoric men and women. We have found their flint and
bone tools, their own bones and those of the animals on which
they fed, as well as remnants of the boats and houses which
they later constructed. But of human relations, and how they
communicated with one another, and the birth of language,
there can be no record. The impulse to mutual help must have
come before language; for example, when there was heavy
work beyond the strength of one human being, and of course,
when men took to hunting animals for food and women with
their children to food gathering. Of their feeling for animals,
they have left us the remarkable cave paintings, which reveal
not only the picture as a means of communication, but by their
beauty and sense of design, show that the impulse to artistic

creation is one of the first and fundamental impulses of human beings.

There has been much speculation as to the origin of language, whether spoken or written. To utter anything beyond cries and growls would not be possible until the tongue, throat and facial muscles had attained a sufficient degree of flexibility and delicate movement to achieve the formation of intelligent word sounds. An interesting feature of early spoken languages is that they are highly inflected, cumbersome, and, one might have thought, difficult for a slowly awakening conscious mind. But it may be that those large mouthfuls carrying meaning by inflection were suited to primitive physical and mental development. Later forms of language, analytic, supplementing and replacing inflection by the use of prepositions and other linking words, may well indicate the growth of a reasoning faculty. Early humans – as we guess – thought in pictures; their transformation into metaphor, and then to symbols, words and concepts, comes with an advanced development of conscious thought. William Golding has written a remarkable novel, *The Inheritors*, in which the characters not only conduct their lives by smell, sight and hearing, but by the thought-pictures in their heads. A highly verbalised modern has much difficulty in following the narrative, but to have written it and got so far into an awakening conscious mind is a fine imaginative feat.

Communication and recording by writing has also a complex history, starting, as seems certain, from pictures. In fact I would hazard a guess that writing came before coherent speech. If you want to tell your neighbour how to get to some place, or warn him or her of the presence of a dangerous creature, and find that gesture and expression do not suffice, would you not draw something on the soil or rock, or a fragment of bark? The cave pictures show that there was no lack of draughtsman's skill. Picture writing, like speech, evolves by contraction – the picture of the animal becomes a symbolic sign, or ingenious combination of signs, and presently mere upright marks in clay tablets show that social groups have begun to need to count their possessions: flocks and herds, sacks of grain. The fact that the Sumerians wrote in clay tablets left a wonderful treasure house of information and poetic myth for the archaeologists to decipher.

What we know of the early thought of human beings about themselves and their world has been pieced together from myths and legends handed down by word of mouth. They lived by light and dark, day and night, phases of the moon, and the changing of the seasons; they had no other measurement of time. As to how fire was discovered, and how to kindle it, there are many legends and myths, the best known being that of Prometheus, whom the Gods chained to a rock where vultures devoured his flesh, as a punishment for stealing fire which belonged to the Gods. The custom of tending a sacred fire, never allowed to go out, may have arisen from the fact that it was very hard to kindle a flame. This is one of the very ancient rituals that we still practise in these days, on the tombs of the Unknown Soldier and, in a lesser way, the torch of the Olympic Games.

Anthropologists have also been able to learn much from the study of peoples still living at the primitive stages. Of recent years anthropology has greatly expanded its scope and attracted many more students. It has also changed its attitude, in that historically the early and primitive peoples are no longer studied from a height of greater knowledge and civilisation, as inferior, strange, superstitious and savage kinds of beings. We study ourselves also and find that in many respects we have much in common with our remote ancestors; we are not immune to superstition and savagery. Above all, we share with them immense preoccupation with the unsolved mystery of the universe.

To primitive peoples the elements, thunder, fire, the rain, the winds, were Gods, as were likewise volcanoes, mountains, trees, rivers and the sea. It is not surprising that these Gods were feared and placated with offerings made to images representing them and worshipped. More interesting is the human refusal to accept the finality of death. They would often bury with exalted dead persons all those objects which he or she still might need, even going so far as to slaughter wives, servants and warriors to accompany them. Possibly it was the re-birth of the life of the world each spring which suggested that a body was not really dead. Nor was it long before, conscious of his capacity for thought, the male of the species hit on the idea that he – as also other living beings, the animals, plants and trees – had within him a spirit, which could depart from his body at death, but also, perhaps, at other times. Possibly, too, the likenesses observed in successive generations of families was the source of the belief that a spirit might be born again, after death, in a different body. These are, of course, mere guesses. But the mystery of fertility in crops, animals and women became surrounded with a huge number of known sites and ceremonies of worship, many of them savage and cruel, such as human sacrifice. Sex, too, became involved with harsh and painful initiation rites at puberty, including circumcision of both men and women, which still survives today, as does, to some extent, the notion of the uncleanness of women during menstruation or after childbirth. The loss or the shedding of blood could never be regarded as of little consequence in the ritual sense, however many enemies a tribe might kill.

The relations of men and women in the very far distant past still determine many of our customs today. How was it that man, from the very beginning, assumed the dominant role, so that whatever we know about prehistory or historical times has come to us from the hearsay and written reports of men? Elaine Morgan has pointed out, in her remarkable book the *Descent of Woman*, that all theories and conjectures about the evolution of our species have centred round what were thought to be the activities of the male.

The time and energy of women were naturally taken up in bearing and nurturing children, and they thus came to be associated with the domestic arts which went with this care; the making of clay pots, agriculture and cooking, as and when these began. Men hunted and fished and, when they deemed necessary, made war. There was also, in the male possession of the female body, an element of submission on her part. Men do seem to have revered women as goddesses on account of their fertility, until they discovered the contribution made by the male sex to conception of the unborn child. Then followed men's desire for certainty of paternity, patriarchy and the further subjection of women.

None of this seems to me to explain adequately why men

and women did not, even in prehistory, regard themselves as equal partners in the struggle for survival of themselves and their offspring. Why has there always been this contempt for women and, even in what are held to be civilised societies, an underlying hostility between the sexes? I believe that this is to be sought in some of the myths about our origins, but still more in the differing attitudes and approach of men and women to sex itself. When sex drives him the male seeks the female and enjoys her. She may also feel pleasure, but she learns that for her there follows a further biological experience. The male, on the other hand, is temporarily liberated from desire, and may experience some recoil from the woman who aroused him, together with a certain element of triumph. This is where what I call the male flight from the body begins. Pride and dignity begin to reside in that faculty by which the male acts and achieves apart from procreation and concern for the female and her young. In this respect the human male does not differ from many other male mammals, who leave the protection, nurture and hunt for food to the female of the species. Man starts to set himself free from biological bondage, a process inextricably entangling woman, to which he feels himself superior, and which, together with her, he comes to despise. This thesis explains so much in the long saga of the relations between men and women, throughout history and to the present time. In Genesis, it is Eve the woman, who, beguiled by the serpent, tempts man; ironically it is she who eats of the tree of knowledge of good and evil, which man forthwith adopts as his privilege. Woman is relegated to the animal kingdom; most of the myths see her as closely bound to the earth. Myths of the creation of the world tell of the division between the sky and the waters, or the earth, in which the God of the sky, sometimes called the father, or no more than a great spirit, is the supreme power, Mother Earth lying beneath. Male and female were, after all, more familiar with the earth on and by which they lived, and with the tribal gods and the spirits believed to inhabit all of nature; it was the sky and heaven above whence came the light of the sun, the rain and the thunder, to which the male aspired. Just because it was above and outside that world in which he found himself, it held the greater mystery. Surely up there above must be whatever power it was that created the earth and its inhabitants. Looking through many myths of the creation I find only one that gives the supreme power and universality to woman. The Kaga people of Colombia in South America assert:

> The mother of our songs, the mother of all our seed, bore us in the beginning of things and so she is the mother of all types of men, the mother of all nations. She is the mother of thunder, the mother of the streams, the mother of the trees and all things. . . . She alone is the mother of the fire and the Sun and the Milky Way. . . . She is the mother of the rain and the only mother we possess. . . .
>
> Our Mother of the growing fields, our mother of the streams, will have pity on us. For whom do we belong? Whose seeds are we? To our mother alone do we belong.

A legend of the Masai women in Africa tells of a time when women were the friends of all animals who came and dwelt with them. In some way, perhaps by eating animal flesh, the women offended the animals, who then all ran away into the jungle. Thereafter, women became the servants of men and had to go with their gourds to milk the men's cattle. From virtually all rituals and deliberations of all tribes women were excluded. The lives of women, whether as property or in a somewhat more dignified position, were ultimately in the control of masculine authority. Such very ancient and deep-seated traditions have had great significance in all places and in all ages.

The early anthropologists found the effigies of Gods, the masks and carvings and tribal customs of considerable interest, but always from the condescending point of view of superior civilisation. Later, living among such simple communities, anthropologists such as Malinowski and Margaret Mead studied the relations of men and women, and how they brought up their children. At times it seemed that some of their customs could bring helpful information on the social problems of far more sophisticated societies. Ruth Benedict's study of the diversity of customs in communities in different lands brought into popular use the term 'culture', to describe the almost unconscious acceptance of habits, rituals and beliefs surrounding every individual within each society from birth. It transpired from her work and that of Margaret Mead that the tone and quality of a culture rested mainly on whatever drives or impulses in human beings were valued by the members of the community. There were harsh and militaristic communities; others gentle and benevolent; others absorbed in ritual, pursuing the golden mean. Admittedly there were wars between tribes, and cannibalism. But the picture of primitive man savagely defending his 'territory' against all-comers is far from interpreting the complexity and depth of primitive life. Starting from those bones and shaped flints we have at first envisaged humans as food gatherers, hunters and tool-makers, then tillers of the soil. We took it for granted that they must have been entirely absorbed in the severe struggle for existence. On the contrary, these lonely and apparently insignificant creatures on the planet were profoundly exercised as to how they got there. They asked the eternal question: 'How did the world begin? How and why are we here?' Recent researches reveal that in every corner of the globe were people who conceived of high Gods above the spirits immanent in mountains, rivers, plants and animals on earth. From the North American Indians, to Africa, Australia, South America, Polynesia, come myths of a Great Spirit, outside the world, able to create from the mind, and having made the world and man and woman. These high Gods are mostly all-powerful, impervious to prayer, and speak to humanity with fire and thunder from the skies. Thus the human male, assuming dominance, early aware of his own consciousness, observed, stored in memory and reproduced in images what he saw about him, realising with pride and some awe this spirit, soul or intelligence within him which enabled him to do these things. Perhaps because of his hard life he felt the need to imagine a power higher than humanity who bestowed especially on him the gift of these faculties. Religion in the sense of a credible interpretation of the universe, which afforded him some guide in life, became essential to him. Religion, so defined, is also something that many men and women of today seem to need, if life is to be worth living. So were born those first visions of the universe, shaping beliefs. For it is by what the male mind believes about the nature of the universe that, down the ages, man has set his course.

CHAPTER 2

The old gods

What is this universe in which, by the mere fact of existing, human beings feel themselves irretrievably involved? Ever since the planet earth became capable of sustaining human life, the eyes of tiny, bewildered, awe-struck men and women have gazed up into the deep, dark blue expanse of heaven, spangled with its myriad stars; rejoiced in the pale beauty of the moon; felt cheered and warmed by the rising of the beneficent sun and the gift of a colourful world brought by its power and light. Who would ever deny being entranced by the eternal mystery surrounding us?

As the millennia passed, scientists claimed to have penetrated some way into this mystery; the philosophers replied that science, based as it is merely upon induction, cannot even guarantee with certainty that the sun will rise again tomorrow. Bounded in space and in our senses, we assume that outside of our persons, around us, exists a 'real' world. There are those who even cast doubt upon taking that for granted. We exist; something about us exists; but what may be its ultimate meaning or purpose we really know no more than those far-off ancestors who, as it were casually, inadvertently, embarked on the perilous and courageous course of beginning to think at all.

'Can one think without words?' was a question I once heard asked on a radio programme. It seemed at first to flummox the panel, who must have been of the educated, academic élite. To become and to feel superior has been an important element in human history.

As they picked up those flints and unearthed those bones,

learned men considered that to achieve so much was remarkable for 'savages' – a description used by even so distinguished an archaeologist as Gordon Childe in much the same way as adults, when in an indulgent mood, have looked upon the play and efforts of young children, as something 'cute' and amusing; whereas children, like 'savages', have their own individual pictures of the world. Superior attitudes to other peoples, classes, children, are, of course, highly significant in the social structure.

Once aware of this conscious power within himself the male expressed it in diverse ways; applied as practical skill, it made tools and weapons, built shelter; a dawning sense of order presently brought organisation and later the concept of law; but possibly the finest and most extensive use of this beneficent faculty was in the flights of the imagination, enabling humanity to interpret sense impressions in so many ways, not only in pictures, but in rhythm, music, song and words; above all to reach out in curiosity and wonder beyond the limitations of the senses into the infinities of space and time.

The tool-maker and builder may be regarded as ancestor of the technologist; the organiser ancestor of rationality; whilst the dreamer is forerunner of the artist, the poet, the utopian, creator of gods, of religions, of faith in the future life, as also of monsters, devils and of every superstition and black fantasy of magic, terror and madness, all those powers of darkness by which we mortals have haunted ourselves from the cradle to the grave.

There have been and still are countless ways of writing human history. The line of thought that concentrated on man the tool-maker has been pursued by applied scientists and economists, preoccupied with the relation to and extending use of material resources, such as the mining of minerals, copper, iron, coal, as well as the settled cultivation of food. Culture, ideas and beliefs are then looked upon as a superstructure on the foundation of the current means of production.

Other post-evolution historians see the mind and imagination as the prime movers of change and innovation, for them human relations and the communications of mankind as a species are pre-eminent. Man makes his world; he is not determined by it. Among these is Lewis Mumford, whose whole life has been given to this aspect of humane studies. In one of his finest books, *The Myth of the Machine*, Mumford challenges the tool-maker thesis, asserting that the human being with a highly adaptable body and brain power, already demanded outlets beyond the mere struggle for survival. He says:

> Through man's over developed and incessantly active brain he had more mental energy to tap than he needed for survival at purely animal level; and he was accordingly under the necessity of canalising that energy, not just into food getting and sexual reproduction, but into modes of living that would convert that energy more directly and constructively into appropriate cultural – that is symbolic – forms. Only by creating cultural outlets could he tap and control and fully utilise his own nature. (p. 7)

Starting from the very earliest times, Mumford endeavours to seek out human values and set them above technics, up to our present day. And whereas Bronowski in his well-known series the *Ascent of Man* sees man, in the advanced civilisations of our time, as the culmination of the evolutionary process, for Mumford, on the contrary, modern humanity's preoccupation with the machine has been a disaster, not merely through errors of choice by misguided statesmen, but akin to the worship of false gods.

His argument is learned and substantially supported by his many years of studying the habits of human communities; it is rich in illustration and absorbing to read.

As far back as 1920, like Mumford, I could see that the preoccupation of urban and industrial communities with the machine appeared to be drifting into a form of worship of which most of them were, so far, quite unaware. During the intervening sixty years, the machine has intensified and deepened its grip on human lives as well as expanding its influence widely over many countries. Its hold on the imagination, as on the conduct of practical affairs, resembles the dominance of the innumerable religions created and served down the ages by male consciousness, expressing as they do successive and changing male aspirations, needs and dreams. Possibly our present predicament can in part be explained by taking note of these exercises in speculation. What do men believe in and why?; how does belief affect their behaviour? Many of the answers are to be found in the insight and wisdom of Mumford's writings, to which very few could aspire. The purpose of this book is modest and, by its very nature, superficial, simply to trace, from some examples, the consciousness of the male as he creates, worships, discards and re-creates his gods. Leaving now, therefore, the speculations of post-evolutionary man, we must return to the birth of consciousness, to the male as he starts to explain himself and the world about him.

Fear must have been the first emotion of human beings. Indeed it may be said that fear eternally dogs us like a shadow – a phantom we have never been able to conquer or dispel. All species are at the mercy of the weather and natural forces; all are on guard against likely predators. Humans, adaptable, inquisitive, adventurous, had also much to fear from wild life about them, and were not, like more restricted species, programmed to one specific type of action, or equipped, like them, in their own persons, with means of defence. Humans had no dangerous teeth or claws or powerful stabbing gear. The human male had to fashion the weapons for his hand and summon the armour of fortitude for his heart. A saga might well be written of the part played by fear in human destiny: of its temporary subduing by martial valour; by passive heroism enduring for faith or principle; by reckless intransigence in the cause of liberty; or simple risk of life to save another; as also of the failure of nerve in a crisis; or pure cowardice; or justifiable retreat in the face of overwhelming odds. Progress towards each civilised epoch in history is a journey out of fear and uncertainty in search of some degree of permanence and security. Fear of an immediate danger, or of impending future perils, may well lie at the root of each civilised epoch's decline.

For the young child security resided in the arms or the near presence of its mother. Primitive women likewise attained consciousness and were as capable as their male partners of its exercise and extension. It would seem that this passed unnoticed by the men; the inferior roles assigned to women did not permit of their advance beyond the use of practical skills to inclusion in joint decisions on the policy and safety of the group. None the less women must have contributed vitally to the men's sense of security as they cared for the children, tended the fires, scraped and spread and sewed the skins, creating a semblance of comfort in whatever cave or shelter became their home. 'Home is the sailor home from the sea and the hunter home from the hill' expresses an almost age-old sentiment. Equally ancient, too, is the male acceptance of this warm blanket of reassurance to his whole being – the gift of female domestic labours – coupled with little regard for the giver and a wilful refusal to perceive within her those faculties similar and equivalent to his own.

Man's first allies in the struggle for existence were therefore other men, who instinctively came together, acting as a group, forming a tribe, but always excluding women in the matter of secret and sacred rites or common decisions. Apart from this puzzling embargo on the female sex, man must have been, from the beginning, a social animal. As numbers grew, more communal decisions were required. To judge by the way Africans,* and the original native Americans and others assembled for palavers and pow-wows to consider united action, there must have been at first some form of elementary democracy. Again, we think of primitive life as hard, which it was, in the sense that it called for physical energy and enterprise. But these requirements have varied enormously according to climate. There were the grim ice ages; extensive droughts that wiped out many; but also more kindly periods and places, where the sun obviated the need for clothing and where food from growing fruit and the catch of fish and birds were plentiful. Man had time to indulge those fantasies in carving and painting grotesque marks and animal totems, or to paint, adorn or distort the shape of his own person; women did likewise and made garlands, necklaces, bracelets, and anklets. And for festive occasions enormous painted decorated contraptions were carried in procession. It is worth noting that the more complex and organised life becomes, multiplying imperative daily tasks, the less leisure, or inclination, there is to indulge in creative fantasies and inventions, whether individual or communal in inspiration.

* In a television film which carried translations of the speech in a tribal discussion, about the movement of their herds, I recall a man in the centre, arguing animatedly like any speaker at a political meeting.

By what is called the neolithic period settled communities were established whose way of life was the fore-runner of, and indeed, evolved into, the mixed farming which has been practised right up to the present day. Students of prehistory seem to regard this period as, at first, more especially belonging to women, because of the contribution which they are thought to have made in work and invention.

'Our debt', says Gordon Childe, 'to preliterate barbarians is heavy. Every single cultivated food plant of any importance has been discovered by some nameless barbarian society. So we find neolithic peoples relying not only on wheat and barley, but on rice, millet and maize and even yams, manioc, squashes and plants that are not cereals at all.' (p. 50)

These discoveries are largely attributed to the activities of women, aided by their growing children; women were almost certainly the pioneers in agricultural labours; in grinding the corn, cooking, making baskets and containers for the collection and storage of food; as also presently spinning and weaving in wool and flax. Mumford suggests that the acquisition of domestic animals began with the encouragement by women and children of playful animal young, attracted by food at the human settlement. These villages, given foresight and adequate harvest, could, with some hunting of game, maintain a self-sufficient existence. It was a time when one might say that man lived within his species, that biological values were predominant, in that members of the family were occupied in co-operative and also creative efforts to attain a tolerable and even pleasant life.

The intelligence of both men and women, one may guess, was devoted to the improvement of the yield of their crops: as the soil became exhausted, a further area would be cleared. Skills and experience would be acquired, then learned by the young from their elders, through imitation, gesture, later word of mouth. Awareness of fertility and human and animal procreation presented new visions to the imagination. The mystery of sex, birth and all these things living and proliferating about him, then declining into ageing and death, affected the male definition of religious beliefs. Reverence for ancestors began to replace animal totems and also to establish traditions. Greater care and ritual were now observed in the ways of bestowal of the dead. It was even thought possible to go to them for advice; quite natural to suppose that the spirits of the fathers might somehow be there to inspire and guide their sons. With this came haunting by ghosts, the magic – for good or ill – of the medicine man; dread of the evil spells that might bring death to men and beasts alike, or to pregnant women.

Though all these express fears, yet tilling the soil, rearing domestic animals and human families, was, in the main, a hopeful and, above all, peaceful way of life. The myths and rites associated with agriculture are universal and so well-known as to need no emphasis: the corn spirit who must die in order to be reborn (which, however, among some people may have meant human sacrifice, later resolved into symbolism); the descent of goddesses – like Persephone, into the underworld for half the year; the decoration with evergreen branches and the kindling of fires in mid-winter in order thus, by sympathetic magic, to ensure the return of the light and warmth of the sun.

A vast lapse of time occurs, during which, presumably through successive generations, or by new types of men and women evolving, human hands and limbs and whole bodies grew in suppleness and skill: a delicate network of facial muscles are said to provide the basis for emotional expression peculiar to human beings – anger, curiosity, anxiety, pleasure, above all the greeting of a smile.

Populations increased, villages expanded, men explored. Communities must have discovered one another; exchange of goods – trade – began. Classes of craftsmen, who were not tillers of the soil, but working in metals, or as specialised potters, now appeared. Such people had to be fed. Communities amalgamated; whether by the large absorbing the smaller, or by predatory conquest of a neighbour's land. However it was, cities came into existence.

As is well known, urban life is only possible if a locality can provide a sufficient surplus of food for those who are not food producers. The classical examples of the rise of cities in the ancient world are Babylon, (the Sumerian) Egypt and the valley of the Indus in India.

To say that the increase of the population represents a serious problem for the administrator is a mere platitude.

When men and women and families are living at close quarters, rules and laws will obviously be required to regulate the conduct of the citizens – that very word derived from the concept of the city.

But what of the effect on the dominant male mind and conscious attitude to his fellow citizens of the change from neolithic style village to urban living? Man had been working with his family group, as also with other households, co-operating against occasional dangers. He had begun to assume control over family relations and matters of kinship, but beyond this his authority barely extended. Despite experience gained and family labours, in the yield of his harvests he was at the mercy of the elements.

> We plough the fields and scatter
> The good seed on the land
> But it is fed and watered
> By God's Almighty hand.

When it came to animal breeding, he could not control the numbers or fitness of his flocks and herds, or of human beings. None the less sheer numbers, either of flocks and herds or of his own offspring, brought a sense of pride and power of possession. The advantage of numbers in work or danger was well perceived; man's 'gods' began to urge on him to be fruitful and multiply that his seed might inherit the earth.

Power over the environment was always a primary objective, lack of power the source of fears. Conscious knowledge of power as well as the motives behind its exercise are an integral part of the human story. Power which comes out of the gifts of good fortune does not bring the satisfaction of personal achievement. The early huntsmen no doubt experienced the exultation of power, but this was contaminated by rage, hate and fear. (The 'Red Indians' in America on the contrary, would apologise to wild animals whom they had to kill for food.) Man began to shape tools and to work in metals, melting copper and making bronze; with actually using the dread element of fire, came the sense of a power due to personal skill of hand and brain. The fullest and purest joy in the experience of personal power resides in artistic achievement. For early man this lay in the work of the craftsman – in fashioning in wood, clay, or

stone, statues and reliefs, the images of gods or the great ones
of his world. It was expressed too in the increasing beauty and
delicacy of household objects and jewelry; it saw also the birth
of architecture.

Human power, however, extends far beyond the impress of
human hands on the materials of the natural world. It comes
in a myriad guises and is exercised above all upon humanity
itself. As the people congregate in cities, the dream of controlling and directing the mass of his fellow men for some purpose
of his own enters the male mind. There will be a few men of
exceptional drive and ability, to whom the possibilities of such
a project appeal. Even before the idea of such organisation or
exploitation occurred, urban life had begun to sort people out
into classes. The scribe whose stencil marks the clay tablets
with records of stores and possessions, as of the history of the
gods who must be believed and worshipped, is already a
literate and numerate bureaucrat, raised above the level of
ordinary men. There will be those who design and those who
oversee the labour of others in building temples for those gods
and the priests by whose interpretation of their commands the
people will be governed.

The coming of words spoken and written must literally have
expanded the mind of human beings like the opening of shut-
ters on to a landscape as yet unseen. Everything about them,
whether person, animal, plant, household utensil, could be
designated by a name. Indeed how could anyone begin to speak
of anything without giving it a name? In Genesis, God gave
to Adam, even before He made Eve, the privilege of naming
all creation. Thus, besides the actual person or thing, there
came into existence a separate entity – the name. It transpired
that there could be names for thoughts and feelings as well as
concrete objects. That people were dimly aware of some great
significance in this new world of bodyless intangibles is shown
by the superstitions that became attached to the use and the
speaking of names. Often aliases were given: to divulge the
names of cherished or sacred persons might lay them open to
danger from the spells of their enemies.

The connection between written picture symbols and spoken
words also presented difficulties, and still does, even after
centuries of inventing alphabets, and translating the sacred

texts and literature of the learned élite into the vernacular of the people. Languages, like the people who speak them, are alive and change with custom and use. In centuries to come people were to do almost incredible things with words, as also with numbers.

Counting does seem to have begun, as might be expected, from the five fingers, and measurement by the length of foot or arm. But from tens the next stage was not necessarily to hundreds; the Sumerians counted in sixties. Other peoples counted in numbers more easily divided by two, sixes and dozens. The evolution of writing numbers was a slow business. The Romans had their elaborate clumsy system of letters with which all students are familiar. Zero and the placing of the digits in the decimal system did not arrive till the twelfth century AD (invented by the Arab mathematician Muhamad-Ibn-Musa).

This digression is a prelude to a brief exploration of the myths of Babylon, which are, however, relevant to language and speech. Cradle of one of the most ancient civilisations, Babylon rose and declined over a period of thousands of years on the fertile delta formed by the Tigris and Euphrates in the Arabian peninsula. Revered by some devout scholars as the origin of the Garden of Eden, it has lived on in their imagination, as in that of our poets. For many it will still have the aura of romance imparted by the tales of our childhood about the Hanging Gardens of Babylon, one of the Seven Wonders of the Ancient World; and the building of the Tower of Babel, which God, in wrath at man's impiety in reaching towards the heavens, punished by imposing the confusion of many tongues. So Babylon has given a word babbling, forever associated with speech and a reminder that, however, or whenever, this awkward event came to pass, we do not all speak the same language. (H. G. Wells, describing radio transmitters pouring out propaganda to control the populace, calls them the 'babble machines'.) As a matter of historical fact it would seem that in the busy city life that was to be found in Babylon, the coming of new settlers, traders and merchants must soon have presented problems of understanding and translation. The Sumerians are thought to have been settled there as far back as 6000 BC and the inscribed tablets show that men of other languages followed. From the mass of layers of material only a modest proportion have been translated, but they have provided a fascinating picture of the whole way of life of our Babylonian ancestors' cosmogony, gods, administration, poetry of feeling and of vision. A Babylonian city, by our standards, was small, but large compared with a neolithic village:

> Ur, with its canals, harbours and temples occupied two hundred and twenty acres; the walls of Erech compassed an area of just under two square miles. A governor of Lagash, one of the smaller cities of Sumer . . . claims to rule over ten 'shars' of men, – a round number, literally thirty-six thousand, and perhaps applying only to adult males. (Childe, p. 84)

As a rule it was only in times of danger that one male had sole power, normally the male elders or priests were in command.

The people of the city states were bound together in the service of their particular god. They could not do otherwise, since the fertile land that they tilled and the animals on the farms were held to belong to him absolutely. Small private ownership in housing at the city centre might be allowed. A part of the land would be portioned out to be farmed by families, but always under the tutelage of special separate gods, occasionally goddesses, themselves subject to the chief god of the region. This god would have a special estate, administered like a huge household; the temple itself raised upon an artificial platform, behind this rose a sort of tower (a ziggurat), close by were granaries, storehouses and workshops.

For the goddess Bau (Childe, p. 84), consort of Ningirsu, the chief god of Lagash, there worked twenty-one bakers, helped by twenty-seven female slaves; twenty-five brewers with six slave assistants, forty women preparing wool from the goddesses' flocks, female spinners, female weavers, a male smith and other artisans, as well as officials, clerks and priests. The temple also owned metal tools, ploughs, wagons and boats. Wages were paid in barley. Thus, while the common people raised the subsistence of the official classes, these were able to dispose of considerable accumulated wealth to purchase the many goods not obtainable at home. Though their clay made good bricks for building, the Sumerians had no forests, or stone quarries, whereas wood, precious stones and metals, gold and silver, were much in demand to adorn the images and temples of the gods.

Administrators and priests were far from idle. They had to account to the god for all his possessions, as well as undertaking public works such as the construction of the temples. In these tasks, among other things, they began to create a phonetic writing script, to make libraries and dictionaries, and to use the rules of arithmetic, as well as the basic elements of geometry. An important consideration of urban life, as well as the measurement of space for building, is the measurement and reckoning of time. Obviously the seasons of the year were observed, and yearly time was checked in moon months, though presently observation of the stars showed the moon-month system to be inaccurate. Day and night the Sumerians divided into twelve two-hourly periods measured by sun dials, and water clocks, similar to the use of hour glasses with sand.

There must have been a well-organised and well-occupied literate class very far removed from the wordless people, of long ago, who thought in pictures. Their minds now took in details of administration, the attractions of mathematics as of the literary expression of poetic thoughts and feelings, and of history. For illiterate people, on the contrary, language was more of a utility for exchanges at the work place or with their neighbours, whilst older ways of thought and feeling would still be their main preoccupation. Music, incense, ritual, beauty and splendour accompanied the ceremonies and processions of the gods and must have gripped the imagination of all sections of the population.

The city states of Babylonia, the name given to this whole region, achieved so much in the arts of civilisation, because they remained without being really devastated by an imperialist conqueror for some four thousand years. But by now the males had succeeded in using power to mobilise citizen armies; the city states fought with one another. But it was the gods, not the armies of men or generals, who won victories, negotiated peace, or suffered defeat. A defeated god was literally carried into exile, and back again in victory or peace.

It will be seen that every detail of the lives of these people was identified with that of their gods, and through them with the cosmogony which it was believed these very gods had created. Every action was related to the cosmological background.

As a recipe for effective urban government this type of religion could hardly be bettered. A minor god was revered, keeping watch on the daily toil of the farm, a higher god over the temple staff, artisans and urban workers. The whole was a perfect device for decentralised control over considerable groups of dissimilar citizens. As a sample of religion employed as 'opium for the people' it holds a respectable place.

What was, then, the origin and what the nature of these gods that made them credible to the people?

The poem known as the Babylonian Creation is on seven tablets, inscribed, according to some scholars, about the twelfth century BC, the time of Nebuchadnezzar the first. The myths which it relates, however, are the product of centuries of previous speculation. Nor is the poem strictly a story of creation, because Babylonian philosophy appears to have consistently maintained that the substance of the universe was eternal, in the sense that it was not created out of nothing, nor did any of it pass into non-existence.

There existed three primordial beings, Tiamat, Apsu and Mummu. The name Tiamat means a stretch of water; Apsu an ocean of great depth; Mummu has been interpreted as mist or cloud, but more credibly, as formless chaos into which things that have form disintegrate through loss of the power or energy that gives them shape. In the poem the gods act and speak like human beings (Sanders, p. 74).

> When there was no heaven,
> no earth, no height, no depth, no name,
>   when Apsu was alone,
> the sweet water, the first begetter; and Tiamat
>   the bitter water, and that
> return to the womb, her Mummu,
>   when there were no gods —
>
> When sweet and bitter
> mingled together, no reed was plaited, no rushes
>   muddied the water,

the gods were nameless, natureless, futureless, then
    from Apsu and Tiamat
in the waters gods were created, in the waters
    silt precipitated,

Lahmu and Lahamu,
were named; they were not yet old,
    not yet grown tall
when Anshar and Kishar overtook them both,
    the lines of sky and earth
stretched where horizons meet to separate
    cloud from silt.

Days of days, years
on years passed till Anu, the empty heaven,
    heir and supplanter,
first-born of his father, in his own nature
    begot Nudimmud-Ea,
intellect, wisdom, wider than heaven's Horizon,
    the strongest of all the kindred.

The gods, though brethren and of succeeding generations, break out into quarrelling: Apsu and Tiamat are both too lethargic to deal adequately with all their issue. Mummu, as befits chaos, advises that all these obstreperous offspring be destroyed. But the 'bright intelligence that perceives and plans, Nudimmud-Ea, saw through it, he sounded the coil of chaos and against it devised the artifice* of the universe.'

Ea destroys Apsu, whereupon Tiamat, enraged, gives birth to a horde of monsters, and appoints a mere rough fellow Kingu to be her Captain. The gods are powerless to deal with Tiamat and her rabble, even the authority of Anu, god of the heavens; he does not improve matters by letting loose stormy winds from all four quarters. But the resourceful intelligent Ea again comes to the rescue; he has now a son Marduk, the arch-type of the young hero, strong, beautiful, skilful and wise. Weary of the tempest, the gods accept that Marduk be asked to deal with Tiamat. Marduk consents, but first of all obtains

---

* N. K. Sanders sees in the word she translates as artifice not merely a 'spell' but the concept of a universe to be created.

a pledge from the assembled gods that they will accept him as chief and overlord forever.

Armed with his own bow and arrow and a net given him by Anu and helped by powerful winds, he overcomes Tiamat, deals her a death blow with his great mace, cleaves her body and from it shapes an orderly cosmos, placing the gods in the heavens, on earth and beneath, in accordance with their rightful powers.

In return the repentant gods agree to build a temple and tower for Marduk, hence it is they, not men, who are responsible for the Tower of Babel. In this legend man is a poor humble creature, created by Ea as an afterthought to give additional service. By a wily trick of Ea, and man's obedience to him, man does not acquire the immortality of the gods.

Marduk received the fifty names and powers of all the gods in a lengthy and repetitive chant which was part of the compulsory ritual at the New Year Festival that took place in the spring, when all the gods came, many by river boats, to take their places and move along the wide processional way admired for many years by visitors to Babylon.

The first female in the Sumerian legend appears in most unattractive guise, in the form of Tiamat: a great blowsy, indolent mother, but also, of course, a great treacherous, heaving watery marsh. The gods do have consorts, who are barely mentioned, though they often symbolise the fertility of the earth. Inanna, daughter of Anu, is the goddess who, as in other legends, undertakes the journey into the underworld, which is ruled by her sister. Inanna's journey is terrifying; she is finally rescued only by the sacrifice of her husband to the destructive devils; whereupon his mother and his sister appear in the story, beside his wife, to weep for him. He does not vanish, but becomes a denizen of the underworld; in some versions, he is the corn harvest.

In the name of Ishtar, Inanna, like many of the Babylonian gods, appears in the mythology of the Assyrian conquerors, in variations of the same legends. She personifies Venus and seems to be the goddess both of love and war. She is shown riding into battle on a chariot and is portrayed as, in all aspects, a tempestuous personality. Though she makes tender promises of protection to kings whom she honours with her courtship, she is definitely sex, not maternity, or fertility. She is attended by sacred courtesans. She will threaten to cause the bull not to mount the cow, but apparently without reference to the 'right true end' of his desires. Similarly, by her love she diminishes the ardour of the male warrior, as also of his war charger.

Thou hast loved the steed proud in battle
And destined him for the halter, the goad and the whip.

By her love she tames animals for domestic use, but may also transform the men whom she loves into leopards.

In these early myths the underworld is a very large and important region. Could it be that the immense growth that came from below, not only the crops, but tall trees and vigorous and ample vegetation, suggested that there was a vast magic palace there below, like the great water abyss of which men were afraid. For thousands of years, it must be remembered, humanity walked on a flat earth. The Sumerians even thought that at sunset the sun went underground and journeyed back during the night to the point of his rising.

What, in effect, does this cosmogony symbolise, if it is not that very land between the rivers where the Sumerians had recently settled? It was flat marshy land, where the silt from two rivers was gradually building up the fertile soil in banks on either side, exposed to every wind that blew and in summer to a fierce sun, just like the arid deserts that bounded what was an expansive oasis.

The gods of this area – the natural forces dominating human lives – at times appeared in conflict with one another. Identifying with these gods, or rather creating them as representing their own situation, did not the males read into them the lesson that there is a powerful instrument in war?

More significant is the figure of Nudimmud-Ea, creative, intellectual, a planner, who ended strife, bound and banished chaos, producing a fine and capable son to carry on with his work. Are not these the gods to inspire or to express what those men and women were doing, who out of a forbidding marsh made a cultivated landscape and cities of dignity and splendour?

This cosmogony shows humanity, predominantly male-directed, increasingly aware of its ability to impose an orderly urban society on a hostile environment, and, while certainly increasing the standard of living, to direct considerable bodies of men in labour and war.

Early Egyptian civilisation, supported by the fertile floodings of the Nile, must have been much similar to that of Mesopotamia, though not imitative, since they would, in the early stages, have known nothing whatever about one another. Early Egyptian remains, deeply buried, could not be excavated, hence the archaeologists' story begins virtually at the urban stage, when already the all-powerful god of the Falcon clan, Horus, had subdued the village communities. As we saw with Marduk, in other countries of the ancient world arising out of the disputes of the gods came the drive towards dictatorship. Rule by one god mirrors the hope of rule by one man who would command both the army and the civilian population. What is more, already in the male mind are the seeds of the eternal conflict between secular and divine authority. The warrior kings, whether of Sumeria, Assyria or Persia, had to walk warily in dealing with their gods, to whom they owed obedience and in whose rites they participated. They even felt obliged to revere the gods whose territories they conquered. Hence the same gods, under various names, people the same myths, when they are, technically, in exile. Besides, there were priesthoods to be placated or intimidated; at all times their accumulated knowledge and wisdom inspired respect. Only they were conversant with the movement of the heavenly bodies, could teach writing and the elements of science. The Assyrian who 'came down like a wolf on the fold', ended up by establishing a library of massive clay tablets.

So Pharaoh, in 5000 BC (unless an early Chinese emperor might dispute his claim) stands out as the first man duly accredited as king and god, invested with powers both temporal and spiritual. He was to have many emulators.

The pyramids, in which dead pharaohs and their wealth were housed, are known to all the world, the pyramidal design of their social system a fruitful subject for scholars. Mumford sees it as already a perfect machine composed of human elements, from the labourers at the base, up through the overseers, servants, accountants, scribes, musicians, artisans, brewers, soldiers, of whom statuettes are found even in the tombs of people of moderate means. In the highest social position is the priesthood; at the peak, the figure of Pharaoh points to the sun, supreme object of veneration.

The use of the term machine in this connection seems to me premature because, while the structure of Egyptian society was inhuman, without regard for suffering inflicted, or individual rights, it was not mechanical in the modern sense. It illustrated how complete and effective a social system may be when absolute power, reinforced by divine authority, is given into the hands of one man. Nor was this the case throughout Egyptian history, which did not lack conflict and dispute for the possession of power.

When in our time, we think about ancient Egypt, we recall all those mummies and relics in the British Museum and visualise things in the flat, without perspective; reliefs in stone, weird inexplicable gods, with heads of birds and animals. And ancient Egypt, as a country, is, to the imagination, a sandy desert, adorned with pyramids and a Sphinx. It is hard to imagine real live Egyptians except a few, such as Aknaton, Nefertiti, or Cleopatra, who are given flesh and blood by romantic and poetic stories of their part in history. Again, the Egyptians do seem to be obsessed with funerals and death.

Turning the pages of Wallis Budge's translation of *The Book of the Dead*, I learned that some excavation of the graves of the primitive inhabitants has taken place and showed not only the provision of food and other articles for the needs of the body after death, but already the wrapping of the body itself as it were for protection, in the hope of its perpetual preservation. The elaborate process of embalming indicates that this belief must have survived for a very long time. He considers that many of the funeral chants and prayers written down by scribes about 3500 BC go back to magic ceremonies performed before historical times. These prayers deal especially with protection from snakes, scorpions, and reptiles, he adds:

Such formulae date from a period when the banks of the Nile were overrun by wild beasts, and when they formed the home of creatures of all kinds which were hostile to man, and which the early dwellers on the Nile sought to

cajole or frighten away from their dead; indeed, there is
little doubt that, before the forests which lined the river
banks were cut down for fuel, Egypt must have resembled,
in many respects, certain sections of the Nile Valley much
further south, and that river monsters of all kinds, and
amphibious beasts which are only now to be found on the
upper reaches of the Blue Nile and near the Great Lakes,
lived happily in the neighbourhood of Memphis, and even
farther to the north.

Here is a completely new picture of the Egyptians, in depth
and colour, as real ordinary primitive people, struggling with
the usual fears and dangers of their lot; presently, as Wallis
Budge suggests, faced with immigrants, armed with metal
weapons, who settle and intermarry. The landscape grows
barer, but order and security increase; urban Egypt emerges.
But the haunting fear of death remains, somehow intensely
powerful among these people, engendering a determination
that at least the soul shall survive, even though, by incanta-
tion, it must be translated into the form of bird or beast. Egypt
thus has its own unique religion, burying its dead with magic
rites and invocations to the gods, seeking, by the preservation
of the body, to ensure the transformation or immortality of
the soul.

The Book of the Dead was copied and re-copied and added
to by one generation after another for a period of nearly
5000 years; and the pious Egyptian, whether king or
ploughman, queen or maid-servant lived with the teaching
of the Book of the Dead before his eyes, and he was buried
according to its directions, and he based his hope of
everlasting life and happiness upon the efficacy of its hymns
and prayers, and words of power. By him its Chapters were
not regarded as materials for grammatical exercises, but as
all powerful guides along the road which, passing through
death and the grave, led into the realms of light and life,
and into the presence of the divine being Osiris, the
conqueror of death, who made men and women 'to be born
again'.

For all its preoccupation with animal forms and Isis and

Osiris, gods of the Nile, there is, in historic urban Egypt, a very marked withdrawal from organic life into an artificial world of duty and subservience, protocol and procedure. Also of overwhelming pride. The title of Pharaoh is made hereditary; there is even incest within the Royal House, since no one less eminent can be accepted in marriage.

The people as a whole seem trapped and imprisoned in the cage of their own fears and superstitions. There is little of the intellect of man here, although the stars are studied and lessons about time and navigation learned from them. Yet the impression is that astrology triumphs over astronomy, and the reading of omens by a powerful priesthood over the worship of Ra, pure light of the sun.

In 332 BC, when Alexander the Great came as a conqueror to Egypt, he was thus far susceptible to the power of this religion as to visit the temple of the oracle of Ammon-Ra set up by the priesthood, in order that the oracle might confer upon him the divine title of a god.

In this rigid, austere, unearthly, obsessional world one longs for a breath of fresh air.

The Babylonian city states and Egypt were settled in favourable regions that provided ample food and stability for development. Peoples who lived on the open plains, or in mountainous areas, had more difficulty in maintaining themselves. This may account, in part, for the predatory nature of the Assyrians. Many tribes were still nomadic herdsmen, living on meat and milk more than the produce of the soil. One of these was a Semitic people, the Jews.

The sacred writings and chronicles of the history of the Jews form the Old Testament of the Christian Bible. Therefore it is extremely difficult for anyone brought up in the Christian tradition to write of them with the impartiality which the examination of historical records demands. Traditionally, all Christians have been taught to accept every word in the Bible as true. But the historian, seeking to disentangle an accurate contemporary report from what may be legends and myths, must, if possible, compare one version of events, in a stated period, with another from a different source. Then again these Jewish records, unlike those of Egypt and Babylon, are, in another respect, contemporary for us, since they have relevance for the view of life and conduct of present-day Jews, as well as Christians. I want to make it clear that I am writing here of the age in which these records first came into existence; moreover I write as a declared atheist, who does not believe in the existence of any of these gods. That is a different matter again from the results that flowed from men's creating the gods and believing in them.

The books collected in the Old Testament were known and probably recognised as important sacred writings about 100 BC. It is difficult to say definitely when any or all of them were written. The later books are accepted as a contribution to actual Jewish history, the earlier ones as a recording of hearsay, legend or myths.

The book starts, however, as if it purports to tell how the world began, and the relevance of subsequent events to the experience of the Jews as Jehovah's chosen people.

Many learned scholars who have studied these ancient records have concluded that the early chapters of the Old Testament were written during, or soon after, the captivity of the Jews in Babylon. Their own history, and that of others, agrees that they were deported by Nebuchadnezzar in 587 BC. They returned to rebuild Jerusalem and their temple in 539 BC when Cyrus the Persian conquered Babylon. At the period of the captivity, Nebuchadnezzar boasted of the splendour and achievements of his kingdom, of the great processional way and buildings, by which he hoped 'to attain eternal age'; it was indeed a time of flourishing Babylonian scholarship and literature which may well have stimulated the Jews to investigate their own. Myths of the two peoples could have become confused.

The Old Testament version of the Creation of the World is very similar to the Babylonian Creation, except that there is only one god in the Jewish version and he creates the world out of nothing. Both have stories of the Great Flood and the building of the Tower of Babel. Another and puzzling similarity is that, in the Sumerian records, Sargon 1, ruler of Babylon about 2750 BC, relates a story of the events surrounding his own birth which is identical with the Jewish account of Moses in the bulrushes. What is more, in the Egyptian records, there is no mention of Moses, the plagues of Egypt, or of a Pharaoh drowned in the Red Sea.

The delectable vision of the Garden of Eden may express what many felt about the amenities of Babylon. But there are vital differences here. Babylonian 'man' is an afterthought, who loses the chance of immortality by blind obedience to a god; Adam, on the other hand, the peak of god's creation, is banished to the wilderness for disobedience; a sin apparently associated with sex. This passage may also allude to what was a burning issue of the time – expressed likewise in the story of Cain and Abel – the conflict between prosperous, settled agricultural communities who were encroaching on pastures vital to the nomad herdspeople – much as, in the United States, the cowboy ranchers were antagonistic to the farmers. Cain, who slew Abel, was a tiller of the soil, whereas it was Abel, the herdsman's, burnt offering of an animal that was pleasing to the Lord.

God the Creator, origin of the Universe and of human existence, is an imaginative concept held in common by the Jews and a vast number of peoples. This god is not, in my view, identical with Jehovah, tribal god of the Jews.

Abraham, sometime between 1900 and 2000 BC, moving about in the open country between Egypt and Babylon with his flocks and herds and the kin of his tribe (assuming that he was a real person), is the father of the Jewish people and their history. Like other nomads, he and his people would come from time to time to the agricultural communities for cereals (corn in Egypt) in time of need. Besides some antagonism to tillers of the soil, nomadic tribes had trouble with rival nomads, disputes and bargains about grazing grounds, sale of cattle, as also the risk of abduction and raping of their wives and daughters. There were no city walls for their protection; tents were the homes of their roving existence. Such dwellers in the open spaces find few objects, or even animals, in the landscape which they animate with dangerous gods. They commune with the heavens above and whatever power abides therein. It is not surprising that Abraham and his tribesmen, like the desert dwellers of today who worship Allah, had no need of a multitude of trumpery images made with hands. Nor did they, like the Babylonians, invent a god who owned the very soil they walked on. Constantly in movement, free rangers, sometimes in danger, they needed the inspiration of a tribal warrior up there and on their side, able if need be to send down pestilence on their enemies, or make the sun stand still in their aid. Jewish history reveals them as a turbulent and aggressive people. It was natural that when Abraham first passed through the land of Canaan and saw that it would be a good place to settle with his clan, his god should have promised him that one day it would be his. Centuries later, his descendants did come into the legacy, for which, however, in fulfilling the prophecy, they had to fight. Those were times when there was a great movement of many peoples, looking for some region of the earth which they might occupy and call their home.

These were also times of wars between peoples and nations, now growing in size, prosperity and power: wars which it would be tedious to describe. What is interesting is why all this happened; what thoughts were in the minds of men; what feelings, what motives lay behind their actions. Some light is thrown on this by the later history of the Jews, which illustrates the conflict, previously noted, between secular and divine power. The Jews were managed by a priesthood, founded by Moses and Aaron; also by lay judges, among whom at least one woman, Deborah, is recorded. But they felt themselves to be constantly under the immediate direction of Jehovah. After a great tragic defeat by the Philistines, the people demand of Samuel that they, just like other nations, should have a king. They in fact feel that their god has failed them. In this extremity, Jehovah advises Samuel to give way, but to explain what a king is likely to do. Samuel told his people (1 Sam 8):

This will be the manner of the king that shall reign over you: He will take your sons, and appoint them for himself, for his chariots, and to be his horsemen; and some shall run before his chariots. And he will appoint him captains over thousands, and captains over fifties; and will set them to ear his ground, and to reap his harvest, and to make his instruments of war, and instruments of his chariots. And he will take your daughters to be confectioners, and to be

cooks, and to be bakers. And he will take your fields, and
your vineyards, and your oliveyards, even the best of them,
and give them to his servants. And he will take the tenth
of your seed, and of your vineyards, and give to his officers,
and to his servants. And he will take your menservants, and
your maidservants, and your goodliest young men, and
your asses, and put them to his work. . . . He will take the
tenth of your sheep: and ye shall be his servants. And ye
shall cry out in that day because of your king which ye shall
have chosen you; and the Lord will not hear you in that
day.

Solomon, for all his glory, in part exemplifies all this, taking
on the role of an oriental monarch, patron rather than servant
of religion. There follow about four centuries of wars in which,
with their kings, the Jews are involved, ending with the start
of their captivity in Babylon.

These words of Samuel spoken about 1000 BC describe very
fully what then constituted the accepted behaviour and power
of a king. It was a new kind of man who exercised this power;
a new kind of people who submitted to it.

Humanity is now far removed from the innocence of primitive simplicity, from spontaneous, unpremeditated acts of
instinct. Urban social life has brought sophistication; desires
are no longer satisfied direct, but with conscious forethought.
Though some of the gods still represent the forces of nature
which are feared, others are symbols created to express the
varying needs, conscious and unconscious, of male or female
personality. Gradually the male especially ceases to regard
the natural, organic world, by which he lives, as the sacred
property of the gods.

By an imaginative process the human male steps out of his
own organic species into a world of concepts in which fantasies
of ambition play an increasing part. Normally it would seem
that to belong to a species must imply concern for its survival,
and acceptance and recognition of the identity of groups and
individuals within it. The dominant male, in his increasing
consciousness, creates differentials and divisions. Social life,
which could be unifying, is split into classes, of whom the least
regarded are women and children, the illiterate, and slaves.

Neighbours of the very same species are turned into enemies; the old instinctive empathy to get together for mutual aid is transformed into the drilling of serried ranks of martial men.

What continued to matter most was power, power residing now in numbers of brave warriors and effective weapons. One would have thought that there was still a great deal of room in the world, but none the less men found it good to overrun the territory of others, destroy the finest of their buildings, take their treasure, kill their fighting men and carry off the rest, with women and children, into slavery. It was more difficult for them to resist than if an attempt were made to govern them in their own land. Wanton cruelty accompanied these wars.

What feeling was there of morality – of right and wrong? Such laws and codes of conduct as existed applied only within your clan and under your own god, or gods. The rest of the world were potential enemies, of whom, as of their gods, you were afraid. People were still plainly in constant fear of the finality of death, but none the less overcame, without overmuch difficulty, the fact of dying, or killing their fellow men. Treasure was already becoming more valuable than people, since the latter were apparently in unlimited supply. But they must be your own, that is, of your tribe, or, in the more personal sense, it must be known what father had begotten them, but rarely who was the mother that bore them.

Morality rested on authority: the authority of the god. But that god would be such as was determined by the will and desires of the dominant males. A people with many enemies, and its way to make in the world, felt the need of a warrior god who would not only fight their battles, but whose leadership would assist in keeping the tribe united, and its morale high.

In Egypt there was duty in your allotted station and obedience to Pharaoh. Beyond this, moral sanctions in Egypt seem shrouded in sinister superstitions; judgment in the underworld before a plethora of gods; interrogation of the soul; weighing the heart in a balance.

Jehovah, in the ancient world, gave his people a comprehensive religion, starting with the Ten Commandments handed down by Moses, which are respected to this day. Around this religion gathered volume on volume of a literature of great beauty.

But Jehovah was implacable to enemies and to the disobedient; dictatorial down to the smallest detail to his people – as to what they might or might not eat, rules for cleansing, keeping fasts or feasts. His religion was savagely exclusive: 'Thou shalt have none other gods but me: I the Lord thy god am a jealous god.'

This exclusiveness belongs rightly to a warrior god, but extends to especial privileges for his people, and racial superiority over others. In the Bible this religion is not ascetic, has concern for the race, but its marriage laws are harsh and strict, and, above all, patriarchal, as witness the volumes of who begat whom, that cover a multitude of pages.

Insistence on obedience is also harsh and repetitive, devoid of compassion. This is the religion that invented the concept of sin, while exhorting the sinner in the tone least likely to bring him to repentance.

Jehovah served well his purpose in supporting and encouraging his people among many trials, not always achieving victory, but ready to blame the sins of his worshippers for their defeats. On the whole this was a good morale-boosting religion in the period and circumstances that created it. That is where it belongs.

Babylon (the Sumerians), as may perhaps be inferred by the amount of abuse heaped on her by her many righteous enemies, comes over as a trifle more lax and tolerant than her contemporaries. Was she not the whore of Babylon, liable to corrupt those who came there? No doubt her citizens were cruel like the rest, but slaves there could own property and buy themselves out; in times of stability, women had some rights. A number of gods answering to many sides of human nature may well be easier to live with, and for, than the one Almighty Dictator who always knows what is best for his recalcitrant children.

Those who served all these old gods, in hopeful mood, saw them as destructive to enemies, but benign to those who bowed down before them. Having attained some degree of security, and first fully tasting the sensual pleasures of life, men simply set out to satisfy and enjoy them: food, drink, sex, luxury of raiment and surroundings. By the use of power such satisfaction could be got irrespective of consequences, or the needs or existence of others. That any human being had 'rights' (in a modern sense) would have astonished these peoples.

Natural empathy for your fellowmen did not die; it survived within family and clan, it began to be hinted at in the visions of the prophets of a new heaven and earth that, under new leadership, might be realised. The tragedy is that, with a very slight shift of emphasis, which was not impossible, these early beginnings could have been very different. As it was, man's first conscious review of the human social condition shaped a class system and very inadequate and dangerous values, casting a mould which was to persist for thousands more years.

CHAPTER 3

Those intellectual Greeks

In the period of history thus far considered there were of course tribes of men and women living according to their own rites, customs and beliefs, in most habitable parts of the world. The first civilisations of the Middle East attracted historians because very many of their records did not perish, were accessible and thus were unearthed and patiently studied with that insatiable curiosity which is the most salient characteristic of the human species. Slowly, by gradual exploration, mankind has been able to fit together the pieces that reveal the puzzle of world history.

For instance, as the small wars of the Sumerian city states broadened out into man's first experiments in imperial conquest, and Cyrus the Persian was at the gates of Babylon, Confucius and Lao Tse are recorded as existing in China, while, in India, Buddha was already teaching. In Italy the story of the Romans was about to begin. Meantime, from about 1500 BC herding tribes of the Hellenes – the Greeks – had been coming down in waves into the Balkan peninsula, spreading out over the islands of the Aegean and into Asia Minor, encroaching on, and possibly helping to destroy, the Cretan civilisation, whose remains have only recently been discovered by modern archaeologists.

The Greek tribes came from what was then probably well-wooded country, but they rapidly became a sea-going people. In those early years they would seem to have had much in common with the Norsemen and Vikings; they were led by brave men of prominent families, who respected valour but did not attach much importance to kingship. They took pleasure in hearing the bards chant or declaim an almost endless saga of their prowess and exploits. The epics of Homer performed for the Greeks what the Icelandic sagas did for Nordic warriors. Chance plays so great a part in what events and ideas survive and are influential in history: it was the Iliad and the Odyssey, rather than the effusions of their Icelandic forefathers, that were to prove the plague of reluctant European schoolboys. What mattered to European and indeed world history was what the Hellenic tribes became as they settled down into city life, and into what channels they directed their conscious thought.

In the Homeric epics the Greeks appear as a people engaged in tribal warfare in which their gods intervene just like other human beings, but with exceptional powers, bestowing their aid on their favourites among prominent warriors. In this aspect of the Greek gods, Odin, Wotan, Thor, Freya and Beltane the smith would have been quite at home among Zeus, Hera, Apollo, Demeter, Athena and Hephaestus. Celebrating the heroic age, Homer is but little concerned with the origin of these gods, or indeed with the creation of the universe in which they play so active a part. There is no divine all-powerful being up above, directing and instructing one favourite belligerent united nation. Nor are there effigies of gods, resplendent in sheaf of gold and jewelled raiment to be carried by a priesthood in victory or defeat.

Replacing these is a vast Greek mythology with an assortment of gods and goddesses; from their serene life nourished by nectar and ambrosia on Olympus, to their every whim, contact and involvement with (and expressive of) mortal desires, lusts, and dreams, gods who have filled whole libraries of volumes, inspired literally countless exquisite vases, statues, and paintings not only in Greece but in most civilised countries; pervaded the imagination of poets and children of all ages, avid for tales of marvels, fabulous monsters, heroic deeds and the hazards of lovers. The fertile imagination of the Greeks fertilised, in its turn, the imagination of Europe.

Homer's epics accompanied the Greeks on their conquests as they moved southwards to their Aegean home. The poems were not written down until much later. Probably 700 or 600 BC. From that century also dates the oldest Greek account of the origin of the gods themselves as also of the universe, Hesiod's poem *Theogony*. Everything starts from chaos, which here means empty space, vast and deep and dark: then appears Gaea 'the deep-breasted mother' – earth, ultimate source of all creation; next comes Eros, not here the god of love, but a metaphysical force of attraction that enables things to come together and take shape. Out of chaos come Erebos and Night; from them Ether and Hemera the day; whilst Gaea creates Uranus the sky, crowned with stars 'whom she made her equal in grandeur so that he might entirely cover her'.

There follows the birth or creation of the endless multitude of inhabitants of the immense Pantheon of Greek mythology, whose names, functions, stories will be familiar to so many Western peoples; the Titans, the Cyclops, the giants, Cronus who devoured his children; the Fates, Prometheus, Pandora and all the rest. These legendary figures offer a whole country of fantasy in which to roam at will and there find whatever thought or emotion may fit the passing whim, or no matter what human predicament.

As to man's arrival on the scene, one legend has it that he was drawn by Gaea out of her own bosom; in another, which, however, seems to relate to the renewal of mankind after the great Flood – (appearing here as in the Babylonian and Jewish story) – Prometheus, with earth and water – or his own tears – fashions the body into which Athene breathes soul and life. Prometheus, credited with stealing fire from the gods, seems to lead an ambivalent existence between the gods and loyalty to men.

Hesiod relates four ages of mankind: the Golden, like the Garden of Eden, in which men, though not immortal, were happy and well provided; the Silver in which men became effeminate, practised agriculture and obeyed their mothers; the Bronze, when they revived to become foulmouthed, and pitiless in war, but skilful in the discovery and use of metals. After the Bronze age, Hesiod writes of a period when the heroes fought before Troy. Thereafter, it would seem, came the contemporary scene of degeneracy, when men cared neither for justice nor morality – in fact the Iron Age.

This cosmogony comes from a people who, at heart, cared more for the pageant and tumult of life on this earth than for whatever might be going on in the heavens, or even for how the earth and the heavens came into being. There must have been interaction with the mythology and civilisation of Knossos and Crete, which I surmise to have been pacific, as well as artistic, which latter its remains have amply proved.

The Cretans worshipped the earth mother, although like other peoples, they also revered the bull as a symbol of strength and virility.

There is an almost prophetic vision in the poet Hesiod's Ages of Man. Apart from the idyllic golden period, one might read into it the stages of the development of all mankind on this earth. From hunter and herdsman, man settles down to a period of peacefully cultivating the soil and revering the feminine attributes of fertility. A sense of masculine power and domination revives as he discovers, manipulates and uses metals for peace and war, and the iron of the industrial way of life enters his soul.

Helen of Troy, the war of the Greeks and the Trojans, the voyages of Odysseus, Penelope and her suitors, survive in the poems of Homer, but of Knossos and Crete, which must have been a very beautiful civilisation, we get only glimpses, such as the tales of Theseus, Ariadne and the Minotaur. All this, what may be called a first Ancient Greece, was past and gone by the time of the Ancient Greece of historical record, when Athens, Sparta, Corinth, Samos, Miletus, were the significant towns and places of the story.

The Greek tribes settled down in their own special areas, islands, or city plus cultivated land; each city state with its own type of government, not large, for the most part not more than 50,000 inhabitants. Athens, the largest city, reached perhaps at its highest about 300,000. These were the settlements of a restless and roving people, not the slow growth of a static soil-rooted peasantry, with a dominant priesthood. There were still plenty of superstitions, with temples and oracles attended by priests or priestesses, and religions, but not an official one. The city states did not fuse into a nation or unite unless against a common enemy. Nor did they focus their worship upon one superior chosen god, unless it were Athene, sprung from the head of Zeus, helmeted and armed, patron of her immortal city and the temples built for her in her rightful place, on the commanding heights.

Athene is credited with so many exploits and qualities that it is difficult to define her special significance. As Zeus' favourite daughter, she did whatever she pleased. Honoured first as a warrior, she fought for the Greeks before Troy; like many of the gods, she was jealous and vengeful. She presided over the building of the ship *Argo* which was to take the Argonauts on the quest for the Golden Fleece. Concerned also with the arts of peace, and patron of sculptors and architects, she is credited with the invention of the potter's wheel, the making of the first fine vases and with teaching women the domestic arts. But she was not susceptible to specific feminine emotions, defending her chastity savagely against potential lovers. Except that she seems to have encouraged olive trees to bear fruit, fertility had little interest for her. She had wisdom; is described as Pronoia the foreseeing; Boulaia the counsellor; and Agoraia, goddess of the Agora, that place in which the Greeks assembled to make their famous speeches. Her emblem was the owl.

Those who honour and study the Greeks would therefore seem to be justified in taking Athene as a symbol of the intellect, not the intellect in quiescent contemplation, but active and challenging, making war on ignorance, stupidity and muddled thinking, in a search for clarity of thought and pursuing enquiries into the realities of the external world, as also the nature of the enquirer, man himself.

There came into being with Greek thought a new use of the aspect of the conscious mind that was distinct from the mysticism of religion, or the dogmas of the priests; this was – philosophy – the love of wisdom, the quest for knowledge, for no other purpose than simply to know.

The Greeks fought many wars on land and sea; they built fleets of magnificent ships to keep contact with their scattered island allies; they even held at bay and then defeated the Persians; their real-life heroes set famous examples of self-sacrifice in wars in defence of home, country and ideals rather than conquest and booty; but nothing that they ever did eclipses the splendour of that brief period in their story when they set the human intellect free to rove and speculate at will over everybody and everything under the sun that they might deem worthy of their attention.

War between sections of man's own species had already long been acceptable. The glorification in the history books of Greek heroism now added a new ethical sanction to wars of national defence. Very many centuries must pass before any notion of abolishing wars between nations began to dawn. The liberated intellect, together with all that it came to imply in man's quest for personal freedom and demand for human rights, sped on its sorely beleaguered path through space and time. But it, too, was to discover within itself seeds of ambivalence.

While each Greek state preserved its independence, the states did associate together for other purposes than defence in war. They came to value the human body not solely in military terms, for sexual potency, or sheer strength, but, whether male or female, for its beauty, style and grace. They instituted the Olympic games, in which they came together for honourable competition in strength, speed and skill, for which the only reward was to be crowned with a wreath of laurel. There is no need to stress what came to be called the classical beauty of their sculptures, of both men and women, embodying their ideal and, as for instance in the Muses, symbols of their culture.

Posterity has reason to be grateful for another expression of their artistic achievement, a beautiful literary language, evolved or shaped over and above varied dialects, which enabled the young Greeks to learn the epics of Homer, their poets to make poems, their great dramatists, Aeschylus, Sophocles, Euripides and the satirical Aristophanes to write plays; their first ever truly literary and poetic historian Herodotus to produce his fascinating and invaluable account of his travels and his times. The Athenians listened with pleasure to Herodotus reading; they had festivals for competition in the performance of poetry and drama.

Language spoken and written evolves wherever there are people; the Greeks gave both to language and numbers a new meaning and dimension. The first use of language had been simply to name a concrete object: a noun. It passes on, as everyone who still studies grammar knows, to adjectives which qualify, verbs which describe action. Plurals and counting are not easy for a primitive mind: a tree, a tall tree, three trees; but many trees must be counted or a new word found, wood, or forest. This is a very elementary observation, but it spells the transition from concrete to abstract thought, from the particular to the general, and thence to the definition of classes. A tree, a tall tree, three trees, a wood, trees as a species. Beyond this the intellect, thinking purely in concepts or numbers, is removed entirely from the organic or concrete world, even outside time and space. Deriving ultimately from practical geometry, this is the domain of mathematics, in which the Greeks not only excelled but were prime creators and innovators.

Later on mathematicians created their own language of symbols; their work became of vital importance to the sciences. But mathematics remains unintelligible to any who lack the capacity for the special type of intense concentration that it demands. All departments of academic study, such as law, medicine, psychology, tend to create their own appropriate abstruse language, thus multiplying the categories of élite bodies or persons. Of course our own language, or any language used for such studies, is full of the new words, coined by the Greeks to make clear the content of their thought, the meaning of the questions they were asking, and the topics they discussed: philosophy, physics, metaphysics, ethics, politics, democracy – our vocabulary, our dictionaries are stuffed with them; the very word 'idea' was invented by Plato.

For their part the Greeks, in their day, playing with these new words and definitions, puzzling over the odd conclusions that may be reached by pure deduction and the peculiar irrationality of some numbers, were experiencing that first joyous flight above the pleasures of the senses into the intoxicating pleasures of the mind.

Logic is the art of deductive reasoning, learning how not to talk irrelevant nonsense, but to estimate correctly what (logically) follows on a statement or event. When it comes to talking about the true nature of man or what the earth is made of, objective events and facts themselves come into the picture, hence the empirical philosopher, and what is called the inductive method, practised in the early stages of science. The intellect collects information provided by the senses on things or events deemed to be objectively real; from these general conclusions are formed. The next task is to collect ever more information, compare and contrast, try to establish an impartial picture of what really is the natural world.

Those almost incredible Greeks, though their chief contribution was the deductive method of reasoning, already, in their theorising, sowed the seeds of most of the basic modern sciences: Pythagoras (532 BC) founded mathematics; Thales (585 BC), Anaximander (546 BC), Anaximines (before 494 BC) wanted to know what the earth is made of; Democritus (420 BC) and Epicurus (b. 342 BC) said it was made of atoms; Aristarchus of Samos (310–230 BC) (see Heath, 1913) actually antedated the Copernican theory by stating that the earth and planets revolved round a stationary sun; Aristotle (b. 384 BC) conceived the idea of the collection of scientific knowledge and facts: With a grant from Alexander the Great of Macedon he had at one time a thousand men scattered through Asia and Greece collecting material for his natural history of the world.*

Although Athens was to become the centre of the arts, culture and civilised living, famous because of Socrates and the founding of the Academy where brilliant men congregated and Plato taught, and for the Lyceum where, after Plato's death, Aristotle set up a school, it was not, in fact, the real cradle of Greek philosophy and scientific thought.

In Asia Minor and the scattered Aegean islands, cities and citizens became prosperous through an ever-growing volume of trade. Here were Greeks, living and travelling within what was still the Persian empire, which by 521 BC under Darius the Mede, successor of the son of Cyrus, stretched from the borders of India over what had been Babylon, Egypt, Asia Minor, even into part of mainland Greece. Many of the Greeks were paid, persuaded or dragooned into the Persian armies; others fled from place to place to escape scenes of conflict. The Persians, however, allowed much local autonomy, and ruled by payment of tribute; communication by land and sea was good and therefore helpful to the spread of information and knowledge.

* H. G. Wells, *The Outline of History*, p. 177, remarks that not for 2,000 years were grants for scientific research again available.

The Ionian Greeks in Miletus (Asia Minor) seem to have been especially lively; they were at first allies of the Persians but also rebelled against Darius. Thales, a native of Miletus, visited Egypt; he predicted an eclipse that must have happened in 585 BC. He might conceivably have met with some of the Jews who had fled to Egypt from Nebuchadnezzar, but, like other Greeks, he did not agree with them that the world was created out of nothing. He thought the primal substance was water. Anaximander, another native of Miletus, held that there was a primal substance, not any of the known substances, but infinite, eternal and ageless, encompassing all the worlds of which our world is only one. This substance is transformed into the substances which we know, and these into one another. He says:

> Into that from which things take their rise they pass away once more, as is ordained, for they make reparation and satisfaction to one another for their injustice according to the ordering of time. (Russell, 1946, p. 45)

Justice in this sense probably meant to the Greeks a natural law of balance between the various elements, such as fire, earth, water: if one element were 'primal' it would conquer the others. The primal substance, basis of all others, must therefore be neutral.

Anaximander also held that living creatures had evolved from the moist element as it was evaporated by the sun. And man must have come from other animals because, otherwise, with his long infancy, he could not have survived in his present form.

Anaximenes, the third of the Milesians, is interesting in his theory that the soul is air; fire rarefied air, and that air can condense into water, and further, into earth or stone. 'The speculations of these Milesians', Russell says, 'are to be regarded as scientific hypotheses and seldom show any undue intrusion of anthromorphic desires and moral ideas. The questions they asked are good questions' (ibid., p. 47).

Owing to a revolt of the Ionian Greeks, the city of Miletus was destroyed by the Persians in 494 BC. Four years later Darius was checked in his attempt at mainland Greece by the lone stand of the Athenians at Marathon.

The Island of Samos, just off the coast of Asia Minor, was about 535 BC ruled by Polycrates, a typical 'tyrant', the name given by the Greeks to men who, by means of wealth, from time to time acquired, and used, military and naval power. Polycrates, playing politics ruthlessly to keep the island for himself and out of the clutches of the Persians, allied himself with Egypt. His fame in history rests on the story that, boasting one day to Amasis, King of Egypt, of his power and consequent happiness, he tempted fate by throwing his ring into the sea. The gods retorted by returning the ring in the body of a fish, a bad omen tragically fulfilled when Polycrates was caught by a Persian trick and put to death. Polycrates had, however, been a patron of men of intelligence and imagination; Anacreon was his court poet.

Pythagoras, son, it is said, of a well-to-do citizen, was born in Samos, and was active there about 532 BC, presumably immersed in proving that the sum of the squares on two sides of a right-angled triangle is equal to the square on the third – the hypotenuse – a feat which earned for him undying fame and the title of the Founder of all Mathematics. No doubt Pythagoras found that life under Polycrates was not conducive to such intellectual efforts. He was also of a mystical turn of mind, and probably had some contact with Egyptian thought, in which sun worship and the immortality of the soul were upheld. He moved to Croton in Southern Italy and thence to other places in order to found communities with sympathisers and disciples.

The atmosphere in which Greek intellectuals somehow managed to survive and think coherently is well illustrated by these events in Miletus and Samos. Another example is Herodotus, who was born not far from Miletus, in Halicarnassus, Asia Minor, under the Persians, in 484 BC, that is, between the Persian repulse at Marathon (490) and the destruction of Athens by Xerxes, followed by his defeat at the great sea battle of Salamis (480). By the time Herodotus was forty-six years old, he had travelled in Egypt, Babylon, indeed all the world accessible to him, and arrived in a rebuilt Athens, to tell the tale of all that his people and he himself had achieved.

The most publicised names in Greek philosophy are those of Socrates, Aristotle and Plato.

In the year 438 BC when Herodotus came to Athens, neither Plato nor Aristotle had yet been born, though it is probable that Socrates was already stirring up discussion among the young. And Socrates was not strictly a philosopher. The first man who introduced philosophy to the Athenians, and lived and worked in Athens, was Anaxagoras, who came from Miletus and was of the Milesian rational way of thinking. He was sceptical as to the existence of gods, saying that mind, 'nous', was the source of life and motion and the sun a ball of fire. He was one of the circle of varied talents encouraged by Pericles. Plato, who was born in 427 BC and lived for 80 years, and Aristotle, who lived from 384 BC to 322, were rather followers and developers than originators. Socrates' date of birth is uncertain, but his trial and death took place in 399 BC. These dates are important because of the influence exercised by the changing fortunes of their country on the lives and thought of these men.

It is usually said that the Athenian victory over the Persians gave them a feeling of power and self-confidence which stimulated their subsequent artistic and intellectual achievement. On the contrary, the sense of triumph that follows victory in war is repressive rather than creative. The climate favourable to creative activity in the arts and sciences is relief from fear, a stable and relatively peaceful period, when a man is no longer obliged, at any moment, to reach for his sword to repulse a marauding enemy. It was some years after the first flush of victory that the Athenians had such a time. In spite of their reputation for heroism, war was not the métier of the Greeks, nor indeed should it be the métier of any people. It was, to a large extent, the métier of the Romans, who much later on, absorbed Greece into their empire, absorbing at the same time Greek culture and Greek gods. At peace, the Greeks turned their ever-active minds to the techniques of tolerant social living, and evolved the first concept of democracy. Government of the city state by all true-born Athenians was, it is true, exclusive of strangers and did not depart from the long-accepted practice of slavery, provided it was not applied to true-born Greeks.

Slaves are, after all, the spoils of war and slavery is power over people. Pride in the power to rule men was certainly among the motives of the Athenians as they extended their commercial and naval strength in the Aegean. Like any other fighting men of their time, they were capable of brutal slaughter of their enemies. But, as their fate in the international power struggle shows, imperialist ambition was no more than a minor trait in their character. Of far greater interest to them were individual personal lives and fortunes and the discussion of ideas.

In truth these people live forever in history as the superb example of the finest and purest use of power by individuals or a community – human and artistic creation – the hand of the sculptor on the marble; or of the architect and builders on the temples; the force of great poetic drama and its performance arousing emotional participation from thousands of spectators; the persuasion of men, not by violence, but by the voice, eloquence and sincerity of orators. In that small country of no more than a few hundreds of thousands of people, and out of the fertile genius of a mere handful among them, a whole new way of life and thought was born.

Pericles, whose personality inspired and presided over this glorious period of Greek history, was chosen by his people as leader about 466 BC, thirteen years after the end of the Persian war. As a young man, he apparently became the classic figure of dignity, beauty and grace, and a cultivated mind, which was the Greek ideal. His vision and encouragement of sculptors and architects rebuilt the city, on which he was accused of spending too much of the spoils of victory. He was, in fact, scrupulous over money and did not even enrich himself, remaining a relatively poor man. His devotion to Aspasia, outside the accepted shape of Greek marriage, is one of the legendary love stories of history. According to laws which he had had a part in making, they could not marry, since she came from Miletus and was not a true-born Athenian.

They were the centre of a circle of fellow intellectuals, who lived in comparative comfort and leisure and must have discussed all topics of the day, among these sex, and scepticism about oracles and traditional religions. They are somehow akin to the post-war questioning engaged in and enjoyed by our own Bloomsbury intellectuals in England, whose impression on our culture still persists! Pericles and his friends were not typical of the average Athenians of the 'establishment' of their day, among whom it was proper still to render honour and ritual service to the gods and women were restricted to home and domestic duties.

The unorthodox citizen risked accusations of 'impiety', which would lead to 'ostracism', which meant exile. In spite of his prestige and position, Pericles was harassed and attacked through those who were his friends or protégés. Among these Anaxagoras, whose theories interested him, was forced to return to Miletus; Phidias the sculptor was imprisoned on a pretext of theft of gold meant for his work; Aspasia was threatened with exile and defended by the proud Pericles in tears.

Peace under Pericles lasted no more than thirty-five years. The next seventeen years, from 431 BC Sparta and Athens waged an idiotic fratricidal war, which ended in disastrous defeat for the Athenians. On a small scale, it was more like a war between two counties. From their city walls, the Athenians could see the flames as the Spartans raided and set fire to their farms in Attica. With what seems to be the invariable habit of democracies, Pericles' fellow-citizens continued their campaign of envy and denigration of their leader. They relieved him of his command. Perhaps Pericles himself, disillusioned by the ingratitude of the people of the city he loved so well, and to which he had brought a splendid dignity, beauty and some wisdom, no longer had much heart for war. Athens was short of food; plague struck and killed Pericles' two sons and then Pericles himself in 428 BC.

Something must be said here about the very male Greek attitude to sex, family life and their ambivalent view of women. In this, as in most things, their frankness is refreshing. Their code of love and sex relations between men and adolescent boys scarcely needs mention; it was part of training and comradeship in battle. As to women, to be honoured, they should be the least-spoken-of, respectable wives and mothers. Social life between men and women, as in Pericles' circle, was not good morals. No attempt was made to bring women into the intellectual discussions or to allow them to take part in the public assembly. Consequently, while men transferred their allegiance from the earth mother Gaea to childless Athene, women remained very much under the influence of oracles, omens, superstitions and magic. Not for nothing did Pythagoras say that women were more pious than men, a common male wish-fulfilment. Women functioned at temples and shrines of oracles; they took part in certain festivals. Little is heard of women's intellectual achievements, apart from the fame of Sappho as a poetess. But women had no position of power.

Within the home, when not actually giving birth to the warriors required of them, women, tended by female slaves, must have felt a monotony of idleness. Aristotle complained of the luxury indulged in by rich, lazy married women in Sparta – a great contrast apparently to the severe upbringing of some of their daughters, who were trained naked in athletics side by side with their brothers.

What did the women of that time think about, secluded and leisured in their homes, while the men were at war, or talked philosophy and politics in the Agora and the streets of Athens? As usual, it is men's picture of women that we get. But this must not be neglected, for of this there is no lack in quantity or variety. The marble figures of women as muses and goddesses still stand there in Athens; the Winged Victory is a woman; women of powerful personality step out of the pages of the Greek dramatists: Antigone, Alcestis, Hecuba, Electra, Clytemnestra, Medea. They are not presented as docile or feeble, but simply as human beings who, like men, are as capable of savage and murderous rage as of passionate love. Note too, by the way, that, as the women in the Babylonian story weep for the death of the beloved Shepherd, Athenian women wept for Adonis. In Babylon too, they knew that women might soften the heart of warriors, or stir men to primitive savagery.

What, then, do men and women do or say about their children? Nowhere so far is there expression of concern about the young, not in the Old Testament, nor, so far as I know, in other ancient records. In war they died or went with their mothers into slavery; in Carthage they were sacrificed to the gods; in Greece, as also in Rome, the unwanted babies were simply exposed on the bare hillside to die or be devoured by animals or birds of prey. Whether this was a remedy for over-population or simply to avoid the trouble of bringing them up, one cannot say. At times, of course, a child who might bring danger to some powerful man when it grew up was deliberately exposed. It is clear that no one, unless it were the mothers, set any value on young lives, and mothers had next to no power over their destiny.

In Greek drama, finally, Euripides shows compassion at the sufferings of women and children and at least attempts, in the *Trojan Women, Medea, Alcestic,* to show what have been their feelings at the wanton waste, whether in babyhood, or as adults in war, of human material, to produce which, for men's use, was apparently the sole purpose of women's existence. Nor does Euripides neglect to notice the self-love and callousness of husbands and fathers. Even Aristophanes in *Lysistrata* shows women on strike against war by refusing to sleep with their husbands, but driven to capitulate by the power of sex.

It is tragic that, when their dramatists could portray so powerfully the passionate realities of the relation between men and women, the men of their time, because of their obsession with their own sex in war and comradeship, were unable to create harmony of life and purpose with their women. Given a longer period of peace this might have happened.

As it was, Greek men had to fight to preserve their liberty, relying only on themselves, or uncertain allies, and gods who were no more than outsize humans. Nor did any Greek, to his credit, want to be a god. Sparta had kings, but the democratic men of Athens had only to see a 'tyrant' rise above the horizon, to conspire in order to bring him down.

They played out their lives like their own dramas, in a theatre in which implacable destiny or fate directed the moves of gods, men and women, bestowing reward or retribution according to their deserts.

What a man's conduct might deserve was one of the riddles, rejecting authority, they sought on their own initiative to solve. Socrates, who was the son of the local stone mason and had also been in the Persian war, was ready to help. He was uncouth and rather ugly, but he had a way of stimulating a young man's talent and thought. He hated humbug, believed in human nature, that men did not knowingly do wrong; knowledge was what mattered. No suggestion of original sin appears in his teaching.

From the time of Pericles, Socrates had freedom to teach and was an important influence. Some of his pupils tended to convert free argument into cynicism. His trial for subverting the young came after Sparta had defeated Athens, a period of repression, when oligarchy was imposed by Sparta, but resisted. Plato, then 28 years old, was present at the trial. His account of Socrates' defence has been an inspiration to all kinds of people throughout history, because Socrates died for what he believed in. He could have accepted exile, but preferred to die by the condemnation of the judges of his own people, even though, these judges, among whom were some of his ex-pupils, were condemned by him.

The lives and works of Aristotle and Plato prove how closely in the Greek mind philosophy was related to practical action. This must be regarded as a new departure, one aspect of democracy, in that authority and morality no longer rested on edicts of gods, but must be evolved and administered by human beings. This is, in effect, what is now called humanism. Democratic government, as understood in Athens, was not delegated, but direct. All men classified as true-born Athenians, but no women, took part. The human face, as well as the limits of such government, is illustrated by Plato's observation that a city or region should not comprise more than 1,000–5,000 persons. Aristotle, in his *Politics*, on justice says:

> For the proper administration of justice and for the distribution of Authority it is necessary that the citizens be acquainted with each other's characters, so that, where this cannot be, much mischief ensues, both in the use of authority and in the administration of justice; for it is not just to decide arbitrarily, as must be the case with excessive population.

This insistence on individual character and human contact, this refusal to 'think big', left the Greeks temperamentally defenceless among the ravening imperialists of their day. It also led to some defects of character, in that an ambitious

Greek, such as Alcibiades, would play politics for his own hand.

Aristotle, born in the North in Thrace, came, when he was 18, to Plato's Academy in Athens, where he studied until the death of Plato in 348–7 BC. Through his father, who was physician to Philip, king of Macedon, Aristotle became closely associated with Philip, who was a man of foresight, deeply impressed with the new ways of thinking, and concerned with plans for good government. In 343 BC he appointed Aristotle tutor to his son Alexander, then aged 13; but discharged him only three years later, having judged his son to be fit for adult responsibility, which, when Philip was assassinated at 45, in his prime, fell entirely on the shoulders of Alexander, then only 20.

Throughout the meteoric career of one who became Alexander the Great, conquered all the world he knew, got himself made a god in Egypt, and died after a drinking bout in Babylon, his tutor Aristotle, who had returned to Athens, remained there peaceably teaching and writing his books until that fatal end of his ex-pupil in 323 BC. Then, as had happened when Sparta defeated Athens, with the result that freedom of thought was under attack, and Socrates brought to trial, so now, in Athens, in reverse, the Greek passion for liberty revived and any persons associated with Alexander, who was, after all, a Macedonian imperialist, came under threat. Facing Socrates' choice between death and exile, Aristotle, apostle of the golden mean in life, took the prudent course. He left Athens, but a year later he died.

Though the Greeks had played fast and loose about support of Alexander, and the lack of stability of purpose in Alexander himself, as well as the inability of the various states to combine, caused the loss of what might have been a far-reaching Hellenic civilisation, Greek ideas did spread and many able and learned Greeks found a home in the town Alexandria, built by the young conqueror in Egypt. Euclid was living there in 300 BC.

Historians have attributed Alexander's erratic and wild temperament to his mother Olympias, who was not only brutally savage and jealous, but imbued with the superstitions and orgiastic rites of some of the cults that flourished, such as that of Dionysus. If that were so, then it was a penalty paid by the men of the time for their failure to educate and admit the female sex to the domain of rational thought by which their male consorts were then trying to live. In the struggle for power most men themselves were still irrational and cruel and did not live up to their new ideals. It may be that, with the usual practice of always blaming the woman, Olympias' character has been maligned.

Aristotle was a born academic professor, to whom his contemporaries and posterity owe his systematic attempt to assess, clarify and pigeon-hole the achievements of his predecessors. His own books cover metaphysics, ethics, politics, logic, physics, an extensive grounding in philosophy for all-comers. It is said that he nowhere mentions his distinguished pupil. Perhaps that is not surprising.

The impact and subsequent influence of the mind of Plato is more significant. When he was born, a year after the death of Pericles and the historian Herodotus, the glory of the great period was not yet lost, though Sparta and Athens were already at war. After the crushing defeat of Athens, the young Plato had seen Socrates condemned by some who, like himself, had been the disciples of a teacher whom they revered. Plato, belonging to one of the more influential and wealthy families, was somewhat dubious about the efficiency of free-for-all democracy, since the more highly disciplined Spartans had won the war. Herein must have been material for conflict in his mind. He lived on to the age of 80, holding seminars and writing, closely associated with Aristotle, and with access to practically all of the new Greek thought. Did he, in his old age, change his views and resolve this conflict, which was already apparent in Greek philosophy itself? Like all men, they wanted to understand the universe, to know what their earth and even the heavenly bodies were made of and what was the capricious force that rebuked what they called 'hubris' – that touch of arrogance in man. At the same time they wanted to find out the right way for men to behave to one another. They began to seek some way of bringing these two quests into harmony, a search which still goes on; as Milton says, 'to justify the ways of god to men'.

Studying their world, they could not bring themselves to

dissociate their wishes from their conclusions, they wanted what was good to be true, what was true to be good, and, over it all, a helpful bonus that everything could also be beautiful. This has become the essence of what the average person associates with Plato: the Absolute in a trinity, Goodness, Beauty and Truth.

Neither the conscious thinking of Plato nor of the Greeks stems from the Absolute. They *began* with reason and mathematics. For Plato, in a world made of fire, water, earth and air, each of these four elements was composed of atoms, of geometrical shape: the earth atoms are cubes; fire atoms tetrahedra; air octohedra; water, icosohedra (Russell, 1946, p. 169. These shapes are perhaps not so odd when one thinks of the shapes of crystals.). Plato's Republic, the very first concept of a Utopia, the first realisation that men need not depend on haphazard biological grouping, but could shape their own society, is, in effect, a pure intellectual concoction, a planner's paradise. Philosopher guardians, suggested by the Spartan system, make all the rules. Romantic people like poets are excluded; only certain kinds of music permitted. Citizens belong to the state, have a tough upbringing, in total ignorance of who are their fathers and mothers. Some persons are obviously superior to others in quality or ability and will be placed accordingly. But the populace as a whole will be taught and persuaded to believe that the system is democratic. A perfect pattern for totalitarianism.

Plato was intoxicated with what, in one sense, is the true outcome of mathematical thought, the idea of perfection. He distrusted empiricism, the evidence of the senses, as giving a distorted view of reality. Looking at a cat, and thinking of the whole genus of cats – a 'universal' concept – he postulated a vision of a perfect prototype of a cat, the 'idea' of a cat to which all cats might approximate. This obviously applied to everything, not only cats. By this sort of reasoning perfection became identified with reality, an ideal world of reality reached only in the mind, outside of the senses.

Here he missed the turning signposted for him by the pure intellect, which would have led to the methods of science. Scientific investigation must perforce disregard human wishes, moral and aesthetic values, in pursuit of objective truth, which is the 'reality' of science. Pursuing the 'ideal' or 'ideas' as abstract entities, Plato seems to have missed the point that human aspirations for the ideal spring from feelings in the body, rather than the mind. In planning his republic, he ignores or overrides the biological family impulses basic to human association. He must concern himself not with what life and the world are, but what men, especially philosophers, would like them to be. So he takes the other turning and joins the Pythagoreans and all others who conceive of an eternal world, which the soul of man may reach the further he removes himself from his body, and in which, after death, his soul will find immortality. In that eternity may reside the mysterious power governing and determining the destiny of all things created: a world belonging to god.

By the sheer power of deductive reasoning men had created for themselves a fascinating region of intense mental activity. Was not mathematics a blessed refuge for men surrounded by the tragic turmoil of war? That they had a dream of final escape from the agony and contradictions of human existence is not surprising. Unhappily, perhaps under the pressure of failure, and through Plato, they seem to have departed from the self-confidence and clarity, and exact application of the intellect which was their great gift to civilised thought. In this departure, though they did not perceive it, they in the end did no more than create a new shape for an old myth.

In the years immediately following Plato, his thought was taken up by philosophers and played its part in shaping Christian theology.

The Greeks had achieved so much in expanding conscious thought. They had begun to see that gods are made by man and that he could do without them. Although they based their way of life on slavery, they also perceived that human relations could not rest only on the power of the strong to rule over all others. They were aware of how love can bring to sex something more than procreation.

They had in very truth a vision of how men might live with pride, dignity and social grace on this earth. The birth of Jesus Christ, which founded a new religion, extinguished the light of their vision for fifteen hundred years.

Gods versus kings or power: temporal and spiritual

While the Greeks had been defending themselves against the Persians and Alexander achieving his lightning conquests, a new power, the Romans, had been expanding in the West. Though they established an elaborate legal system and created their city life, the Romans were neither intellectual nor humane. They learned about democratic government from the example of the Greeks and established their senate. Greek gods and goddesses appeared under Latin names, Roman architecture followed the Greek style. Nor were they drawn to the kind of mysticism that affected the people in Egypt and the Far East. The Roman type of intelligence was rather that of the organiser; or man the tool-maker. Romans are famous, of course, for their road-making, water conduits and the designing and heating of their homes for comfort and convenience. Above all, they were military men and in the end the love of power and glory set them on the road to empire.

An attempt was made to placate the Plebeians by installing tribunes, but in the end democracy was lost in the internal struggle for despotic power and the imperial crown, in the course of which Julius Caesar was assassinated.

The Emperor Augustus (30 BC–AD 14), heir and adopted son of Julius Caesar, brought about a time of peace and calm and was revered by his people as a god. From then onwards there seems to have been hardly one Roman emperor who did not aspire to divine status. The Romans had slaves; the famous Spartacus revolt of the slaves was brutally suppressed, as, more than once, were rebellions of conquered peoples.

In the patrician classes, women had a position of dignity not previously accorded. But marriages were very much a matter of bargains and arrangements between influential families. Nor did women fail to learn from, and take advantage of, their men's political intrigues and tactics. It was said of Julius Caesar that, when he wanted to discover the plans of his enemies, he would get on sleeping terms with their wives. He will not have been the only one, male or female, to use sex as a means to personal and political power. The decadence of the Roman Empire is not edifying in what it reveals of the sheer cruelty and vileness of which human beings of both sexes are capable. The Pax Romana is said to have been a benefit to those subject nations on which it was imposed. As to that, I have my doubts. Aristotle and Plato, with their concern for the character of individuals and a reasonable size for states, would not have approved of it. Yet, for at least two hundred years, those who submitted to, or were held down by, the Romans did have peace and security. But the emphasis on the military type of organisation, treating people like things or numbers, assessed by quantity rather than quality, resembled the Egyptian pyramidal society, mechanical, though strictly not machine-made.

In assessing the direction and expansion of man's conscious thinking, I have not so far taken into account the meditation and mysticism of the religions, or religious temperaments of the Far East. This is because I am not concerned here with all expressions of consciousness, but mainly with the type of thought that led up to the creation of machine civilisation. This type of thought is not characteristic of early thinking in the Far East, in China, or India, although the tremendous researches of Professor Joseph Needham and his colleagues have recently shown that there was more aptitude for science in China than superior minds in Europe have admitted as possible. Roman engineering and technical advance led the way, as did the Roman habit of dealing with populations, rather than people. But the mathematical intellect was a critical and indispensable element in the machine's creation.

It is a long journey from primitive peoples 'thinking in pictures' to the precision of mathematical concepts. I have tried to indicate the stages of this advance, through the use of words in speech and writing, and then through the measurement of space and experimenting with numbers. But just why did Plato and his followers apparently turn to the pursuit of the Good rather than the True?

There were, perhaps, two main reasons. The young male who 'thought in pictures' sought power over his surroundings, at first through fear. Next, like every young child ever born, he saw no reason why he should not do, take, or grasp whatsoever his desires moved him to do, take, or grasp. Experience taught him both the exercise and then the limits of his power. It taught him to submit to the strong, rule or destroy the weak, and, presently, to accept rough rules of justice arising out of social life. Morality rested in his gods, who were really quite simply the expression of his powers, hopes and aspirations, or the basic needs of his tribe. Reasoning, intellect, this new aspect of conscious thought, had looked at the character of individual man himself. It had made him aware of his own identity, as a person who both thought, *and* acted on impulse. Was he not personally responsible for his actions and what went on in his part of the world? This was a very hard notion to accept (as it still is) amidst the violence of power rivalries and war. Obviously, in that hard school, a man must learn certain virtues, such as courage and loyalty to comrades, though even that had its limits.

Over and above the need for food, and shaping the necessary tools, the human imagination had always afforded strange dreams of splendid or monstrous beings or events. But this world of numbers was something different; it was serene, perfect, above the urgent pressure of desires and rivalries, the trials and tribulations of this mortal life. Moreover, it was not just a dream; the calculations worked; it seemed real. In some way, too, through astronomical studies, the concepts of this new world seemed to be linked with the heavenly bodies and the stars.

What then was more natural than to accept that this was the ultimate eternal reality, the home of god, an all-powerful spirit ruling and maintaining all, a home that might also be the resting place for the troubled soul after death, or even, by spiritual communion, during mortal life? The mystics of the Far East, who had created many fantasy gods, also came upon this concept of an ultimate eternal reality. The disciples of

Buddha sat in complete stillness for meditation, so that they might attain contact with this world soul or eternity, Nirvana, into which the human soul could 'slip like the dewdrop into the shining sea'. The transmigration of souls was even a part of the mystical side of the teaching of Pythagoras, while he also taught that the world was made of numbers.

Mystical contemplation had one thing in common with the practice of mathematics. It existed outside of, and had nothing to do with, the impulses and desires of the body, or sense perception. Philosophers coined for it the term 'a priori' in contrast to 'a posteriori' or empirical judgment. It became the pride, indeed the whole essence of being, defining what was human, to live within the soul, spirit, reason, intellect, imagination, by whatever name, so long as it was outside of and rose superior to the desires and functions of the body. Plainly, if he so decided, this might serve as a definition of the soul or essence of man, but hardly that of the essence of woman.

Unhappily, the one essential unique characteristic of the mathematical intellect was not perceived. The exercise of that intellect in its own sphere of calculations might inspire in a man the pure concept of perfection, and lift him into a state of contemplation above the body and outside of space and time; but this was an ecstasy of reason, in the quest for truth, not a mystical aspiration for unity with a world soul. It had, strictly, no part in morals, in human assessments of right and wrong, or in any way with the human longing for security and peace and hunger after righteousness. The confusion and interaction of these two strands in male consciousness, the rational intellectual, and the irrational, mystical imagination, constitute the tragic history of the next centuries in the Western world.

The Emperor Augustus was still presiding over his Roman peace, and the Roman writ ran in Palestine, when Jesus Christ was born. It is doubtful if Augustus heard much of the troubles experienced by his administrators with some of those Jewish sects and potentially subversive agitators. Taxes had to be collected, and reasonable order among subject peoples maintained. The Jews had preserved their archives and their traditions and shaped their religion into a creed with special rites and laws, as well as privileges accorded to them by their god, including the promise that he would send them a prophet, the Messiah, who was apparently to rule the world.

Argument goes on to this day as to whether Jesus Christ ever existed, whether, if he did, he was god as well as man, a spiritual teacher, or an agitator prepared to lead his people in a revolt against Roman rule.

It is best simply to take account of the ferment of ideas that was going on in most places under the Romans in this time of two centuries of peace. There was still the school of philosophy founded by Plato in Athens; in Alexandria was a library and university, where people of different ways of life argued and taught. Rome had ruthlessly and cruelly destroyed Carthage, but Roman occupation brought some prosperity to parts of Northern Africa and Egypt. There was bound to be a sense of frustration and impotence under the authority of the Roman administration and pattern of life, as occurs under any imperialism alien to the habits of peoples whom the overlords govern, but do not understand. To be born or accepted as a Roman citizen still had a prestige above all others. None the less, slaves and subject peoples began to have ideas about democracy, as of liberating themselves from paying tribute to Rome.

Those who felt themselves oppressed and frustrated under Roman rule, though of varied languages, religions and native customs, must have had in common a growing compassion for the under-dog. Even young children began at last to be included in that category.

The later Greek philosophers, Epicurus and the Stoics, had been much concerned about human happiness – the pursuit of pleasure and the avoidance of pain. Epicurus (341–270 BC), opposed to magic and superstition and indifferent to the gods, shows compassion for the human predicament in his advice to live modestly and prudently, with due avoidance of pain. A remarkable disciple of Epicurus was the Roman Lucretius, born in 99 BC, contemporary with Julius Caesar, when Epicurean maxims were popular in Rome. Lucretius' poem *On the Nature of Things*, coming from a Roman, is rare for its melancholy at that period, but also for his advice 'first study to learn the nature of the world' and feeling for growth and development, even in children (de Hause, 1976, pp. 81–2).

If things could come from nothing, time
Would not be of the essence, for their growth,
Their ripening to full maturity.
Babies would be young men, in the blink of an eye,
And full-grown forest come leaping out from the ground.
Ridiculous! We know that all things grow
Little by little, as indeed they must
From their essential nature.

He notes grown-up irritation over the tiresome habits of children:

> Kids wet the bed
> Soaking not only sheets, but also spreads,
> Magnificent Babylonian counterpanes,
> Because it seemed that in their dreams they stood
> Before a urinal or chamber pot
> With lifted nightgowns.

but he associates their troubles with the common fate of their elders:

> When nature, after struggle, tears the child
> Out of its mother's womb to the shores of light,
> He lies there naked, lacking everything,
> Like a sailor driven wave-battered to some coast,
> And the poor little thing fills all the air
> With lamentation – but that's only right
> In view of all the griefs that lie ahead
> Along his way through life. The animals
> Are better off, the tame ones and the wild,
> They grow, they don't need rattles, they don't need
> The babbling baby-talk of doting nurses,
> And just as children, fearing everything,
> Tremble in darkness, we, in the full light,
> Fear things that really are not one bit more awful
> Than what poor babies shudder at in darkness,
> The horrors they imagine to be coming.

Lucretius died by his own hand only fifty-five years before the birth of Christ. Only one manuscript of his poem survived the Middle Ages. His importance has only been recognised since the Renaissance and, in modern times, largely through the masterly translation of R. C. Trevelyan.

Philo, the neo-Platonist philosopher, who was contemporary with Christ, seems to be one of the first to condemn the horrors of the exposure of infants.

> Some of them do the deed with their own hands; with monstrous cruelty and barbarity they stifle and throttle the first breath which the infants draw or throw them into a river or into the depths of the sea, after attaching some heavy substance to make them sink more quickly under its weight. Others take them to be exposed in some desert place, hoping, they themselves say, that they may be saved, but leaving them in actual truth to suffer the most distressing fate. For all the beasts that feed in human flesh visit the spot and feast unhindered on the infants, a fine banquet provided by their sole guardians, those who above all others should keep them safe, their fathers and mothers. Carnivorous birds, too, come flying down and gobble up the fragments. (ibid., p. 28)

It goes without saying that there were doctors and nurses with some knowledge, able to officiate at childbirth and also not ignorant of suitable nutrition for such babies as were allowed to survive. The point is the uses for which they were reared and the scant value attached to human life, more especially at its weakest and most vulnerable.

These two voices from the ancient world are quoted in anticipation of the birth of that religion that was also the birth of a child; in circumstances which, according to the gospel story, drew the Wise Men of the East to journey far in search of him; a child to whose mother some importance was attached; who, as he grew up, showed qualities of leadership in his own country; a child, moreover, who, as a man, was the first preacher to say 'Suffer the little children to come unto me', and who remarked that only by emulating the innocence and simplicity of children could their elders hope to lead good lives.

The words that were handed down from the sermon on the mount were something which, in that age of fading Roman glory, emphatically needed saying and have never been irrelevant to the ages that have followed.

To me the arrival of Jesus Christ in human history has none of the meanings attributed to it by very nearly all of his followers and disciples. To me his significance is quite simply that he spoke to the human species of the way in which they both could and should have lived together in tolerable peace on earth ever since they came into existence.

They could, and should, have loved and cared for one another and for the children born to them, not by holy inspiration, nor by intellectual appraisal, but by the elementary biological fact that they were one flesh, organisms in whom rested the power of creation.

Here was, indeed, in the age of the Caesars, the prophet of the slaves, the under-dogs, the mass of the people; no respecter of the rich and powerful; who might even then have proclaimed the slogans of a far distant future age, 'liberty, equality, fraternity'. This is in no way to see him as a revolutionary leader in his times, even though he might have become so. Rather he was the voice which spoke what was in the minds and hearts of thousands and thousands who were looking for guidance and inspiration in their quest for a new way of life. They had had their fill of power and conquest; spiritual meditation and contemplation of infinity was no more than an escape from the responsibilities of living; the dialectical exchanges of the philosophers, however entertaining, seemed to lead nowhere. Of course the Greeks, followed by the Romans, had seen the value of democratic government, but only as the privilege of a civilised people or nation, exclusive of the conquered or barbarians.

No one had ever said – though perhaps in the very dawn of human history, *before* speech, it had been *felt* – every man or woman is your neighbour, why don't you love and help one another? But once there are some men who seek or have acquired power over others, this 'dangerous thought' of love and mutual aid becomes intolerable and subversive and must at all costs be suppressed.

What of the other elements in Christ's teaching – to love god the father, the promise of eternal life? Jesus was a Jew, his own faith had long held the tradition of a personal god in close touch with his chosen people. Belief in one god was current in his day among very many of the Gentiles. The hope of life after death had also been widespread for centuries. In all these ways I see Jesus as very much the voice of his times, the voice crying in the wilderness of the bankruptcy of human desires and aspirations, the eternal tragedy as, men saw it, in that period, of the human condition.

There is no need to go over the well-known story of Jesus Christ's brief life and brutally cruel death, as told in the Gospels, or to enter into argument as to what is verifiable historical fact. What matters is what about half the human race have made of that story of his life and his teaching.

It is said that, at first, the Romans regarded the spread of some odd faith and superstition among the slaves and subject populations as inoffensive and absurd.

Since, however, the essence of this new faith was not mere passive contemplation, but active communication of its hope and promise, Jesus's disciples were very soon openly preaching the gospel in Judea and in Jerusalem; while groups of converts began to form, passing the simple message of love and brotherhood from neighbour to neighbour and holding their goods in common.

The disciples spoke first of all to the Jews, even in the synagogues. When two of them were beaten by orthodox Jews and threatened with stoning, a Rabbi called Gamaliel, a Pharisee, came to their rescue, warned them to move off and at the same time also admonished and warned off their opponents.

Meantime some trouble arose among the converts in Jerusalem over the distribution of food; there were Greeks among them complaining of unfairness by their Jewish comrades. Underlying this dispute was the question which had already arisen, as to whether Christ's message was for the Jews only, or also for the Gentiles.

The apostles, saying that they were busy with preaching and could not concern themselves with the matter of communal food, appointed several eager young converts to settle it. Among these was Stephen, Hellenic in origin, obviously one who had travelled and was well informed. It seems clear that he must have been arguing for the wider dissemination of Christ's teaching, which caused him to be accused of blasphemy and brought before the Sanhedrin. Stephen defended himself passionately (Acts 6:5, 7:55), also by showing his full knowledge of all the historical record of the Jews, including the promise of the Messiah; but he intimated that some things 'dwelt in temples not made with hands', implying thus his support for the wider project; he ended by claiming that the Messiah had come and had been murdered.

Enraged, his judges ordered his death by stoning, which took place immediately outside the gates of the city. The law required that the accusers should be the executioners, also that they remove their clothes and that one among them stand by the clothes while they did their bloody work. The person who undertook the stand-by office was a young man from Tarsus, called Saul, who was at this time most active in opposition to the new teaching. This man was, of course, later St Paul.

Stephen, in these circumstances, was the first Christian martyr. I would hazard a guess that the conversion of St Paul was due to his remorse over his participation in this appalling slaughter of a sincere and innocent man, rather than to a vision of Jesus on the road to Damascus.

This first tragic incident is the kernel of everything that went wrong with the Christian religion.

When people of some conviction set up a new sect or party, the first step is, obviously, to make it known and get support. Eloquent speakers are required, but also a good organiser to travel about and establish branches. Then it is essential that those at the centre should be able to keep in touch with what goes on at branch level, more especially that what is being preached to the public accords with agreed principles and policy. To ensure this, there must be a statement of aims, a manifesto, or, should we say, doctrine. There must be rules governing membership, hence a constitution will be needed, which, to tidy legalistic minds, should come first of all.

The disciples of Jesus Christ were simple men, they had been overwhelmed by the personality of this man who had called them to his service. They believed he had performed miracles, of which they felt they had witnessed some. They revered him as a god, or, by his own statement, the son of a Father god who was in heaven. However all that might be, and in spite of his cruel execution by the Romans (they knew that the Romans, in any case, executed people, with scant justice, on all sorts of charges), this man had inspired them with a new optimistic, creative way of living with their fellowmen, with the hope that there might be peace and justice on earth and that death would not be the final end.

Paul, when he came to join them, was already a person of some standing. It is calculated that he was probably born some time in the first five years AD.* He was an intellectual, a scholar, studying under the Rabbi Gamaliel. Though born a Jew, he could claim Roman citizenship. He was fluent in spoken and written Greek. He was well versed in the philosophic and theological discussions which were going on in various centres of learning. The Academy in Athens was still functioning; in Alexandria there were teachers of Greek philosophy and mathematics; there was also, in that city, quite a colony of Jews.

Once convinced of Paul's sincerity, the Christian brethren must have looked upon him as a very valuable acquisition; perhaps his Roman citizenship had special advantages. He became their organiser, missionary, and teacher by correspondence. His missionary journeys (facilitated by good Roman roads – and perhaps his Roman 'party card') in Asia Minor, and also to Greece and the islands of the Aegean, are documented. He often remained for a considerable time in one of the important cities, such as Ephesus. Apart from the famous poetic exhortation to love in an epistle to the Corinthians, it must be said that, on the whole, Paul was concerned with doctrine. Beautiful as are the words on love, it is a spiritual equality that he extols. He enjoins marriage only if a man cannot bear a life of abstinence. Carnal love was not much favoured, even by the philosophies emanating from the neo-Platonists, Stoics and others. Nor did women derive any benefit from the natural birth of Jesus from a human mother. On the contrary, women were firmly told that they must submit and keep their place, whilst, before long, they were to be bitterly and obscenely reviled by the fathers of the church.

Paul, and following him the early Christians, preached Christ crucified, the shedding of his blood as a sacrifice in atonement for sin. The Jewish notion of God in anger punish-

---

* Smith's *Dictionary of the Bible*, John Murray, 1907.

ing his sinful people lay behind this teaching, as also the age-
old propitiation of the gods by sacrifice which was common to
both Greek and Jewish cultures. But Jesus had protected the
woman about to be stoned to death for adultery; he spoke of a
god who was not a revengeful tyrant but a father, creative in
the natural world, who cared for the fall of a sparrow and
adorned the lilies of the field with their radiant colours.

Just as the old mythmakers pounced upon the new religion,
so did those intellectuals who loved hair-splitting argument.
What was the precise difference between the Father and the
Son; which should have precedence? Were the souls of unbap-
tised babies damned? Long before the teaching of Jesus had
become an established institution and church, the very heart of
that teaching had been not only distorted but literally turned
upside down. What was intended to promote life and creation
had focussed on death and destruction; what was to encourage
human beings to do good, was turned into the assertion that
they were inevitably wicked and born in sin; what was meant
to bring peace, tolerance and justice, became a crusade to
destroy all pagans, and unbelievers, and to approve and
promote just wars. This is not to deny that, as the gospel
spread, there were thousands and thousands, and presently
millions, who lived lives that were morally superior to the
lives of those who rejected conversion.

On his many journeys Paul found himself more than once
in collision with Roman pro-consuls. As the Christians became
more numerous, Imperial Rome, in alarm, persecuted and
sought to suppress the movement. It was evident that the
cement of brotherly love could render communities of men and
women dangerous to despotic power. Roman soldiers began
turning Christian: in the Roman army, as among the Greeks
who fought for their country, fellowship and affection came
natural to men engaged in a common purpose and at risk of
death. It is said that this was the reason why the Emperor
Constantine accepted Christianity as the official religion. With
a crucifix as the emblem of the Army, 'In this sign we conquer.'
Centuries later 'Onward Christian soldiers', 'with the Cross of
Jesus going on before', became a favourite hymn.

It was in 312 AD that the Emperor Constantine, fighting
for his life and the defence of his city, Rome, rallied his troops

in the name and sign of Jesus Christ. For just on three hundred years therefore, the Christian faith had been expanding its influence and the number of its converts. How had this come about? Why did not Jesus, after inspiring a generation or so, simply take his place among other gods as a beautiful legend or myth that would ultimately pass into history? From this particular period of history, which is somewhat obscure, some reasons do emerge. First of all there was the intense missionary zeal of the converts, which went on at two levels, that of the theologians and philosophers and that of the emotional and physical needs of the illiterate and down-trodden. Roman law and order lay like a great crust over the distress of subject peoples. Corruption, strife and degeneracy had destroyed whatever respect or idealism it might have inspired as a system of government or pattern of culture. The crust itself was cracking; moreover Rome was now threatened, not only by her own dissensions, but by the incursion of barbaric tribes.

There are various ways of achieving community life or social cohesion. The barbarians were held together by the old organic links, plus sufficient hardihood for war-like adventure; Rome had the static, bureaucratic organisation of the imperial coloniser. The Jews were very much on a racial, though no longer primitive, tribal basis; the Greeks, and others, who had defended the territory of small nations, might be said to be united by chauvinism (though not in a derogatory sense). All had a superstructure of culture, of greater or less value or depth.

A new kind of social cohesion was evolving in Christian communities: cohesion by faith or ideology. The followers of Jesus were, at first, certainly to be found among the slaves, the poor and illiterate. They did not arise out of family ties, they were of any race or nation, their background urban rather than rural, a mixture of types and skills, often foreigners, working in the cities of considerable size in Syria, Asia Minor, Italy, and Rome itself. They were, in fact, what might be called the proletariat, of which, should it become a mob, those in authority might well be afraid.

At the level of literacy and higher education, as time went on, those who were aware of the size and strength of this new movement were deliberating how it was to be guided and controlled. That there was controversy is shown in St Paul's writings. Toward the end of the first century there is extant the treatise by Origen (AD 185–234) refuting the opposition to Christianity of Celsus, whose script is unfortunately lost. But it is clear that the relative importance or rightness of Jewish teaching or Greek philosophy was in question. Origen was in Alexandria, where a great deal of the learned dispute took place.

There was, so far, no organised church, with final authority as to doctrine. Presently in the cities there were bishops elected by the local Christians, who took charge of the monies held in common.

It would seem that the Emperor Constantine must have hoped that the Christian communities would supply the cohesion and willpower needed to arrest the dissolution of all that Rome had built.

Unhappily, although he found plenty of willpower, even obstinacy, bitter controversy reigned among these learned men. Athanasius was the bishop in Alexandria, Arius a foremost and, it would seem, a somewhat turbulent priest, of the same city. Arius insisted that Jesus, as the son, was not the equal, but created by his father; Athanasius that they were equal and separate, but of the same substance. Constantine had to call a Council at Nicaea (AD 325) to try to settle the question. According to Eusebius, old Arius was struck in the face when he rose to speak and many covered their ears or ran out in horror at his heresies. Constantine, who had little Greek, could barely guess at what it was all about. He had not yet been baptised a Christian, or he might have understood. In any account of the early years of Christianity, this quarrel must be noted, since its ultimate result was the recital of the interminable and awful Athanasian creed by unfortunate worshippers, young and old, every Sunday in church.

Other fathers of the church soon came on the scene. Ambrose (b. 340 AD), who became Bishop of Milan, St Jerome (b. 345 AD) and St Augustine (b. 354 AD), Bishop of Hippo (near Carthage). Authority, if not complete unity, was established. Further, the bishops soon began to assert priestly directives as regards the conduct of emperors, and were to continue the attempt to do so for the next few hundred years, over kings and emperors alike.

To chronicle the many religious schisms or temporal wars would be tedious; in the end there was the Christian church beyond Constantinople, voicing god's will in Greek, whilst in the West and from Rome he spoke in Latin. It was of course a long time before the words of Jesus in the Gospels would be read and heard in their native tongues, by those of his worshippers who 'had little Latin and less Greek'.

The views of these first founders of the church, and also the doctrines they imposed, are very well known. Not only did they record their teaching, but, in correspondence, much of their lives and actions. What they laid down as belief and dogma, even before the final fall of Rome, was, in fact and content, the very 'shape of things to come' – the medieval world.

All three exemplify the struggle in men's minds between the régime of the old world and the new, and how the final victory of the new influenced their actions.

Ambrose had legal standing and a position in the secular world before his conversion; when he became bishop of Milan he gave away his possessions to the poor. He used his ecclesiastical position to admonish the sins of secular imperial power.

Jerome was among the many desert fathers, of whom, in the third and fourth centuries, there were vast numbers, according to some reports more even than the population of the towns.

These holy ascetics condemned themselves to a life of near-starvation, dirt, disease, even self-mutilation. Jerome's letters eloquently describe his agonies of sexual lust and, among his many sins, his inveterate appetite for continuing to read his pagan authors, which he carried with him into the wilderness. Later, in a more congenial environment, in Rome, he translated the Hebrew scriptures into Latin and busied himself in converting distinguished ladies to the Christian faith and chastity. He accepted the carnal institution of marriage as a means of producing women to become virgins.

Augustine, a man of fine intellect and considerable learning, details his struggles with his pagan self, together with what he knew of the speculations of pagan astronomers and philosophers about the nature of the universe. His chief work, *The City of God*, became world famous and of major influence.

The hallucinations of the desert were already productive of a new type of mythology – some very real-seeming devils with their temptations. According even to Augustine the pagan gods did exist; they too, were devils. He also chronicles some new immortal beings, with a special type of body, angels, both good and bad, and the devils of hell.

St Paul's teaching about women's duty and place is on permanent record. But it seems advisable, having regard to their powerful influence in centuries to come, to quote some of the utterances of the desert and early fathers of the church, more especially where they relate to women and sex. It should be noted that, at their time of writing, these fanatical converts believed that Christ's second coming was not far distant. Even so, their alienation from life is extraordinary.

Clement of Alexandria on how woman should dress to go to church:

> Let her be entirely covered, unless she happens to be at home. For that style of dress is grave, and protects from being gazed at.

On hair-dressing:

> Head-dresses and varieties of head-dresses, and elaborate braidings, and infinite modes of dressing the hair, and costly mirrors in which they arrange their costume, are characteristic of women who have lost all shame.

On the crying of infants:

> Why, O mother, didst thou bring me forth to this life, in which prolongation of life is progress to death? Why hast thou delivered me to such a life as this, in which a pitiable youth wastes away before old age, and old age is shunned as under the doom of death? Bitter is the road of life we travel, with the grave as the wayfarer's inn.

Cyprian on cosmetics:

> Are sincerity and truth preserved when what is sincere is

polluted by adulterous colours, and what is true is changed
into a lie by the deceitful dyes of medicaments? Let your
countenance remain in you incorrupt, your head
unadorned, your figure simple; let not wounds be made in
your ears, nor let the precious chain of bracelets and
necklaces circle your arms or your neck; let your feet be free
from golden bands, your hair stained with no dye, your
eyes worthy of beholding God.

Tertullian is brutal and extreme, almost to nihilism.
On having children:

Further reasons for marriage which men allege for
themselves arise from anxiety for posterity, and the bitter,
bitter pleasure of children. To us this is idle. For why should
we be eager to bear children, whom, when we have them,
we desire to send before us to glory (in respect, I mean, of
the distresses that are now imminent); desirous as we are
ourselves to be taken out of this most wicked world and
received into the Lord's presence.

Let the well-known burdensomeness of children,
especially in our case, suffice to counsel widowhood –
children whom men are compelled by laws to have, because
no wise man would ever willingly have desired sons.

What has the care of infants to do with the Last
Judgment? Heaving breasts, the qualms of childbirth, and
whimpering brats will make a fine scene combined with the
advent of the Judge and the sound of the trumpet. Ah,
what good midwives the executioners of the Antichrist will
be!

Relieved at the absence of his wife, he also rejoices that, at
the day of resurrection, they will no longer need to copulate:

Let us ponder over our consciousness itself to see how
different a man feels himself when he chances to be
deprived of his wife. He savours spiritually. . . . There will
at that day be no resumption of voluptuous disgrace
between us.

Finally his verdict on woman:

Nothing disgraceful is proper for man, who is endowed with

reason; much less for woman, to whom it brings shame even to reflect of what nature she is. (Langdon-Davies, 1928)

By the fifth century under St Cyril, patriarch of Alexandria from 412–444 AD, Christian intolerance flamed into persecution of Jews and pagans. One example, recorded by Gibbon in his *Decline and Fall of the Roman Empire*, is the fate of a woman who was also learned in philosophy and a Greek. Hypatia, a lecturer at the university on neo-Platonism and mathematics, was:

> torn from her chariot, stripped naked, dragged to the church, and inhumanly butchered at the hands of Peter the Reader and a troop of savage and merciless fanatics. Her flesh was stripped from her bones with sharp oyster shells and her quivering limbs were delivered to the flames. The just progress of enquiry and punishment was stopped by seasonal gifts! (Russell, 1946, p. 387)

That last tragedy belongs rather in the category of religious persecution, though it happens to be directed against a woman.

The founding fathers of the church seem totally unaware that their uncompromising condemnation of sex was, in effect, a repudiation of life itself, the source of their own existence. Since their hopes were set upon life after death and their belief that Christ's second coming was imminent, possibly what mattered most to them was exemplary conduct and devotion to god in the brief interval.

The collapse and dismemberment of the Roman Empire, apparent all around them, might well suggest that they were on the eve of a new era, it might even be the Day of Judgment. While in 429 AD St Augustine lay dying in his bishopric of Hippo, near Carthage, the Vandals were about to overrun it. A period of appalling turmoil and destruction, accompanied by sicknesses and plague; quarrels between one sect and another; wars between the divided halves of the Roman Empire – all leading to the rise of new kingdoms – spanned the next five centuries and more. The growing body of Christians, distressed though they might be at the suffering about them (but apparently more concerned with the shaping and maintenance of their faith) did hold together and expand. Side by side with the emperors, there were bishops in Rome continuously from the first century onwards. Since Christ did not reappear, the Christians dreamed of replacing the defunct imperial power by a Holy Roman Empire, ruled by the Pope, whom they did establish in Rome, destined ultimately with the power of religion, to rule over the world. Already, with the Emperor Constantine, hand in glove with military power, conversion with or by conquest proceeded apace. Religious belief and dogma henceforward began to be one of the most effective incentives employed to make war. But studious and holy men could take little part in violence and struggle. Their self-denial and asceticism stood them in good stead, as they sheltered in caves, or, in secluded and remote places, set up communities in which sheer physical survival and preservation of their learning and their beliefs were combined.

The dark ages in Europe were not merely a scene of destitution and bloodshed. Millions died, but many grew rich and powerful. Where there was no actual fighting, work went on in rural areas and in towns. Travel and trade did not cease. In what was to become the Christendom of medieval Europe, however, the division between the two aspects of Christianity persisted – the one militant and persecuting, appertaining to royal rulers and the higher dignitaries of an institutional church, the other ascetic, literate and learned, evolving into the monastic orders which comprised women as well as men.

The shape of things to come – that medieval world – issued from the thoughts and illusions of the handful of third-century bishops and preachers. By the fourth century it is all there, this cosmogony – the universe according to Judaic Christianity. It must be emphasised, however, that this cosmogony no longer represents the speculations of enquiring philosophers; on the contrary, it enjoins articles of faith, which to disbelieve – (or even fail to be baptised) – is to be damned. What is more, this is a revealed religion, it has been laid down following the incarnation of god in his son upon earth. Any further speculation on these matters is now blasphemous and will be severely punished. God, as accepted in this faith, is external to the universe, which he alone created out of nothingness and he alone maintains. Starting with the creation in Genesis, practically the whole of the Jewish archives and prophesies together with the Christian gospels (albeit in Latin or Greek) are laid down as holy writ and thus indeed command belief as 'gospel truth'.

The vision presented to the medieval mind is of God in the heavens above, seated in majesty, with his son Jesus at his side, attended by the angels; below, on earth, are the priests to whom by the Holy Spirit God's will is imparted, as well as the power to celebrate the sacramental rites of the faith; secular power, also by divine right, is vested in emperors and kings. Should sinful men have need to plead for mercy when punished for their wickedness, it is on the compassionate intervention of the son of God, himself a sacrificial lamb, that they must rely. Unhappy men did, much later, try to call in the help of the Virgin Mary, or even the saints.

Under the earth is hell, whose various stages of torment were later elaborated, but the main conception was of a pit of everlasting fire in which souls would burn in eternal agony, harassed by devils with tails and pitchforks. Fires, too, would presently be lit upon earth to burn heretics, blasphemers, witches, any who sought knowledge not sanctified by God and his church.

The righteous, in heaven, would praise God eternally for their salvation. This is a true picture of the social system which, after the Dark Ages, was to emerge in the Catholic Christian West and the Orthodox East. By imposition of this divine hegemony, in the years to come, multitudes of illiterate peoples, and even some of their powerful rulers, were intimidated and held in subjection.

If those early converts could have foreseen all this, would they have so eagerly adopted the new faith? As already indicated, neither this nihilism nor this institutional exaltation of power was what Christ taught. Those who were alive during his life, if they heard anything at all about him, must have learned of his teaching and the story of his resurrection. Longing for immortality perpetually haunts mankind. Again, in a world of military conquest, Jesus had spoken of loving your neighbour, of being a maker of peace. He had referred with contempt to money tribute to Rome: his only – and modest – act of violence had been to attack those who were making profit on the threshold of a place of worship.

Conscious thought, in that period of unrest and uncertainty, had already turned from racial or national pride towards the conduct of the individual. Could you not be a good, happy or creative man or woman without seeking wealth or power? If others did likewise, might not human life be very different, more especially with this hope of life hereafter? For the first time in history the words 'peace on earth' had been spoken and were being interpreted to the world through the strength of passive resistance, displayed, to the amazement of all, by the Christians in their martyrdom. In all this there was much in those times to inspire hope, faith and courage.

What incentive or inspiration was there in medieval Christian Europe that might lead ordinary men and women to live according to the peace and brotherhood enjoined by Christ? Their physical environment was, as it were, a box with three shelves, in the middle the flat earth with some mountains and seas, whose boundaries spelt the extent so far explored; beneath was hell, and above was God's heaven. Astronomy, or curiosity about God's region, was not ruled out. The vision of a round world, which had dawned on the Greeks, had been completely lost. When it began to reappear, it was a dangerous heresy. But observation of the stars, as always, could stir the imagination and led to useful aids to navigation.

Such studies were, however, for superior learned people; ordinary men and women, illiterate, were either peasants in their villages, or, later, also artisans in the towns. The fertile earth, which in the ancient world men and women had once tended as belonging to their gods, now appeared to have been leased or given by the Almighty to overlords who took possession of the land together with the men living upon it, serfs who worked for their lords and could be called upon to fight in the wars of barons or kings. Women were subject to their men. A remarkable example of this ownership is how, after 1066, William the Conqueror took an inventory of everything in Britain that was now his and distributed parts of it as gifts among his Norman followers.

The upper strata, the Kings and Knights, whose favourite pursuit was jousting and fighting, could also not read or write, or even sign their names. Popes and their ecclesiastics were, of course, literate, using Latin, which greatly helped communication at top levels and was the basis of the medieval consensus of general beliefs about the world and human destiny, providing a unity which some historians have admired. It could only have had meaning for the very few at the top in the universities or among such rulers and courts as patronised learning. To ordinary folks even the church services, which they were more or less obliged to attend on Sundays and Feast days, were unintelligible in Latin. But these occasions were used by the priests to convey in sermons what the authorities wished the people to know and to believe. The confession of their sins to their priest, who could give them absolution in God's name, was obligatory before receiving communion. Sin was inescapable: the very act by which their parents had conceived them and their own birth were sinful. The soul's sojourn in the body was, in any case, purely temporary, to be endured with duty and obedience till death gave release into eternal life. 'For here we have no abiding place, we seek one to come.' The soaring lonely liberating flight of the imagination and the intellect into that supersensual realm of perfection – the Greek empyrean – had been translated into eternal life in God's heaven with the harp playing angels, or, if pursued while on earth, confined within the limits of communion in prayer with an omnipotent god in constant command of the soul.

Happiness and enjoyment were not to be found, should not even be sought, in life on earth. These doctrines and the system created by them was a prison of mind and body, claustrophobic, stifling past endurance. Small wonder that human energies, pent up and damned by prohibitions, burst forth into hatreds, wars and persecutions. Of course people sinned and sought pleasure, but they usually paid for it in some way if they did not keep the rules. Those who could not endure fighting and violence could and did take refuge in the monastic institutions. Even this required the vows of poverty, chastity and obedience. They did obtain a life of seclusion, which was, it is true, not always secure from predatory barons and royal persons. But learning and teaching reading and writing, as well as very many other creative pursuits, went on behind monastic walls.

Founding a religion can be an exciting as well as a profitable enterprise. Mahomet, next in line of prophets seeking to found a faith which would conquer the world, was born in 570 AD in Mecca, in Arabia, which was still a country of nomadic Bedouin tribes who, in spite of some contact with Jewish and possibly Christian thought, still revered idols as gods.

Mahomet was poor, no more than a shepherd or camel-drover until he married Kadija, a well-to-do widow who employed him. At the age of 40 he began to assert a belief in the one true god, and a future life, as well as rules for righteousness. He composed poems which he claimed to have come to him from an angel. His wife and a few friends, among them Abu Bekr, supported him in his prophetic mission, but he was at once the target for hostility, including a threat to his life, from the devotees of the old gods and goddesses. In 622 came his famous flight, known as the Hegira, together with Abu Bekr, to Medina, where he and his beliefs were welcomed. He was now 52, and his wife had died. In 623, with Abu Bekr at his right hand, he sent letters to all the monarchs of surrounding kingdoms, calling on them to worship Allah, the one true god. Most of these communications were, naturally, treated with scorn.

Mahomet had had some hopes that the Jews and Christians would realise that all worshipped this one true god. These hopes were not realised; hence some persecution and killing of Jews occurred in the small tribal wars that saw the start of campaigns by the belligerent disciples of Allah.

To be brief: the opposition of Mecca was overcome, Mahomet returned there and died of a fever in 632, master, by then, of most of Arabia and succeeded by Abu Bekr, the first caliph (which means successor). Abu Bekr was followed by war-like caliphs, good generals, who within twenty-five years conquered Persia, Syria, Armenia and Egypt. By 750 AD, the Moslem empire extended from the borders of India in the East through Asia Minor and the whole of North Africa into Spain and the fringes of southern France. Haroun al Rashid, the caliph reigning in Baghdad from 786 to 809 AD, a legendary figure even in real life, was immortalised by romance in the Arabian Nights.

The rapid spread of the Moslem faith was by conquest rather than persuasion. At the same time, the peoples who became converts were oppressed and disgruntled and would seem, like

the peoples north of the Mediterranean, to have been waiting
for some new inspiration that would make life worth living.
What Mahomet offered had something in common with what
Jesus actually taught, but there were significant differences
between the Moslem faith and Christianity, as the latter was
presented by Christ's followers. Mahomet revered Christ as a
prophet, though not as a god. His god, Allah, was outside the
world and had no immanent presence on earth. Allah, of
course, totally rejected the worship of idols: any image,
painting, or representation of a human-like figure, was – and
is – utterly banned from Moslem places of worship, which were
called mosques.

The Moslem attitude to the natural world differed fundamentally from that of the Christians. Since Sumerian times,
tradition had seen matter as something that was already
there, not created out of nothing, but given shape by the power
of the gods. Nor had the natural world with all its contents
and living beings been placed by god at the disposal of man.
There was a certain degree of sanctity about nature. But all
men were brothers and equal in the sight of god; no priesthood
was set up to dictate god's commands to man. None the less,
men must always be mindful of Allah and obey the call to
prayer to him so many times a day.

There seemed to be no suggestion that men were inherently
wicked and born in sin. A code for righteous behaviour was
set forth in the Koran. Though there had been ascetics in
Persia and elsewhere in what was now Moslem territory, sex
was now treated by the Moslems as part of natural life and
not as a disgusting animal pursuit. On the contrary, a man
might have several wives, and, as is well known, such wives
might be beautiful and graciously adorned. There were several
laws about adultery, while the code as to other breaches of the
law which occur in society were equally severe. Some foods,
such as the flesh of pigs, were ruled out and, perhaps surpris-
ingly, the drinking of wines, or any intoxicating liquors,
strictly prohibited. Women, of course, remained little more
than chattels – men might enclose them at will in the harem,
though men were exhorted to be kind to their women and their
slaves, as also to give alms to the poor.

The average man – and woman perforce – could accept the

tenets of this faith far more readily than that of the Christians. It gave ordinary people self-respect and a far greater degree of liberty of thought and personal conduct. They could, with a clear conscience, develop normal sex and even love relations, and, though believing in a future life, none the less really savour the loveliness of the natural world, create and enjoy beauty and worldly pleasures. They were not forced to believe (or even risk disputing about) such theological problems as the nature of the Trinity, the virgin birth or transsubstantiation. Possibly the ban on intoxicating drink was a sign of respect for a clear, unconfused, unclouded intellect. However that may be, greater liberty of mind and thought in Moslem countries did mean that learned men were able to speculate about the universe, read Greek and Latin works, though perhaps in translation. They followed on the work in Greek medicine, were even able to use anaesthetics and perform some operations; pursued chemical knowledge and above all mathematics. They invented algebra, the decimal point and decimal system of notation, devices bringing with them zero and infinity, with all the radical consequences of these for future work in this field. They acquired knowledge of how to make paper, probably from the Chinese. The value which their scholars attached to learning and their approach to many problems had that element of frankness, zeal for enquiry and truth, which had been lost by the diversion to religion since Plato. This is not to extol the Moslem civilisation as perfection; on the contrary, it had its rivalry and wars, and its decline. Haroun al Rashid was reputedly a wine-bibber. But in the year AD 732, when the Arabs were first checked in their threat to the South of France, they were probably far wealthier and, at least in their cultured élite, more civilised than their Christian adversaries.

CHAPTER 5

Christendom in Europe

Europe had continued to impoverish itself in intellectual as
well as material wealth by tribal, temporal versus spiritual,
and sectarian warfare. At long last Charles the Great (Charlemagne) as king of the Franks, fighting enemies apparently on
all sides, came at the request of the Pope Leo III to his aid in
northern Italy and was recognised as secular ruler of Rome.
Then, in 778, he led the expedition into Spain against the
Arabs. In the fierce battle of Roncevaux, forever renowned in
history, Oliver and Roland were hard pressed as they covered
their army's rear, but Roland forbore to sound his horn to call
for help. The epic legend of the death of Roland and Oliver
was immortalised in the *Song of Roland*, sung by minstrels in
one of the first uses of the newly evolved French language.
The Arab threat to France was ended: this was, however, only
the first skirmish in the wars between the two religions that
were to come.

In 800 Charlemagne was crowned emperor by Pope Leo in
Rome, when, on Christmas Day, he went to hear mass in the
basilica of St Peter.

Beyond the great arch, the Arch of Triumph as it was called,
behind, in the semi-circular apse, sat the clergy, rising tier
above tier around its walls; in the midst, high above the rest
and looking down past the altar over the multitude was
placed the bishops' throne. . . . From the chair the Pope now
rose, as the reading of the gospel now ended, advanced to
where Charles, who had exchanged his simple Frankish
dress for the sandals and chamys of a Roman patrician,

knelt in prayer at the high altar, and, as in the sight of all,
he placed upon the brow of the barbarian chieftain the
diadem of the Caesars, then bent in obedience before him,
the church rang to the shout of the multitude, again free,
again the lords and centre of the world: 'To Charles
Augustus, crowned by God, the great and peace-giving
Emperor, be life and victory'. On that shout, echoed by the
Franks without . . . from that moment modern history
begins. (Bryce, 1907, p. 49)

But Eginhard, biographer of Charlemagne, had a different
version. According to him, Charles was taken by surprise and
said 'he would not have entered the church if he had known
what was to happen, great festival though it was.' It seems
that Charles may have entertained hopes of making himself
emperor, but had no desire to accept this title as a gift from
the pope. This further estranged Rome from the church in
Byzantium, whereas Charles had been contemplating their
union by marrying the Empress Irene, then reigning in
Constantinople (Wells, 1920, p. 346).

Charlemagne had interests other than fighting. He enjoyed
hearing music and reading aloud. The epics of heroes were
frequently sung, and lengthy romances read aloud to relieve
the tedium of dark winter evenings. Charles could apparently
read – which must have been in Latin – but he could not write.
He kept a lively court, and invited men of learning, who were,
of course, all Christian churchmen. Yet his relations with the
Moslem world were not unfriendly. Haroun al Rashid sent to
him, by his ambassadors, the gift of a water clock, a tent, an
elephant, and the keys of the Holy Sepulchre.

When Charlemagne died, his realm was divided between his
three sons in 843, in the terms of the document known as the
Strasburg Oaths, the text of which was not only in Latin, but
German as then spoken, and the Lingua Franca – or early
French.

As the material empire again fell apart, new countries of
Europe, with more settled native populations and diverging
customs, began to emerge. They were still mosaics of small
bellicose tribal kingdoms, but they spoke varieties of their
own evolving vernacular languages; French, Italian, Spanish,

German, Anglo-Saxon and so on. Where the Moslems still prevailed in Europe, there was Arabic. For the rest, only the church and the learned, using Latin and the still-handwritten books, had a literate culture which dispensed with frontiers.

> The ancient world found an end to anarchy in the Roman Empire, but the Roman Empire was a brute fact, not an idea. The Catholic world sought an end to anarchy in the Church, which was an idea but was never actually embodied in fact. Neither the ancient nor the medieval solution was satisfactory, the one because it could not be idealized, the other because it could not be actualized. (Russell, 1946, p. 51)

None the less, centuries long, the ghost of the Holy Roman Empire haunted the minds and policies of monarchs and prelates; frustrated and failing in Europe, it first took ship with the Catholic colonists to the New World. It has never lost sight of, or abandoned, its ultimate goal.

The Christian religion steadily acquired a firm and profound grip on the hearts and minds of the peoples of Europe. By its doctrine about sex it reached down to control those deep sources of creative and generous emotion which lie within the body. The conscious self also, intellect and imagination, were held locked in its medieval dungeon. These qualities would have to find outlets. Physical fear was an impediment to both; the secular arm and the ecclesiastical one were equally powerful and ruthless. The intense fear of death, which has been noted in the psychology of the Middle Ages, may well have owed as much to the dread of hell fire as to the menace of plague and pestilence, from which the people suffered.

What the power of a religion, which offers faith in a future life, may do to overcome fear was amply and tragically demonstrated when, in the year 1073, Peter the Hermit, on the rumour that the Turks had destroyed the Holy Sepulchre, preached his crusade. Thereby he unleashed the destructive impulses of the people and sent forth, like a stampeding herd of cattle, a mass of unorganised, leaderless devotees, to the rescue of the sacred places. Ignorant of geography, distances, foreign languages, large numbers of them perished in Hungary, which they mistook for the Holy Land. A few got as far as the Bosphorus. Crusading was then taken up by the holders of power. In 1097, largely inspired by the energetic Normans, most of West Europe launched the first organised military operation, achieving the capture of Jerusalem, after a bloody campaign and appalling slaughter, on 15 July that year. Retaken and again besieged, the city was the centre of five crusades – though with declining zeal – an overt holy war, declared on both sides between Christian and Moslem, which lasted close on 130 years and ended, in 1212, with the shocking event of the Children's Crusade. Nearly eight centuries later, Jerusalem is still the prize for which religious sects compete. But we speak here of religion in the hands of the medieval mighty, who were, as yet, not 'put down from their seat'. What then was to happen to 'exalt the humble and meek'?

If the body might not indulge its pleasures without sin, nor the mind play freely with ideas, what should man do? He could use his hands. The peasant on the land, the artisan in the workshop, had been doing this long before recorded history, expressing their conscious life as 'tool-making man'. Through them the food supply and amenities of daily life had much improved. While Adam delved and Eve span, the gentlemen of the ruling élite, well supplied by those labours, did not need to bother about the tools of daily toil. Royal minds were exercised about the requirements of warfare, roads, perhaps bridges, weapons, swifter transport; priestly minds about offerings and grandeur for the temples, or weaving and entangling men's minds in their sacred mysteries. It was left to ordinary men and women to grind the corn, to keep the fires and smithies going to make swords, spears and shields. Wheeled chariots and carts and well-schooled horses were useful to civil and military alike, but, in other respects, technology had shown practically no advance since about 600 BC in Sumerian Babylonia.

Now in medieval Europe, from about the eleventh century to the thirteenth, comes a period of history fascinating by reason of the kind of mental and physical development that took place. Tool-making man had begun to use wind and water power to turn the grindstones. Forest and woodland were being demolished to make the charcoal that kept the fires of the smithies going. Wood, which began to be in short supply, was also needed by the builders, who were now more highly skilled in carpentry and joinery. Skilled masonry, quarrying, mining for lead, coal, tin and iron began to improve the economic position and prestige of the workers.

Water mills had been known to the Romans, but in southern Europe water itself was not too plentiful; moreover, the Romans preferred the labour-intensive solution, since they had no lack of slaves or indigent freedmen.

The old Quern Song is eloquent of the constant arduous toil demanded to produce man's daily bread.

> Maids at morn, grind the good corn,
> Each in her mill, with a will,
> In go the oats, wheat and pearly barley,
> Down, down in a shower, falls the flour.
>
> Those hands that are strongest
> Will find a welcome here
> And they who work the longest
> Shall have the best cheer.
>
> Winding, winding strong, winding all day long
> Round, round and round goes the mill
> Winding turn about, till the meal is out
> Must never ne-ever stand still.

So great a boon were the water mills that they spread like wild fire along the rivers of Europe, even in the towns and under bridges. The Doomsday Book listed 5,624 water mills in England alone, dotted all over the map along the rivers (Gimpel, 1977, p. 24). Water and wind mills – of the latter there were very many in Holland – could yield a profit from the clients who brought their grain to be ground. Monasteries had their own mills and at times competed with the independent local miller, who might 'Care for nobody, no, not he'.

Medieval hand-copied books on parchment, exquisite illuminated manuscripts and missals, which are valued treasures of libraries and museums, have given a misleading impression that these aesthetic creations were the main occupation of monks and nuns, when they were not kneeling in prayer, engaged in ritual celebrations in church, or ministering to the poor. In actual fact learned ascetics who sought a quiet life in self-sufficient communities had to turn their hand to anything and everything. To learn the necessary skills they went to the peasant and artisan. Though relations between abbot and peasant were not always harmonious, mutual learning and mutual respect were beneficial to both. Agreement as to belief in the established religion and what to think about the universe left room for practical invention. There is ample evidence of inventive minds active in agriculture and technology.

No more nonsense about earth goddesses, it was the Lord to whom prayer must be offered for a good harvest. All the same it was prudent to study yields and costs and apply new methods. The hundreds of monasteries existing now all over Europe acquired land which they farmed; in addition they were lords of manorial estates and even larger ones. The heavy plough with wheels was used, its share, now edged with iron, if not entirely of metal. Horses gradually began to replace oxen in pulling wagons and ploughs. Their task was made easier by the use of the horse collar harness; their hooves, previously shod with rough sandals, were now provided with nailed on iron shoes. Such shoes,* together with the requisite nails were also in demand, thousands upon thousands, for the knights who jousted or went crusading. Iron was, of course, in demand for the armourers, but it received increasing use and attention in civil life, serving to strengthen masonry, make strong sharp tools, but what is more significant, it could be used to make machines.

The use of wind and water power to drive a mill was one of the most important influences on the *direction* of man's conscious thought, which is the main concern of this book. While the Crusades were in full swing the consciousness of the truly powerful was, as ever, concentrated on power rivalries and war. The privileged exemption of the monastic orders from warfare naturally fostered that close relation to peasant and artisan which thus enabled them to pursue the arts of peace. Hence the expanding monasteries steadily increased in wealth but also in productivity. Though each single monk was

---

* The horse collar, which seems to have come from the China-Siberian borders, was not used in Greece and Rome. Their horses wore straps which pressed on the jugular vein and windpipe, making them less efficient for work, but causing that arching of the heads of great beauty, as shown in Greek sculpture (Gimpel, 1977, p. 44).

vowed to poverty, the living standard of his community had practically all the amenities of civilisation then available. Abbots presided over hives of near-industrial activity. Water mills not only ground corn, but, fitted with the appropriate camshaft, caused the fall and rise of heavy wooden mallets or hammers: they tanned leather, fullered cloth, produced the first ever machine-made paper; may even have forged iron. For the first time the machine revealed its potential for lightening human labour.

Machine production, however, also increased employment. Some monasteries, notably the Cistercians (founded 1098, and later, under St Bernard, a strictly regulated order) took in numbers of lay brethren, who were obliged to take the vows, but not allowed to learn to read and write. This prohibition is very significant in that it indicates a resolve to uphold a class distinction between workers by hand and brain that has never been abandoned. There is another aspect: the literate minds of that day certainly wished to prevent the uneducated from access to the holy scriptures, which were in Latin or Greek, but they also originated that cleavage between the two cultures, literary as opposed to the technical and scientific, which has likewise persisted. The literary and learned were not men of the hands or tools, neither did they become men of the machine.

Ordinary people lived the average human life of work, with their children, finding, in spite of poverty and harsh overlords, some all-round enjoyment, expressing their religion – and with some humour and horseplay – in their mystery plays.

But what could occupy the intellect and imagination of a man or woman vowed to poverty, celibacy and obedience? Deprivation of sex and children inevitably caused atrophy of the warm generous feelings that accompany these natural human functions. Nuns might be encouraged to feel themselves the brides of Christ, men to reverence the Virgin Mary, but men's nightly temptations were the work of the devil. Since all literature not proscribed was Holy Writ, there was not much relaxation there. There were the arts, holy pictures and tapestries to adorn the churches; fine embroidered raiment for the priests, a great solace in church music, perhaps? In our own time, may it not have been the loss of any meaning in verbal communication that drove our younger generation to express their resentment in strident, violent pop music? Authoritative words from elders whose values you have come to despise, propaganda words, double talk, generate the search for a different medium. For the medieval mind, on the contrary, the verbal communication that came from authority conduced rather to monotony and boredom.

So it was that the medieval intellect and imagination conceived of an enterprise that could have magnificence and permanence – an enterprise that also called in man's third conscious faculty, the use of his hands – this was the building of the cathedrals in a new gothic style.

The American Henry Adams* sees the Virgin as the inspiration of Chartres and other cathedrals, but, in the chapter headed 'The Dynamo, or the Virgin', he perceives the existence of her formidable rival. Those austere cloistered intellects, who sponsored and sought rich donations for the rising spires, were also intrigued by the tricks of mechanism, the movement of wheels in machines, as they were still fascinated by the movement of the stars in their courses. What seems specially suited to them, too, is their interest in inanimate and inorganic substances, glass and the behaviour of metals. Unlike most other clerics, St Bernard did not approve of the use of stained glass in church windows. But glass in the form of lenses that magnified and could make spectacles was acclaimed by all as a boon (the telescope came later).

Such was the enthusiasm for building cathedrals that a competition arose as to which would achieve the tallest spire, in which Strasbourg was the winner. Why do men want to build high? This ambition existed already when they erected the Tower of Babel, for which, as the Bible tells us, they were rebuked by Jehovah. Were they reaching up to the domain of the one true god, or of the many gods which, to them, were the stars and planets, or were they seeking an escape from the earth? Men may often have dreamt of exploring the uttermost depths of the sea, but they feared too much to attempt it.

---

* *The Education of Henry Adams*, covering many years, was published in 1906. Concerned with various stages of the motivation of man's energy and actions, he sees the years 1150–1250 as the point in history when man had the highest idea of himself as a unit in a unified universe.

Regions imagined under the earth they tended to regard as a place of punishment or judgment of the soul; but the underworld of the ancients was more spacious and dignified than that conceived by medieval fantasy, until Dante arrived.

One architect of our time, possibly in jest, remarked that, in Freudian terms, our skyscrapers are symbols of male virility. It would seem that to build tall does express some kind of religious aspiration. Is it a coincidence that the classical style of the more rational civilisations of Greece and Rome and eighteenth-century Europe is solid, wide, dignified and imposing, without human dwarfing by its height, and dizzying grandeur soaring to the skies?

The architecture and methods of building the cathedrals brought many inventions, as for instance the flying buttress: space forbids a detailed description of all these. The architect engineers were justly honoured by their contemporaries, more so than the profession in our own day. A circular or octagonal plaque on the cathedral floor would be prominently inscribed with their names. They and their master masons were in great demand, well travelled and well rewarded. Skilled workers were by no means servile; in addition to the wages which they were not slow to demand, they received special concessions, such as the special courts of the stanneries, given by charter from King John to the Cornish tinners, by which the miners were exempt from the jurisdiction of the local magistrates and coroners. Some stalwarts in Cornwall are at present claiming that this charter is still in force.

A sketch book of one of the great architect engineers, Villard de Honnecourt, survives and is in Paris in the Bibliothèque Nationale. Honnecourt, near Cambrai in Picardy, where he was born, is not far from the then building site of the Cistercian monastery of Vaucelles, where as a boy he began his work; his main professional life lay between the years 1225 and 1250. In a brief foreword to his notebook he writes:

Villard de Honnecourt greets you and begs all who will use the devices found in this book to pray for his soul and remember him. For in this book will be found sound advice on the virtues of masonry and the uses of carpentry. You will also find strong help in drawing figures according to the lessons taught by the art of geometry. (Gimpel, 1977, p. 126)

Villard must have been familiar with the works of the Roman architect Vitruvius, as also with Greek handbooks of geometry. Sketches and designs, rather than words, fill these precious parchment pages. It is significant that in all this technical work pagan sources were not regarded as subversive; they did not entail theological or philosophical discussion.

Villard's notes reveal the contemporary delight in experimenting with mechanical movement. He drew designs for making a water-powered saw and for a mechanical angel who would rotate on the roof of a cathedral so that her finger pointed continuously at the sun. Like all engineers, he was obsessed with the dream of a wheel which would give perpetual motion, and drew sketches. On this dream another famed scientist of the day, Peter of Maricourt, astounding for his pioneer work on magnetism, remarked: 'I have seen men floundering exhausted in their efforts to invent such a wheel.' Villard tried the device of hanging bags or objects of different weights on either side of the wheel. While this did not succeed, it was the source of the mechanical clocks driven by rising and falling weights which were finally successfully invented during the century, the first public clock appearing in Paris in 1300.

The aim of the first makers of mechanical clocks was not merely to tell the time, but to achieve an astronomical clock, that is one which could forecast the movements of the sun, moon and planets. The first such astronomical clock was built in China in the eleventh century by Su Sung. In China the calendar and astronomical observations were held as imperial bureaucratic secrets. In 1126 the Su Sung dynasty was driven south by the Chin Tartars. The clock remained in use in the north but, unrepaired, fell to pieces. Meantime, in the south, the plans for the clock still existed but no one there had the skill to build from them.

The astronomical clocks, that of Giovanni di Dondi in Italy, and of Richard of Wallingford in England, date, strictly, from the fourteenth century. (See Gimpel, 1977, ch. 7.) A working model of the Dondi clock was made in recent years by an

Englishman, Alan Lloyd, from Dondi's drawings; this model is in the Smithsonian Institute in Washington and a similar replica in the London Science Museum.

Richard of Wallingford was Abbot of St Albans, son of a smith, orphaned at the age of 10. The church took care of his education and sent him ultimately to Oxford where he studied theology, philosophy and some science for nine years. He caused money and labour to be spent upon his astronomical clock instead of some rebuilding of his abbey, because, as he explained, when rebuked by King Edward III, only he had the knowledge to complete this special work, whilst others could do the rebuilding. He also invented instruments for astronomical studies. The record of his achievements is important in that it shows that it was the scientific studies of well-educated clerics which were the source of these mechanical inventions, which were carried out in close association with their artisan assistants – a class from which, like Richard of Wallingford, many had risen – hence a true alliance existed, for a time, between hand and brain.

Mechanical gadgetry was a medieval amusement: these men were scarcely aware of what they had created. In the words of Lewis Mumford: 'The clock, not the steam engine, is the key machine of the modern industrial age.' To measure time was of practical utility, this had been done by various means such as hour glass, sundial, water clock. A water clock had been a gift from Haroun Al Rashid to Charlemagne. Any measurement of time beyond a brief duration must take account of the changing length of day and night. Water clocks could be adjusted to work from sunrise to sunset and vice versa. But it was difficult to solve this problem with a mechanical clock. It must be remembered that the concept of time, ever since men's first observation of the stars, had had for them a metaphysical and religious significance. There were many brilliant minds among these thirteenth-century monastics, mathematicians as well as astronomers, meditating on more than one problem of time. They were much exercised, for instance, by the fact that they had begun to realise that the Julian calendar, by which their years were measured, was inaccurate. People lived more or less according to time belonging with their work. The monks lived by monastic time, the sounding of a bell according to the hours in which the religious observances of the day were divided.

The mechanical clocks were finally set according to what was the only possible compromise – by the equinoctial hours. Before long every church tower in Europe was to have its striking clock, by whose chimes the citizens learned to know and to keep time.

The coming of the clocks in Europe had far-reaching consequences. It led to a gradual departure from living according to natural time from dawn to dark; it marked an overriding by the rational, secular viewpoint of the religious strand in human consciousness. It was as if an iron hand now closed upon men and women compelling them to be ever more mindful of time, even to treat it as something substantial that could be divided and subdivided down to the tiniest fraction that could be recorded:

> 'The bells of the clock tower,' says Lewis Mumford, 'almost defined urban existence. Time-keeping passed into time-saving and time-accounting and time-rationing. As this took place, Eternity ceased to serve as the measure and focus of human existence.' (Gimpel, 1977, p. 155)

It might be said that the first conscious humans had lived, as it were, in space-time. But, as they counted the days and calculated the years, and became more 'highly intelligent', they came to imprison themselves more and more within the limits of a time of their own manufacture.

The Greek Orthodox church, indicating a considerable difference between religious opinion of East and West, refused to place clocks in its churches, regarding it as blasphemy to divide eternity. They were also slow to alter their calendar when it was changed in the West.

Relaxation into peace and timelessness, escape from the self-imposed division of time, is still sought by weary men and women in varied ways; through religious or purely mystical contemplation; or simply by retreat from cities or towns to a remote place in the countryside, where one may wake with the sun's rising and sleep when it sets, and where winds and waters, birds and animals provide the only background of sound.

The cloistered men (as well as women) within the monasteries, had peace and quiet – and to spare. The men presently
became aware that the faculty by which they invented the
clocks and other devices was not identical with the mystical
insight by which they expressed their religious devotions.
Peter Abelard, 1097–1142, who openly defied the monastic
rule of celibacy by his famous love of Eloise, was also justly
famed for his enthusiasm for asking questions. He wrote a
treatise *Sic et Non* (Yes or No). He observed the difference
between men who could make things and those whose theories
sparked off such inventions; that men studied creatures and
events in nature, but not their causes – how, for instance, did
bees know how to make honey? Abelard, and other men like
him, were supported or inspired by the knowledge that was
coming into the Christian world from their fellow scholars
among the Arabs. The Arab university of Toledo, in the twelfth
century, was prolific in translations into Latin from the writings of learned Arabs and Greeks (Gimpel, 1977, pp. 160 ff).

Toledo was visited for its teaching in arithmetics, geometry,
music and astronomy by Christian scholars, who also, like
the Englishman Adelard of Bath, and the Italian Gerard of
Cremona, learned Arabic there for translation purposes.
Groups of scholars, Christians, Moslems and Jews joined
together in Toledo to work on translations.

Space forbids the listing of these works, which were mostly
of a scientific nature. The philosophies of Aristotle and Plato,
however, must be mentioned. Their works, together with those
of the distinguished Arabs Averroes and Avicenna, were the
catalyst that provoked those intricate and bewildering disputations about universals, realism, nomenalism, that were the
favourite pursuit of Christian medieval scholastics.

In the study of the development of human consciousness in
the twelfth and thirteenth centuries, so many important
names and fascinating disputes appear that it is not possible
to do them justice in what is, unavoidably, a brief survey.
Christian and Moslem minds were exercised by the same
dilemmas, which essentially derived from the fundamental
thinking already undertaken by the Greeks. No one was able
to escape mathematics, whether in ambitious building, or

simply as an agreeable exercise for the intellect. All this was a great stimulus to the cause of reason.

St Thomas of Aquinas, probably among the most prevalent influences now in theology, was Italian, born not far from the Monastery of Monte Cassino; Italian was also St Francis of Assisi. Peter Abelard was among the liberal-minded thinkers and teachers at the University of Paris; a similar group of near-humanists existed in the cathedral school at Chartres. In fact statues of men of eminence, who were not Christian, figure on the cathedral itself. In England, Oxford became a centre of unorthodox thinking, and there were Roger Bacon, Duns Scotus, William of Occam, Robert Grosseteste.

There was a constant exchange of ideas and visits, which is not surprising, for it must never be forgotten that this was a European élite literary culture of churchmen, conducted for the most part in Latin, Greek or Arab translation. These scholars were apt to be fairly high in the church, at about bishopric status; moreover they, as well as their Arab colleagues, tended to come from upper-class families. Their numbers, in relation to the whole population, were exceedingly small, which makes the contemporary and lasting influence of their thought the more remarkable. John of Salisbury, when secretary to St Thomas à Becket, was a frequent correspondent; he wrote to the Archbishop from Chartres, in 1154, about a visit to Paris, expressing his immense admiration at the respect with which scholars were treated, as well as their brilliance: 'Happy exile it is for the one who has this city for abode.' (Gimpel, 1977, p. 166) John of Salisbury was later himself elected as Bishop of Chartres.

Of the two Arab scholars, Avicenna (980–1037) lived and taught in Persia, settling finally in Teheran. For centuries in Europe he was regarded as an authority on medicine; he was also concerned with problems of philosophy. Like previous Moslem scholars, his work, both in medicine and philosophy, derives from the Greeks. Averroes (1126–98), born in Cordova, lived and worked in Spain. He studied law, mathematics, theology and medicine, in which last he also practised. He made a special study of Aristotle. Neither he nor Avicenna were quite orthodox according to their own faith, so both risked and suffered some persecution. Averroes, for a considerable period, was exiled to Morocco.

Averroes asserted that the active intellect is in essence separate from the soul. He regarded the intellect as an immortal pervading reason, in which all men participate, though it is not, as it were, a unique possession of one man. On the other hand the soul is unique to the individual and is not immortal. He held that intellect, or reason, was proof of the existence of god.

His influence, at that date, was very great, because clerical scholarly intellects, as we have noted, had been extremely active in matters which were not strictly concerned with God. What was, in fact, the liberation of the intellect contributed to the excited atmosphere observable in Paris. Via Aristotle, plus Arabic thought, philosophy could be set free from religion. What is more, introspection, engendered by the cloister, was leading men to analyse the differing strands of their own consciousness. St Thomas, for instance, in his later attempt to restore more orthodox thinking, stated that there are not three souls in men, but only one, and that the intellect is a part of the soul, which is immortal.

If the rapid spread of new ideas was not surprising, neither was the background of the intellectuals from whom the ideas came. They were almost without exception, of the Order of Friars. St Francis of Assisi (1181–1226) started a new movement when he encouraged the monks out of the monasteries into the open air and to the poverty and simplicity of the life of Christ. More important was his love of birds and animals, the growing trees, the light of the sun. A man who required his followers to live and sleep outdoors must himself have had considerable energy and vitality. Before making himself a friar Francis had lived a worldly and even luxurious life and knew all about 'the world, the flesh and the devil'. Possibly others who joined him had worldly experience too and were not typical shrinking, devout, adolescent novices. In other words, they knew what it was to feel and live like ordinary men, were of the extrovert temperament that does not seek all wisdom in books, but enjoys noticing what goes on around it, whether men's work, or things and events of common or unusual nature.

Robert Grosseteste (1173–1253), a Franciscan friar, was born at Stratbrook in Suffolk, educated at Oxford and perhaps in Paris. He was the first Chancellor of Oxford University, and first lecturer to the Oxford Franciscans in 1224; and bishop of Lincoln from 1235 till his death. His voluminous works seem to have been underrated until quite recently. He knew Greek, and translated some of Aristotle. He held that mathematics and experiment were essential to the understanding of the physical world. He made an important contribution to the question of the reform of the calendar, arising out of his keen study of astronomy and considerable thought about cosmology. In a treatise, *Compendium Spheraerae*, he stated that the earth and the stars and planets are all spheres, as can be proved both by natural reason and astronomy, by observing the sky by men in different locations. His theories derive from his study of light and optics. He already had the idea of lenses to magnify small objects, or to use for distance. Light was his main interest; he held it to be the first corporeal form, whose characteristic property was to be able to propagate itself instantaneously in straight lines in all directions without loss of substance. In this way light had generated the universe (Gimpel, 1977, p. 169).

God had, in the beginning, created uniform matter out of nothing, but then light, automatically diffused, produced the dimensions of space and all things. Such a combination of the passion for astronomy, mathematics and the study of light, reads like a faint far-off prophecy of Einstein. Perhaps it was as well for Grosseteste that he did not, apparently, attract so much attention from papal authority as did his disciple Roger Bacon.

Roger Bacon (1214–1294) came from a well-to-do English family, from whom he actually received some financial help for his experiments. He was educated at Oxford and in Paris before joining the Franciscan Order. He made no secret of his belief in science, which, in his case, was tinged with interest in astrology and magic, derived largely from the Arabs. He does not hesitate to quote both Avicenna and Averroes. Like Grosseteste, he shows an interest in lenses, perspective, the rainbow, all possibly from the Arabs, indicating also knowledge of the splitting of light by the prism.

All accounts of Roger Bacon describe him as quick-tempered, tactless and impatient of fools, as of traditional authority. He was even prepared to scrap the idol Aristotle if necessary. His passion for scientific knowledge was a consuming fire within him, erupting like a volcano. Wells says of him: 'Roger Bacon shouted to mankind, "Cease to be ruled by dogmatic authorities, *look at the world!*" ' To Henry Osborn Taylor (in *The Medieval Mind*) he resembles a hero of Greek tragedy. Russell, on the other hand, chides Bacon as a braggart for his intemperate enthusiasms and exaggerations, apparently unbecoming in a man of science.

Roger Bacon's views were also well known because, more than once suspected of heresy, he was by papal orders required to explain his philosophy, which he at once proceeded to do in three books. He had at that date (1257) been placed under surveillance in Paris, by the order of the then general of his order St Bonaventura. For eleven years, till 1268, Bacon was not allowed to return to Oxford, where, with continuing intransigence, he produced, in 1271, the book *Compendium Studii Philosophiae*, deploring the ignorance of clerics. From 1278, his books condemned, he was in prison for fourteen years; released in 1292, he achieved but a year or two of freedom before his death.

Roger Bacon's greatness is revealed not only by his courage in persisting – and by the methods he thought right – in the search for scientific truth, but rather for his wide-ranging imaginative insight and his admiration and lack of jealousy for comrades such as Grosseteste in their common endeavour. His eulogy of Peter of Maricourt (writer of the study of magnetism) as the greatest experimental scientist of his day is extant, but unhappily so little is known of this valued colleague. Bacon's words about him, however, reveal much about Bacon himself:

One man I knew, and only one, who can be praised for his achievements in this science. Of discourse and battles of words he takes no heed: he follows the work of wisdom and in there finds rest. What others see dimly and blindly, like bats in twilight, he gazes at in the full light of day, because he is a master of experiment.

He goes on to stress Peter of Maricourt's lack of concern for wealth or fame, and his insistence on looking into all sorts of things 'known to laymen and old women, soldiers, ploughmen, of which he is ignorant', such as work in metals, weapons, agriculture.

Peter of Maricourt's own advice bears this out. He writes: 'while the investigator in this subject [magnetism] must understand nature and not be ignorant of the celestial motions, he must also be very diligent in the use of his own hands. . . .' Philosophy and mathematics alone, he adds, without manual experiment, will not solve problems.

Roger Bacon's own science fiction prophecy is not often quoted:

Machines for navigating are possible without rowers, so that great ships suited to river or ocean, guided by one man, may be borne with greater speed than if they were full of men. Likewise cars may be made so that without a draught animal they may be moved cum impetu incestimabili, as we deem the scythed chariots to have been from which antiquity fought. And flying machines are possible, so that a man may sit in the middle turning some device by which artificial wings may beat the air in the manner of a flying bird. (Wells, 1920, p. 401)

Of the other schoolmen, both Duns Scotus (1270–1303) and William of Occam (?1290 or ?1300–1349) were of the Franciscan Order and both studied at Oxford and Paris; Aquinas also studied in Paris, but was, however, a Dominican friar and thus tended to a greater orthodoxy. All these Christian scholars rejected Averroes' concept of the intellect as a universal faculty common to all men, but the personal property of none; they asserted the property rights of each man to his own intellect. With the exception of Aquinas, as we saw, they did agree with Averroes' distinction between the intellect and the soul, thus separating theology from philosophic or scientific thought.

This seems to be the moment to consider the relevance of what these men were arguing about, to the development of human consciousness. It had been a great discovery that, with speech, man could give names to concrete objects, instead of having to deal with them in thought pictures. Giving names had then extended to understanding two facts: one that you could think of an object in your mind by its name, thus have an *idea* of it; two, that a whole group of objects, such as cats, or trees, contained individuals that differed from one another. Which of these two concepts – the *idea* of an object in the mind – or *universals* – groups or classes of objects – came first would be hard to determine. But to both of these concepts the Greek philosophers Plato and Aristotle had given much thought.

Medieval schoolmen were much occupied with spiritual realities: for them, angels and devils (which might now be deemed the products of their imagination) had a real existence. But they were aware that this existence was somehow different from a man's perception of, and his thought about, an actual solid object under his nose in the material world. Their doctrine of transsubstantiation decreed that the wine consecrated at the celebration of the Mass actually became the blood of their Lord. On this many schoolmen began to have doubts and were, in consequence, accused of heresy. It was also heretical to believe in magic. Yet, to a modern mind, belief in transsubstantiation must itself be regarded as a belief in magic.

When it came to using the intellect on matters non-spiritual, introspection showed that the use of names was ambiguous. The human mind tends to exaggerate resemblances and differences and to assume that all objects called by the same name are identical, and those by different names, of necessity dissimilar. We generalise about women, or Russians, without noting or accepting individual differences. Medieval men used descriptive words like 'essence', 'substance', 'individuation'. Are all things or people of one name identical 'in essence' and so on. The problem of universals, which arises out of this, is one which philosophers find it hard to solve. The schoolmen used the term *realist*, oddly enough, to represent generalisation, lumping all certain objects together under one name. *Nominalists*, on the other hand, were those who sought out and clarified individual differences.

Since, in our times, the term realist stands for the scientific view of our world, it is important to understand what realist meant to the medieval mind. The thought of a realist might start from universals, in the sense that he would be aware of a group – cats, trees, men, what you will – whose existence he notes and to which he gives a general *name*. But all things which exist begin in the mind of God, who creates them. Hence, according to Plato, since universals exist first in the mind of God, then there must be a perfect *idea* of each object, or person, in God's mind, to which the form or character of the object or person appearing on earth merely approximates. Man, becoming aware of these less perfect objects or persons, may see them at first as a whole group – cats, trees, men – or else group them together after meeting one after another of their kind. Conversely, knowing that cats, trees, men, exist as a class, the mind begins to perceive how different one cat, tree, or man is from another, and thus the mind adopts *individuation*, and therefore approaches the *nominalist* point of view, each object or person being known also individually by the given name.

To the modern rationalist all this may seem childish, but it played a great part in the way men divided and directed their thought. Men who believed in God, either implicitly, or by compulsion, of necessity also believed that anything in the mind of God must be perfect; when therefore men perceive on earth the actual material (and hence imperfect) objects or persons, they then carry them as ideas in their minds, and cherish the hope that things or persons on earth may with time, or effort, approach perfection.

Whether in the mind of the believer, or the atheist, the ideal of perfection, attempted either by means of the intellect, or imagination, has never departed from human consciousness.

These deliberations echo down the centuries, are heard, for instance, in Shakespeare: 'What's in a name? A rose by any other name would smell as sweet. O Romeo, Romeo, wherefore art thou Romeo?' (Are you the unique young man whom I love, or no more than just one of your horrible family?) And in search of perfection:

> Earthly power doth then show likest God's
> When mercy seasons justice.

The schoolmen were much confused by what we might call different spheres of reality. They became aware of the differing aspects or levels of their consciousness. They could no longer easily escape from the dominion of the one omnipotent god whom, on the guarantee of the incarnation of Christ, they had accepted and institutionalised. With him they accepted also the fantasies of angels and devils, just as men had previously believed in the gods whom their imagination had created.

Then there were these *ideas* in their minds, which some held to be actual material *things*, not merely concepts. There was this intellect, separate from the soul. Intellect having stirred in them scientific curiosity, they could not help noticing how much they, together with men of all classes, achieved with their hands and bodies, as well as with their minds. Among the peasants, as they also knew, there still existed instincts about the old gods, spirits in nature, spells and charms, that were evil and must be suppressed.

In all this confusion, on what element in their consciousness should they rely for guidance; what was real or unreal, what was the truth that came from their god?

Solid material things seemed real enough. Among the non-corporeal though, there was time. Time was felt to be very real, you could begin to divide it, almost as if it were something solid, and, into the bargain, by means of solid manmade contrivances. More and more the function of the intellect began to appear as the instrument used to examine, to differentiate, to divide, to analyse.

The word commonly used by scholars to describe this analytical faculty was quite simply 'reason'. The long wrangle began as to whether by reason alone the existence of God can be proved, or whether, beyond reason, belief is required even to postulate God. The argument is still going on. Reason was also seen as a faculty distinct from feeling; to be employed, in fact, to control or regulate excess of feeling, whether of hatred or even of love. Reason as 'charioteer of the passions' was much later so described by philosophic hedonists. The schoolmen, aided by Arab and Greek thought, had established for themselves, and emphasised, its importance to clarity of thought.

However much the schoolmen have agreed or disagreed in philosophic argument, the dates show that Duns Scotus and William of Occam were of a younger generation. Aquinas died in 1274, Bacon two years later. The younger men, even supposing that both, by the age of 20, were voicing their opinions in Oxford and Paris, which had continued to be the centres of unorthodoxy, this could hardly have been before the turn of the century. They were operating in an already greatly changed political climate.

After the death of St Francis of Assisi in 1226, the friars continued in good odour, but presently were in some conflict with papal authority, by which in 1233 the Inquisition for dealing with heretics had been established. The men of the commanding heights – ecclesiastics, royals, emperors – had more or less abandoned their campaign against the infidels for the Holy Sepulchre; in 1244 Jerusalem fell to the Moslems and was not recovered for Christians until 1918 by the English General Allenby.

Turning back to home affairs, those in power found that the infernal doctrines of those infidels had been infiltrating the minds of their scholars through the back door of their own universities. A crusade against home-grown infidels and heretics began. The ban on Roger Bacon, already noted, was a part of this campaign. In 1277, the bishop of Paris, with due papal authority, condemned 219 heretical doctrines. Supporters of Averroes' theories hastily fled to take cover under whatever régime was likely to afford protection. Some went to Italy; it was not quite so bad, perhaps, in England. Some were excommunicated, but this was no great matter just then, for the church itself was in disarray. The secular powers – the kingdoms – and the ecclesiastical were in a state of bitter warfare; besides this each group was at war within itself. Pope Boniface VIII, accused of Averroism, repudiated by the French, was protected in England; the puppet pope set up by the French in Avignon summoned the English scholar, William of Occam, among other heretics, to Avignon to answer for his sins! William escaped and prudently took refuge with the German Emperor Louis in Munich.

Among these turbulent monastics, democracy even began to rear its ugly head: they ventured to suggest that the tenets of the faith should no longer be settled only by the pope, but by the learned community as a whole in council.

The political events of these wars between European nations, the struggles of various monarchs with papal authority, mostly for personal ends, as well as Protestant dissent and risings of the peasants, are well known to all students of history. Their relevance here is simply to illustrate how deeply and widely the conclusions of abstract conscious thought, whether expressed as dogma or freely in open discussion, influence the conduct of public affairs and human destiny.

The church succeeded in suppressing the dangerous move towards scientific enquiry. The relentless persecution by the Inquisition was carried out by orthodox authorities who themselves, including the monastic orders, were by now largely corrupted by their own power and wealth. It was convenient to be able to seize the property and land of condemned heretics. Heresy hunting was not confined to doctrine; it covered astrology, alchemy, occult sciences, anything that could be condemned as superstition and the work of the devil. Records of the inquisitors themselves boast of the numbers whom they had burned, and reveal the horror, foulness, pornography, of their minds. Carnal lust in women was alleged as the source of witchcraft. Thousands of young women must have been burned on the denunciation of rejected lovers, who could accuse them of stealing the potency of men by their spells.

The activity of female consciousness, persecuted under the title of witchcraft, is not specially dealt with in this book, because, as is evident, it was associated with the general horror of woman as a sex. Male consciousness was dominant. Witchcraft has been studied by historians: it was a part of the undercurrent of the old 'nature' religions, already referred to, in which women were involved. There were wise women, who could foretell the future, who made potions and spells. Much of their knowledge came from the discovery of medicinal and healing herbs, with which they ministered to the sick and the wounded in battle, being rewarded, if denounced, by burning at the stake, according to the edict of the Inquisition. Orthodoxy held that life and death are in God's hands, and to be sought only by prayer.

Doctrinal heresy hunting was seen at its worst in France, which then had the papal power in its control. A famous example is that of the Cathari, better known as the Albigenses, in southern France, where heretics were numerous. The extreme asceticism of their view, that all matter was evil, might surely have recommended them to the Inquisition. Unfortunately they showed remarkable perception and temerity by rejecting Jehovah as evil, and proclaimed that the New Testament alone revealed the true God. They were literally extinguished, put to death by their persecutors.

In spite of the great risks, some of the priesthood, freed from monastic vows, as well as seclusion, assisted the expansion of education and discussion, which now began to concern itself with the rights and wrongs of civil government. William of Occam held and wrote political views; Wycliffe (1320–84), an ordinary priest, for a time Master of Balliol, lectured in Oxford on civil government and began to translate the Bible. There were, as yet, no printed books, these did not appear before 1446 at the earliest. Wycliffe was in danger, but protected by the growth of popular opinion and the influence of the young queen, wife of Richard II, who came from Bohemia, where the heretics that followed Huss were in sympathy with Wycliffe. The tragedy of the fate of Huss himself is well known. Summoned to the Council in Constance (1414–18) for discussion, on a safe conduct, he was seized and burnt as a heretic. The Council, which had been called to deal with disorder and disunity in the church, took its revenge on Wycliffe by ordering the disinterment and burning of his bones. Is there not a strange parallel here between the story of Huss, and that of a young lecturer in present-day Czechoslovakia, persecuted for holding seminars on the philosophy of Plato and Aristotle, who is, furthermore, in close touch with his academic colleagues in Oxford?

The early years of the fourteenth century had seen the beginning of a time of death and destruction in Europe. There were changes in the weather; heavy rains destroyed crops; famine ensued. There were plagues, their contagion greatly helped by the squalor and dirt of the congested, growing cities. About mid-century came the Black Death, striking down a population already weakened by malnutrition. The people of whole villages simply perished and with them the villages themselves, which were completely lost until, in recent times, the traces of some of them have been discovered by aerial reconnaissance.

In spite of natural disasters, men went on making wars; the

Hundred Years War at last came to an end when the French defeated the English in 1453. But nearly two centuries elapsed before the population of Europe reached the numbers it had been before the Black Death struck.

As Italy revived and became more prosperous, Greek refugees from the Turkish incursion into Constantinople stimulated that great literary and artistic revival known as the Renaissance. Owing to the Wars of the Roses in England the full tide of the Renaissance was delayed there until the time of the Tudors.

By then the character and basic beliefs of the peoples of European Christendom had been cast in the mould prepared for them by the fathers of the church in 300 AD. Bitter sectarian and ritual differences still existed and led to being burnt at the stake. But a basic orthodoxy accepted: Jesus Christ as God, his resurrection; ritual mass or communion; birth in sin, the evil of sex and the body; salvation and a future life for the baptised and virtuous.

Old and New Testament were the Word of God, who had created the world and given the use of everything upon it, even before the creation of Eve, into the hand of man. This hard shell of Christianity – its missionary, proselytising aspect – enclosed what may, in this context, be called the soul of Europe.

In the age of expansion, and voyages of discovery that now dawned, this European soul went forth in many guises – but always thoroughly indoctrinated, deeply impregnated with the myths of that religion and the words of the Holy Book – to convert the infidel and heathen peoples. Where conversion was not accepted, conquest by force inevitably followed.

Following the discovery of America by Columbus in 1492, in 1519 Cortes arrived on the shores of Mexico, a land perceived as rich in all the varieties of life which the natural world could provide. He was greeted by natives who brought fish and other foods. Presently he and his soldiers were standing at attention while a lengthy disquisition in Latin was read to the assembled populace, in which he commanded their immediate conversion to Christianity and announced that he took possession of them and their country in the name of the Father, the Son and the Holy Ghost and the king and queen of Spain. A translation of this rigmarole by a Jesuit priest, professing to know the native language, followed. Conversion rejected, slaughter and despoiling began. With consummate treachery, an almost identical procedure was repeated in 1530 by Pizarro in Peru.

When, much later, Protestant settlers arrived in the cold inclement north, while thanking god for their deliverance from storm and danger to reach safe landing, in their hearts they cherished their Bible stories and identified themselves with the people of Israel entering, according to the promise of the Scriptures, into their Promised Land.

So began that iniquity which has been called the 'development' of two great, rich continents, continuing to this day. There is nothing here resembling the Marxist theory of the inevitable natural growth of a civilisation by means of gradual changes in the means of production. These conquests and similar events in very many other regions of the world derive from the fatal words of those first chapters of Genesis, almost, as it were, engraved in the skulls of the Judaic Christian – that God created the earth and gave it to man to do with as he willed. The religion of Christ has many other aspects, but there have been none more formidable and dangerous in their effects.

The minds of those monastic men in thirteenth-century Europe lay like a kernel in the heart of that savage outer shell. More important than all the turmoil of violence that surrounded their relative quiet were these seeds – alas both bad as well as good – of a future civilisation. The achievements of that period are often cited as an example of the beneficial effects of consensus – which means a general agreement about the universe, man's place and conduct within it – an argument, it may be said, for dictatorship, oligarchy, or totalitarianism. The flaw lay in how to handle dissent, which may prove – as it did in that age – the road to violence and war. This dilemma still awaits solution.

One merit of that period was the vision of co-operation and co-ordination between men as imaginative artists, scientific thinkers, artisans and tillers of the soil – a classless state, not achieved but at least seen as possible and in small part attempted.

But there was a fundamental falsity about the whole package of this consensus – its lack of understanding (until St Francis) of the values of organic life, with its implication, the outlawing of sex as sin. Of course people of that day enjoyed sex and the beauties of nature about them, but, by command of their religion, these were forbidden pleasures. Women were in that category, except for the procreation of children. Women still had no legal rights or power. Women of aristocratic or bourgeois birth were property used in making suitable diplomatic marriages. Such women could manage, by sex wiles, by intrigues, like men, to achieve some of their aims for themselves, or their sons, within the system. Signs of their self-assertion appear in the cult of romantic love and the serenading of the troubadours conceived by the lively ladies of Provence. Only at great risk could such love have found physical expression. Indeed love, now increasingly the theme of poetry, song and drama, retains the spiritual, unearthly quality of its religious definition, like Dante for his Beatrice.

Medieval times make mention of the ducking of scolding women. Socrates was said to have been nagged by his wife; the voices of women in protest are heard in Greek drama. How far were they heard in real life? Was perhaps the medieval bourgeoise and peasant woman more active in giving her man 'a piece of her mind' than her sisters of antiquity?

Most significant result of the introspection so diligently undertaken by the schoolmen was the definition of reason – the intellect – as a faculty differing and separate from the soul. That St Thomas Aquinas did not agree with that separation, but held that reason was contained within the soul, is significant of the stand which religion was to take on this issue. Religion seeks to offer a comprehensive view, as controlling guidance for the whole of life; strictly it would prefer not to admit the existence of the secular arm. It might be said that in early tribal life subservience to the gods, plus democracy, provided a basis for harmony; advance to organised government brought temporal and psychic leadership and hence the unending conflict between kings and priests. The church might accept that for centuries common sense – reason – had been operating in many spheres of human thought and action, such as government, diplomacy, law, decisions of daily life, not directly related to religious precepts and considerations; but divided counsels within their own flock between reason, exerted and applied by man, and soul, which belongs to God, were quite another matter and equivalent to subversion.

In fact what the schoolmen had done was to disentangle the two strands in human consciousness which Plato and his disciples had twined together and confused. In his excitement at the height and power reached by the mind in mathematics, Plato, followed by others, had identified the exaltation which belonged to that activity with the mystical longing and aspiration of what in man they called the soul towards a being in the universe, whom they postulated and called God. The intellectual discipline demanded by mathematics was of a totally different order from mystical aspiration. Applying the intellect to the study and analysis of the material world, as intended by Grosseteste, Roger Bacon, and Peter of Maricourt, was something different again, though it had shown signs of emerging in the work of one or two of the Greek philosophers.

Had the church accepted the pursuit of scientific enquiry, the direction and quality of the resultant researches might well have been different. The quest of that perfection which is truth might have been seen in alliance with that perfection which is goodness. Once again the words of Genesis, warning against the forbidden fruits of knowledge, barred the way.

Although the word reason has been used for centuries in disputes between theologians and philosophers, the word intellect, now commonly used in the context of science, is more correct. Reason is certainly defined as a conscious faculty of man, but it has acquired many associations and connotations, as, for instance, that of the art of persuasion. Reason may be used as a check or curb on excess of feeling, either of love or hate. Intellect, on the other hand, a keen-edged tool, stands for an element in consciousness which seeks to establish facts and truths about which, so far as evidence goes, there can be no compromise. Mathematics, from which it derives, is devoid of feeling, apart from the joy of achievement. Applied in scientific exploration, and conclusions arising therefrom, the intellect does not merely serve as a curb, it must, in the interest of exactitude and impartiality, entirely exclude feeling.

The intellect clarifies, divides and analyses; it tends to be the enemy of synthesis. In almost all those sciences that deal with the natural world, it takes substances to pieces even down to the very last, finest particle. It is not so easy to put them together again, for this something more than pure intellect is required. It can dissect all the contradictions of a problem in economics or in law, but, at the end, offer no solution or decision. It can demonstrate to the emotional patriot that within the Russian nation exist highly differentiated individuals, but it cannot compel any American to love any one of them or the totality.

What theologians and philosophers did not realise is that mystical longings and aspirations are born first of all from feeling, which comes from the body, not the soul. Together with, and through, these emotions the creative imagination comes to life. Without these, in total isolation, the intellect, except in the sphere of mathematics, has limitations almost prohibitive of creation. Feeling and imagination are required to create any work of art, for dealing with people, for uniting them, for any generous or creative action.

The medieval monastic, for the most part within four walls, isolated from the organic life outside, forgoing the companionship of sexual love and family life, suffered sensual deprivation. The absorption of his active mind in mathematics was predictable. With what he could learn of its practical lessons about forces, strain, balance, in the manipulation of inorganic materials, in this barren state and alone, the intellect of man did achieve a new unique possibility. It began to make the first real machines.

Why, since the Moslem philosophers had so clear a concept of a universal intellect, did not they also make machines? Perhaps for the very reason that they had not deprived themselves of wives and families. What is more, they had a reverence for nature that the Christians had discarded. For them, in some way, the universe had always been there; it was not created by God out of nothing for the use of man. Nor, although they believed in a future life, did they therefore regard their passage through this mortal one as a mere penance. For good or ill, for the future of the world, Europe in its period of ascetic Christian belief gave birth also to faith in mechanism.

At the close of the Middle Ages what might be said of the state of the minds of the peoples of Europe? It had changed very little, as expressed in action, since the fall of the Roman Empire.

Cities and means of communication had grown, there was a new distribution of powers, both spiritual and temporal. What might be called law and order had been established within the new separate kingdoms. In spite of doctrinal schisms between the now differing ecclesiastical authorities, the basic tenets of Christianity as a state religion had been firmly imposed on the peoples, its dogmas and myths deeply implanted in their hearts and minds. Wars between the secular kingdoms continued; the belligerent element in Christianity was uppermost in violent suppression among its own adherents, as in slaughter of the infidels.

The cult of the Virgin which had begun and was growing, brought to the imagination new images of woman, her beauty, gentleness, femininity and piety, a valuation existing only in the minds of men, bearing little relation to what woman really was, or might be, and which resulted in no change in her enslavement as male property. Indeed, entire freedom from woman, as from all sensual delights, had shown the mind of man at its coolest, keenest and potentially most powerful.

Was it then proving true, as Christ had once warned, that he was come not to bring peace, but a sword? Surely in Christian Europe there had clearly been an immense expansion of love and charity, caring for the poor, building almshouses for the old? Were not many of those who endured persecution, torture and death by burning, true followers of Christ, suffering as he suffered for his beliefs? It is true that the monasteries gave food to those who came for it; it is also true that corrupt priests and friars exploited the fears and superstitions of the people, while the charitable, who endowed the building of cathedrals and abbeys, paid no more than lip service to the gospel that they professed to follow. To martyrs, who claimed to suffer in the name of Christ, must be accorded the honour of accepting that they felt themselves true believers; and that they vindicated the right of a free man to follow the dictates of his conscience.

But what in essence and truth did Jesus Christ really say?

Or rather, first of all, what did he NOT say? He did not say that man must make war on unbelievers; he did not forbid man to use his mind for the observation and understanding of the natural world; on the contrary, he loved and admired the variety, beauty and colours of nature, drew from these in his parables – from fishing, growing the corn, the vineyards. He did not say that sex was a sin and man would be better advised to try and do without carnal knowledge of woman. On the contrary, he made clear his disgust at the cruelty, especially as regards sex, with which women were treated. Rare among prophets, he spoke of the existence and natural disposition of children.

For the rest he simply stated that wealth, power and violence are so much nonsense, since they prevent the one thing needful for man, that he should love his neighbour as himself. Peace, persuasion, compassion, generosity, passive resistance, were not only the most creative, but the most powerful, forces in the world. He asked no more than that men and women should behave like human beings. That message, obscured and perverted by those purporting to follow him, and welcomed by the power-drunk who delight in ruling docile populations, has not yet fully penetrated the consciousness of humanity. None the less, it has gone on working there as a continuous expanding leaven, stirring wherever oppression, accident, hunger and want, or natural disaster, bring men and women together in brotherhood and sisterhood. It may, even yet, achieve fulfilment.

CHAPTER 6

Consciousness expands

With the Renaissance came a mood of enterprise and expansion to the peoples of Europe. It brought with it the full meaning conveyed by Greek and Roman culture in literature, the arts and political thought, to add to what was already known to scholars about their mathematics and, in part, their philosophy. Assisted by rising prosperity, all the arts, literature, poetry, drama, painting, architecture, began to flourish in Europe as never before or since. The known world was expanding too, in response to the adventure of travel; fine ships were built, and navigation aids diminished the dangers faced by seafarers. Weapons of war were not neglected, they were improved; the cannons got larger.

In describing the Greeks we have already noted the profound and lasting influence of classical culture in all the arts as it passes into the European heritage. The grip of its mythology on the imagination, equally profound, was more subtle and pervasive. But of prime outstanding and enduring significance were the two languages, Greek and Latin themselves. Because the literate and educated few had hitherto spoken and written in Latin, and read Greek, these two languages provided the basis for the teaching in schools and universities as these began to be established in Europe. The two classical languages became the main part of the requirement for entry to the university, but also, much later, in upper-class England they permeated down to junior school level. What is more, in various sciences, we still have Latin names for cultivated and wild plants; in physiology; for medical drugs. A great many of the Greek and Latin words that became part of the English language itself, known as the 'learned borrowings', came into our language at that period. But learning Greek and Latin and Christian doctrines was far from the whole story. Just as the horizon of the earth widened, so also did the horizon of the mind. Nothing is more impressive about those times, when books began to be printed and distributed, than the exultant joy which people felt and showed in the use of their very own modern – not classical – languages.

English, born from Anglo-Saxon with Norman intrusions, had been shaped over many years into an instrument of great beauty to which the sixteenth and seventeenth centuries were to make a superb contribution. From the rhyming songs of the mystery plays, from anonymous folksong, from Chaucer's Canterbury Tales, English poetry flows on in a widening, shining river to burst forth into the great sea of rolling billows of Shakespeare and the gentler ripples of the Elizabethan lyric poets. Later come the words of the Authorised Version of the Bible and the English Prayer Book to sound in English ears and engrave themselves in English hearts for countless generations to come. May it not be that poetry and myth are what truly moves nations? They are interwoven with the fabric of people's lives. In the early summer of 1939, in a preface to his new edition of the Oxford Book of English Verse, Sir Arthur Quiller Couch wrote:

> The reader, turning the pages of this book will find this note of valiancy – of the old Roman 'virtue' mated with cheerfulness – dominant throughout, if in many curious moods. He may trace it back, if he care, far beyond Chaucer to the rudest beginnings of English Song. It is indigenous, proper to our native spirit, and it will endure.

The first two poems in the book are:

Cuckoo Song (1226)

> Sumer is icumen in,
> Lhude sing cuccu!
> Groweth sed, and bloweth med,
> And springeth the wude nu –
> Sing cuccu!

Awe bleteth after lomb,
Lhouth after calve cu;
Bulluc sterteth, bucke verteth,
Murie sing cuccu!

Cuccu, cuccu, well sings thu, cuccu:
Ne swike thu naver nu;
Sing cuccu, nu, sing cuccu,
Sing cuccu, sing cuccu, nu!

and

The Irish Dancer   (1300)

Ich am of Irlaunde
Ant of the holy londe
of Irlande.
God sire, pray ich the,
For of saynte charité,
Come ant daunce wyth me
In Irlaunde.

The first was still sung in girls' secondary schools about
1912; secondary school boys probably imbibed more patriotic
verse: whilst prep school boys construed poetic effusions in
Latin. How far traditional poetry plays its part in schools
today may be in question. But there is no doubt about the
emotional need for poetry which our people still feel. 'Q.', in
his preface, on the eve of the Second World War, evokes the
deep old traditions of that system of English education born
in the age of the Tudors. Does this note of 'valiancy' – of poetry
– still endure? And does not the Irish Dancer's invitation still
await acceptance?

To discern what went on in the conscious mind and imagination of the Renaissance period, little more is needed than to
plunge into Shakespeare, plays, sonnets, lyrics and all. Of
course, he is more than this; he has become in most parts of
the world a genius in whom may be found the voice of almost
everything in the human condition.

He speaks to us from a time when man had begun to realise
the whole of himself, regaining some of what humanity had
lost from the age of the Greeks, even the Romans; at the same

time enriched by the growth of knowledge and the opening up of new worlds to explore. There was a growth of courage, too, of a robustness, that overcame natural inherent fears. Man descended from the heights on which his religious mentors had required him to live; he was no longer intimidated about caring for beauty, charm and the pleasures of the body. Because it seems to include and take into account the whole of man, this period has been regarded as Humanist.

In that age a man of the privileged classes, who possessed physical health, strength and swordsmanship, a warrior willing and able to fight for his sovereign, was endowed also with all the graces of the courtier, the lover and the poet; he might well be conversant with what was happening in the arts in Florence and Venice. Where war in progress did not intervene, travel in Europe, as education, began to exist, besides seafaring for discovery and plunder. Though our histories recount events in the different countries of Europe, these were still not, in any real sense, nations. The only persons who counted were still royal, imperial, or ecclesiastical, together with the dominant families, landowners, who might still command private armies.

In England, from Magna Carta onwards, the conflict between the barons and the king had resulted, under Edward I towards the end of the thirteenth century, in the beginning of a constitution and a representative Parliament. The rapacity of the papacy, through its power over drawing funds through the English churches, produced some sort of cohesion between the nobles and the crown against foreign extortions. Under Henry III in England, the climate of opinion towards Europe somewhat resembled that towards the Common Market of today.

The struggle for power between king, church and nobility was continuous. But, in the main, in England, the king held on to the ultimate advantage, consolidated under the Tudors.

With the Renaissance the Greek concept of democracy as an ideal re-entered the consciousness of those scholars who were partisans of the new learning. Sir Thomas More wrote his *Utopia*. Spontaneous real-life democracy by the peasants, so often brutally put down, had astoundingly succeeded and survived in a small pocket in Europe. In Schwyz, a small canton (now part of Switzerland) peasant farmers had broken away from subservience to Rome and to overlord landowners. The story is shrouded in legends, how they burnt down castles and slew tyrants. The fact is that the conflict went on through the latter half of the thirteenth century, culminated in a League between Uri, Schwyz and Unterwalden, consolidated by 1315 as a democracy, joined later by other cantons and existing as a democratic republic of the people to this day.

Meantime the top-level people in the larger European countries, while still prepared for war, were turning towards alliances, diplomacy, religious intrigues, as ways of holding or attaining power, though they, too, were prepared to consider theories about the conduct of government. Machiavelli's book *The Prince* had a considerable and not very desirable influence. Royal marriages and alliances, entered into for short-term considerations, were apt to have unforeseen long-term consequences. For instance, Henry VII, frugal and cautious, after making himself secure on the throne against the pretensions of one claimant after another, looked with foresight to the security of his country in the international scene. He married his eldest son Arthur to Catherine of Aragon, the Spanish princess, when both were about 10 or 11 years old. They were being educated with great care for an august destiny. Unhappily, a year after the betrothal, before the final ceremonies were completed, Arthur died. As is well known, Henry, who did not want to lose Catherine's considerable dowry, after long negotiation, arranged for her to be married to his second son, Henry. Henry VIII's desire for a son and heir, his divorce and matrimonial tangles, cost a great many lives. But it was the long-drawn-out dispute between both sides about the church's doctrine that a man may not marry his deceased brother's wife, which finally led to the break with the pope, the founding of the Church of England, with the secular power of the king as the head of the church and the articles of faith ultimately determined by act of Parliament.

Henry VII married his eldest daughter Margaret age 14 to James IV of Scotland, who at first refused, but later accepted her. The plan was to attach Scotland to England. It was laid down that, should the throne of England have no heir, then the

Scottish king should reign, Scotland, however, taking second place. This marriage presaged the tragic life and death of Mary Queen of Scots, those who served her and her cause, exacerbated the controversy between Catholics and Protestants, both sides of the border, as well as the unhappy rivalry between the two queens, Elizabeth and Mary, and placed on the shoulders of Elizabeth the appalling responsibility of signing Mary's death warrant.

Men and women in positions of power played for high stakes, forever gambling with life and death, their personal agonies providing the stuff of great romantic poetic dramas, as Shakespeare and those who followed him were well aware.

Schiller, in his *Maria Stuart*, imagined and created the dramatic meeting between the two queens, which, in fact, never took place. Schiller also sought to immortalise a very different heroic figure, William Tell, of the canton of Uri. His unerring arrow severed the apple poised on his son's head, and also slew one of the tyrants – a story that has thrilled very many young children's hearts. No matter that William Tell probably never existed; a myth of humble men striving for their home and freedom is potent and long lasting.

While the Swiss, so early in the history of Europe, had been able to lay the foundation of a democratic republic, the English, by the sixteenth century, at last emerged from the power of the feudal barons only to find themselves subject to an absolute monarch. What is more, their king now wielded both spiritual and temporal power. Henry VIII, as the head of his church, now owned the wealthy abbeys and monasteries with their productive lands and fine buildings – those centres of peaceful and civilised living from which had issued both learning and invention. Their sale was highly profitable to the king. He was able to use them, through gifts by favour, or for merit and useful services to their sovereign, to build up a new aristocracy, who, in a society expanding in enterprise and trade, were bourgeois rather than feudal in temperament.

The minds of this and coming generations turned increasingly towards the affairs of this world; the motive prompting hostility to the pope and Catholic dogma was due as much to rivalry with Spain in commerce and military power as to any deep concern with religion. Henry's young son Edward VI, reared as a Protestant, by building and endowing colleges, fostered and extended education, thus stimulating and expanding the consciousness of the English people and their awareness of themselves as a society.

None the less the eleven years that followed the early death of the young king, and the reign of Mary up to the accession of Elizabeth, were the scene of tragic religious and personal suffering and conflict. The attempt to prevent Mary ascending the throne led to the execution of the innocent young Lady Jane Grey. After this thousands who could no longer accept Catholic doctrine (mainly on the interpretation of the Mass) fled to Europe. Archbishop Cranmer, and two younger men, educated in Cambridge and familiar with the newer ways of thought at home and abroad, Nicolas Ridley, bishop of London, and Hugh Latimer, who had felt themselves able to teach and preach more freely under Edward, could not save themselves by flight.

They and hundreds less eminent were burnt at the stake. The story of how Cranmer thrust into the fire the offending right hand that had signed his previous recantation, and how Latimer, as the fire was kindled, called out to Ridley, 'Play the man, Master Ridley, we shall this day, by God's grace, light such a candle in England, as I trust shall never be put out', renders an unforgettable tribute to the heroism of those who die for their firm conviction of what they hold to be the truth. So the heretics burned, but Mary's government conveniently forgot to return to the church the lands confiscated by her father.

And Hugh Latimer was right: his words have been repeated ever since to the pupils in all non-Catholic English schools. That these words were recorded as a landmark in history is due to a remarkable book known as *Foxe's Book of Martyres* (Haller, 1963). Foxe was among the hundreds of Protestants exiled abroad. In Strasbourg he began publishing in Latin stories of victims of persecution in the fifteenth and sixteenth centuries. By 1559 in Basle he produced a large volume, including the martyrs under Queen Mary. By 1563, after Elizabeth's accession, he appeared in England and published a still larger book in English, embellished with woodcuts. The relevance of this book here is the great contribution which it made to shaping the English national consciousness. Among the Protestant exiles, anxiously watching events at home, stories of the martyrs played their part in building up the concept of Elizabeth as the one hope of a settled, independent future for their country, and the dream of England as the elect nation with a princely ruler who cared for her people. In 1570, when the Papal bull excommunicated Elizabeth, Foxe produced yet another enlarged edition, which was ordered to be placed alongside the Bible to be read in churches. Somewhat similar, as Bernard Shaw suggested, the leadership and martyrdom of Joan of Arc was the inspiration of the consciousness of the French in beginning to realise themselves as a nation.

Once Elizabeth was on the throne, the English people began to be glad of the relief afforded by her religious compromises. After all, she herself had lived in fear of the executioner's axe, or of burning. Foxe's propaganda on the Protestant side may well have been needed at that stage to effect a respite and stability of opinion. However, honest reporting must admit that it has become part of the teaching of our history, endowed with a glamour almost impossible to resist, since it now lies far down below our consciousness in personal and national feeling. If we look squarely at the truth, all this brutal sectarian fanaticism was the very reverse of Christian brotherhood. It did not stop; it went on, it was the source of wars between nations, as of civil wars, and has continued on its abominable destructive course until this very day. What lies behind it and still does, is the male obsession with the concept of one all powerful god whom he has invented, and whose interference in human affairs each person or sect interprets in its own peculiar way.

The Renaissance was the period when humanity should have divested itself of this myth of divine control. It was a time of awakening to a sense of purely human values, as of the human ability to implement them and opportunity to live a full life in harmony with themselves and their expanding natural world.

Tragically, human consciousness had still to grow before reaching for a clarity of thought which could make that possible.

Quiet rational thought was not entirely lacking, especially among what were now the secular priests, or clergy, neither monks nor friars, who had come into existence through the dissolution of the monasteries, and were now to be found in charge of their flock in parishes. They speak of 'reason' and, while giving glory to God, 'consider the works of man on earth' and 'his excellent dignity'. English clerical thought from Wycliffe and even Duns Scotus, had shown concern with the 'here and now' of society and government. Richard Hooker, a distinguished sixteenth-century graduate of Oxford, chose a peaceful country living in which to write his *Laws of Ecclesiastical Policy*, still unfinished when he died in 1600. This passage reveals his accord with the mood of his times:

> forasmuch as we are not by ourselves sufficient to furnish ourselves with a competent store of things needful for such a life as our nature doth desire, a life fit for the dignity of man; therefore to supply these defects and imperfections which are in us living single and solely by ourselves, we are naturally induced to seek communion and fellowship with others. This was the cause of men's uniting themselves at the first in politic societies, which societies could not be without government, nor government without a distinct kind of Law. Two foundations there are which bear up public societies; the one, a natural inclination whereby all men desire sociable life and fellowship; the other, an order expressly or secretly agreed upon touching the manner of their union in living together. (Rubinstein, 1960)

The glory of the Elizabethan Age in England was precisely that her people did begin to feel that sense of fellowship. It restored them to self-confidence, courage and an enthusiasm for adventure, which overcame the state of fear and anxiety in which they had been living. So they went out and defeated the dreaded Spanish Armada. A rapid growth in trade and prosperity brought people flocking to London, which grew in size and soon became a cultural centre, in which poets and dramatists celebrated the achievements of popular heroes, men of destiny, past and present. Shakespeare, in his middle twenties, was almost certainly in London to join in the exultant mood of victory over the Spaniard.

What Shakespeare gave to the minds and hearts of all human beings – their moods, tragic or comic, their flights of fancy or folly, their soaring imagination, cannot be overestimated. But what he brought to the spirit and consciousness of his own people was the finest gift of all. Completely in tune with them and the times they were living in, he saw 'all the world a stage' for dramatic action. The theatre was open to all, rich or poor. Masses who flocked to it could neither read nor write. Shakespeare, literally creating for them the marvellous poetic instrument of the English language, unrolled for them in stirring drama the panorama of their own history; into the bargain he showed them how those old Romans conducted their politics and wars, and what those Italian gentlemen in Verona or Venice might be up to; even how, in past ages, there were kings who actually swore by the Apollo oracle at Delphi. Nor did he leave out the antagonism between Christian and Jew, or the relations between white and coloured peoples.

Some of the great compassionate pageant of human beings, thinking, feeling, hating, loving, succeeding, failing, presented by that magician on his simple, modest stage made its permanent mark on the English character, as on the spirit of all through history who read his plays or see live actors perform them, or listen to the cadence of his verse, the music and tenderness of his sonnets. Every contribution of genius to human consciousness is valuable, but that of Shakespeare has a special universality and power that will only pass away with the passing of our history itself.

The Renaissance period in other European countries was more aristocratic than in England. Many separate small states still existed, and the 'national consciousness' growing in England had not so far been created in France, Italy and Spain. The minds of all the European peoples were still concentrated on their one Christian God, but the face which he now presented, which differed from principality to principality, was no longer a uniting but a divisive force.

Temporal and spiritual power have been our theme: in Europe monarchs versus popes presented yet another divided allegiance to the peoples. Was it the fusion of the two powers in one royal figure, in England, stifling or muting the voices of Catholic and Protestant alike, which, ironically, contributed to the growth of that stubborn English democracy which in the next century caused the king to be executed for the crime of asserting his 'divine right'? When that happened, though the king was the sacrifice, their God still reigned supreme.

While imagination and the romance of real-life adventure were uppermost in the Elizabethan psyche, the undercurrent of speculative scientific thought continued. As also in Europe, that intellect which, according to Averroes, was common to all men but the private property of none, did not cease from observation and deliberation.

In England the finest intellect during the latter part of the reign of Elizabeth and into that of James I was Francis Bacon (1561–1626). His father was Sir Nicholas Bacon, Keeper of the Great Seal; his mother one of the distinguished learned women of the time who knew both Latin and Greek. Under James I Francis Bacon rose to be Lord Chancellor and was Baron of Verulam and Viscount of St Albans when he died.

Bacon's frequently quoted apparently boastful remark, 'I have taken all knowledge to my province' was in fact true in scope and achievement. He was distinguished as a statesman, lawyer, judge; a patriot loyal to the sovereign, but concerned with reconciling class as well as religious differences in his own society; one who could also perceive the prospect of imperial power; yet, beyond that, inspired by a vision of what man might achieve by scientific knowledge – a vision that embraced the world and all peoples. Francis Bacon has traditionally been regarded as the initiator in England of the application of the mind to the methods of science, but some recent researches, already mentioned in previous chapters, show that he must have been acquainted with and followed on the thought and discoveries of his predecessors in that field. In addition Bacon was an accomplished writer in both Latin and English, is looked upon as the creator of English prose, as Shakespeare was of English verse. These two men are massive complementary figures, matching a great period of history; the one a rich, universal temperament expounding the wayward passions of man; the other, almost devoid of feeling, expanding only in the regions of the intellect and dominated by legal and moral duty.

Francis Bacon went to Cambridge University at the age of 14, as was the frequent custom then for able young scholars. In his studies there he became disillusioned with the current teaching, based upon the philosophy of Aristotle, and indeed with the inadequacy of the philosophic mode of thought itself. He left Cambridge and at the age of 17 spent two years in France, which resulted in his pamphlet on the *State of Christendom*, in which he noted the dissensions among the French both in matters of the state and religion. For some provision or advancement he was relying on his father, whose sudden inopportune death brought him back to England and obliged him to take to the law as a profession, in which he was active and distinguished for forty years. In the intervals of studying law and scientific reading he found time to initiate and direct the laying out of extensive gardens around Gray's Inn, still existing, though probably very few of us are aware to whom we owe this very pleasant oasis in the heart of London.

Bacon would have preferred to devote his whole life to what he named the 'new philosophy', the 'mechanical arts'; but, of necessity, his time and energy were consumed by affairs of state. He sought endowment for scientific studies in vain from two sovereigns. The first to take such a step was to be Charles II, who founded the Royal Society. Science was Bacon's constant theme in voluminous writings, even in a masque performed on a royal occasion. Above all it was by the vision of science, his one passion, that he desired to be remembered by posterity, a wish which, unlike the fate of many other aspirants to fame, has been amply granted to him.

Seeking the origin of the male passion for science, the present writer came to, and put forward, the conclusion that it might derive from the sense deprivation of the medieval monastics. Amazingly, on next coming to study Francis Bacon, in his *Novum Organum* (i, 80, in Crombie, 1952, pp. 187–8) she found his remark that science 'has scarcely ever possessed, especially in these later times, a disengaged and whole man *unless it were some monk studying in his cell*, or some gentleman in his country house'. This would seem to confirm the present writer's guess.

As Bacon said, in 'these later times' which were his own the 'whole man' of the Renaissance was engaged in multiple activities. Though therefore Bacon, as devotee of science, is our concern, justice must be done to his far-ranging intelligence, his many-sided, enlightened political and social views, and his impartial judgment. In helping to unify the Established Church he wrote: 'God grant that we may contend with other churches as the vine with the olive, which beareth best fruit, and not as the brier and the thistle, which of us is the most unprofitable.' As a Member of Parliament, which he became at the age of 24, his defence of the people in the matter of taxes did not always please his queen. And as regards taxes, his contention that the Commons should not be in consultation with the House of Lords, has helped to preserve that right for the Commons to this day.

On class and economics he thought it unwise to have a large wealthy aristocracy, since this must mean poverty and serfdom for most of the population; moreover, if wealth were distributed more widely, a nation would the better stand up to a state of war with its enemies. He studied the Roman habit of granting citizenship in the context of what this meant in forming an empire.

Had Bacon been able to obtain an endowment for scientific studies, he might well have specialised and forsaken a public career and advancement. But for a man of his temperament and period this is doubtful. He must have enjoyed pouring out all those learned works and essays on all kinds of topics, just as posterity today enjoys plunging into their wit and wisdom. Expansive in all things, Bacon invented the idea of a zoological garden with animals and birds; lakes, one of salt water, one fresh, to contain fish; also varieties of soil and produce. Together with these there would be a museum for arts and crafts and inventions, a library and a laboratory for experiment. Such was his dream of a mythical kingdom ruled by an enlightened sovereign who would bring all these things to pass in perfection.

Bacon's legal mind could turn equally well to detail, to dissecting the problems of the schoolmen. But what attracted him above all were the empirical experiments in science of such men as Grosseteste, Roger Bacon, and Peter of Maricourt. Criticising the inadequacy of philosophy he wrote: 'Plato corrupted natural philosophy by his theology, as thoroughly as Aristotle by his logic.' And in the masque for the birthday of Queen Elizabeth in 1592 he contributed the speech 'Mr. Bacon in Praise of Learning'. In this he says, among other things:

Are we the richer by one poor invention by reason of all the learning that hath been these many hundred years? The industry of artificers maketh some small improvement of things invented and chance sometimes in experimenting maketh us to stumble upon somewhat which is new; but all the disputation of the learned never brought to light one effect of nature before unknown.

All the philosophy of nature which is now received is either the philosophy of the Grecians or that other of the Alchemists. That of the Grecians hath the foundation in words, in ostentation, in confrontation, in sects, in schools, in disputations. That of the Alchemists hath the foundation in imposture, in auricular tradition and obscurity. The one never faileth to multiply words, and the other ever faileth to multiply gold.

He goes on to suggest that all this should be replaced by a 'true science', 'the happy match between the mind of man and the nature of things'. He instances the benefits brought by inventions, the compass, artillery. Though he certainly saw science in terms of these benefits, which were such as to appeal to the mind of a ruler, he was no utilitarian. Like those brilliant thirteenth-century heretical minds he could perceive that in scientific knowledge lay a power beyond that yet dreamed of by priest or king.

Therefore no doubt [he continued to Elizabeth]. The sovereignity of man lieth hid in knowledge, wherein many things are reserved, which kings with their treasure cannot buy, nor with their force command, their spials and intelligence can give no news of them, their seamen and discoverers cannot sail where they grow. Now we govern nature in opinions, but we are thrall to her in necessity; but if we would be led by her in invention, we should command her in action.

Clearly the masculine mind was now set upon the search

for the 'real world' as understood by science. How best to apply those faculties of consciousness of which intelligent men were now also well aware? Deductive reasoning had given them mathematics; now the uncertainties of induction and empirical observation indicated the usefulness of experiment. Francis Bacon, in his famous Aphorism 95 *Novum Organum* Book 1 offers an analysis of method and advice to the aspiring scientist:

> Those who have handled sciences have been either men of experiment or men of dogmas. The men of experiment are like the ant; they only collect and use: the reasoners resemble spiders, who make cobwebs out of their own substance. But the bee takes a middle course, it gathers its material from the flowers of the garden and of the field, but transforms and digests it by a power of its own. Not unlike this is the business of philosophy; for it neither relies solely or chiefly on the powers of the mind, nor does it take the matter which it gathers from natural history and mechanical experiments and lay it up in the memory, whole as it finds it, but lays it up in the understanding; altered and digested. Therefore from a closer and purer league between these two faculties, the experimental and the rational (such as has never yet been made) much may be hoped. (Crombie, 1952, p. 388)

This was really the method which Grosseteste had already been pursuing; experiment, deduce conclusion, then verify or falsify by further experiment – in fact the practice of alternating between hypotheses and experimental tests which has become the foundation of Western science.

Bertrand Russell thought Bacon was 'somewhat unfair' to the ants! As regards the analogy with the bees: we may recall that Abelard, of Paris, was intrigued by 'how doth the busy bee' set about its business; the bee recurs presently to be rejected and misinterpreted by Descartes.

One world-famous figure, with the characteristic wide-ranging Renaissance temperament and intellect, was Leonardo da Vinci. Born in Florence in 1452, his death in 1519 precedes the birth of Francis Bacon by forty-two years. The reason that Bacon has been considered before him was simply in order to complete the picture of Elizabethan England. In the Italy of Leonardo there was, in his time, no such unity as in England.

In the towns and states of Italy only a limited number of the upper classes were influenced by the incursion of Greek literature and learning. Leonardo first became famous in Italian cities, as later in the world at large, as a brilliant artist. Since he was not, as was Francis Bacon, very much a man of words, and publicity agent for his unusual ideas, Leonardo as scientist has only been revealed gradually by the discovery of the astonishing notes and drawings which he left, but which currently passed between and were known to men of his type among his contemporaries in Italy.

No doubt the censorship of Papal dominion counselled secrecy. It was difficult and dangerous for Leonardo to obtain the bodies which he wanted in order to study muscle and skeletons for his art. A meticulous observer, with the eye of both art and science, Leonardo studied the problem of how the eye sees. When, like Archimedes (whose work he now knew), he was called upon by belligerent men of power to invent more powerful weapons of war, he busied himself with mechanics, more especially that of projectiles. He drew the wings, the feet, the heads of birds and animals. He was the first to observe, high up inland, the perplexing existence of fossils of marine creatures.

Like other men of his time it was the natural world about him that captured his imagination and stimulated his curiosity – 'the happy match of the mind of man and the nature of things', as Bacon said. Though in some respects he may be regarded as the forerunner of Galileo, and though he did, like Roger Bacon, envisage the possibility of machines for flight, he was little occupied with the universe and appears to have rested content with the cosmogony accepted by faith in Christian teaching. Thus Leonardo da Vinci has his place as the finest example of Renaissance consciousness – a love and concern for both mind and body of human and animal life, movement and purpose, here on earth.

One remarkable European starwatcher was his contemporary: Nicholas Copernicus, the Pole, born in 1473, dying in 1543, a man who dared not publish his findings until he died, the man whose vision of the universe was to burst asunder the walls of that tightly enclosed medieval world. Copernicus and his fellow starwatchers belong to the next stage in the story of the application of human consciousness to science. Before we move on it should be noted that there would appear to be no change in the ultimate values and purpose of those to whose hands human destiny was committed. Despite their professed belief in a god of peace and compassion, men were still in pursuit of power and wealth; by means of war, by acquisition through discovery and conquest, or invention. Whatever the creative mind and imagination of rare individuals might devise, the men of power demand and seize for their ends.

Women were, and continued to be, in subjection. But now there existed more women – of the upper class it is true – who took pleasure in study, more especially of languages, both ancient and modern. Among them was the figure of a queen, who, however much courted and tempted by her own feminine inclinations, had steadfastly refused to abdicate her sovereignty by accepting a consort in marriage.

What Francis Bacon wrote of her, five years after her death, to her grudging successor James I, does not seem to have found much place in the books of historians:

'On the Fortunate Memory of Elizabeth, Queen of England', 1606.
Elizabeth both in her nature and her fortune was a wonderful person among women, a memorable person among princes. . . .
    The government of a woman has been a rare thing at all times; felicity in such government a rarer thing still; felicity and long continuance together the rarest thing of all. Yet this Queen reigned forty-four years, and did not outlive her felicity. . . .
    Observe too that this same humour of her people, over eager for war and impatient of peace, did not prevent her from cultivating and maintaining peace during the whole time of her reign. And this her desire of peace together with the success of it, I count among her greatest praises;

as a thing happy for her times, becoming to her sex, and
salutary for her conscience. . . .

Upon another account also this peace so cultivated and
maintained by Elizabeth is matter for admiration; namely,
that it proceeded not from any inclination of the times to
peace but from her own prudence and good management.
For in a kingdom labouring with intestine faction on account
of religion and standing as a shield and stronghold of
defence against the then formidable and overbearing
ambition of Spain, matter for war was nowise wanting; it
was she who by her forces and her counsels combined kept
it under; . . .

Nor was she less fortunate in escaping the treacherous
attempts of conspirators than in defeating and repelling
the forces of the enemy . . . and yet was not her life made
thereby more alarmed or anxious . . . but still secure and
confident, and thinking more of the escape than of the
danger, she held her wonted course. . . .

With regard to her moderation in religion there may seem
to be a difficulty, on account of the severity of the laws
made against popish subjects. But on this point I have some
things to advance which I myself carefully observed and
know to be true.

Her intention undoubtedly was, on the one hand not to
force consciences, but on the other not to let the state,
under pretence of conscience and religion, be brought in
danger. Not even when provoked by the excommunication
pronounced against her by Pius Quintus, did she depart
almost at all from this clemency, but persevered in the
course which was agreeable to her own nature. For being
both wise and of high spirit, she was little moved with the
sound of such terrors: knowing she could depend upon the
loyalty and love of her own people, and upon the small
power the popish party within the realm had to do harm, as
long as they were not seconded by a foreign enemy.

As for those lighter points of character – as that she
allowed herself to be wooed and courted, and even to have
love made to her; and liked it; and continued it beyond the
natural age for such vanities – if any of the sadder sort of
persons be disposed to make a great matter of this, it may

be observed that there is something to admire in these very things, which ever way you take them. For if viewed indulgently, they are much like the accounts we find in romances, of the Queen in the blessed islands, and her court and institutions, who allows of amorous admiration but prohibits desire. But if you take them seriously, they challenge admiration of another kind and of very high order; for certain it is that these dalliances detracted but little from her fame and nothing at all from her majesty, and neither weakened her power nor sensibly hindered her business: – whereas such things are not infrequently allowed to interfere with the public fortune.

But the truth is that the only true commender of this lady is time, which, so long a course as it has run, has produced nothing in this sex like her, for the administration of civil affairs. (Rubinstein, 1960, p. 11)

CHAPTER 7

Alone in the face of the universe

With the death of Elizabeth in 1603, the balance which she had endeavoured to maintain between contending forces within her realm and in diplomacy between nations did not long survive. The power-seekers, royal or religious, persisted in their confrontations, savage persecutions and wars. Underlying these were two great movements of human consciousness, which held promise for the future. These were the growing belief in democracy as the rightful basis for human association in society; and the steadily expanding scientific knowledge of the world. In the next two centuries these two purposes, or directives, of the male conscious mind, exploded with devastating force in the English and French Revolutions, and in the revolt of scientific man against his gods.

For the time being the Renaissance imagination was fully occupied with, and somewhat bewildered by, the strange lands and peoples, the rich forms of life revealed when exploring a world that proved to be so much larger and afforded so much greater opportunity than human thought had ever hoped or dreamed. Enchanted with their earth, men no longer looked so often skyward. The stars were good to steer by, but their nature and meaning was of little moment. As Shakespeare put it, equating love with the inspiration of life's voyages:

> It is the star to every wandering bark
> Whose worth's unknown although his height be taken.

The perpendicular aspiration of the cathedrals had expressed one aspect of human ideals; in this age of expansion men might be said to have a horizontal mind. To penetrate those newly found lands in the West, to take ship and sail on and on in search of riches or plunder, or to find out what lay beyond the horizon – on one such adventure Francis Drake, in 1580, after three years' absence, was back where he started from.

Magellan had perished on a voyage of discovery. For it had begun to dawn on men that their earth, so long accepted as flat, might turn out to be round. But busy as they were with their quarrels, their quest for riches, power, glory or adventure, the vision of their wonderful world as a tiny globe spinning and whirling through infinite space would be the last notion likely to appeal to a Renaissance mind.

Yet the pursuit of scientific knowledge in other countries had differed in many respects from that of England and even France. The stimulus of the exciting period in the universities of Oxford and Paris of the twelfth and thirteenth centuries – the works of Grosseteste, Roger Bacon, Peter of Maricourt, Abelard – had focussed attention on the newly devised experimental methods to achieve practical results. Knowledge spelt invention and power. Such aims, it is true, were never absent: Leonardo da Vinci, like Peter of Maricourt, had been called upon to assist the war campaigns of overlords.

Copernicus the Pole (1473–1543), Tycho Brahe the Dane (1546–1601), Kepler the German (1571–1636), and Galileo the Italian (1564–1642), all of them accounted devout believers, had diverted their gaze from worldly affairs to the works of the Lord in his universe. It should be noted that the theories of Copernicus had been available and current some fifteen years or more before Francis Bacon was born. Galileo, born three years after Bacon, was his contemporary. Yet Bacon definitely did not accept the views of Copernicus and seems to have taken no interest in the activities of Galileo. In fact Bacon, undervalued by the queen, whom he near-worshipped, and rising to eminence at the right hand of her successor, might almost seem to have sought to continue to serve her by carrying on the ambience and principles of her reign. But religious and civil forces were sharpening for renewed conflict. Ironically Bacon lived on into the first year of the ill-fated Charles I, and died of a chill caught through impetuous experiment, on a bitter cold day, in freezing a fresh-killed chicken by stuffing it with snow.

Nicholas Copernicus, like so many of his time, astounds by his learning, as by his mobility in its pursuit. Educated at Cracow University, he next studied law in Bologna, while working at astronomy; went on to Rome, thence to Padua, to study medicine and to Ferrara to complete his studies in law. He settled down as a canon of Frauenburg cathedral in East Prussia, busily exercising his talents as cleric, doctor and diplomat. He reformed the currency. Mathematics was his passion and hobby. In this field, which was highly respected and had been associated with religion ever since Plato, Copernicus acquired a very considerable reputation. There was nothing strange in this elderly canon finding some time in his busy life to improve calculations, and apply them where they seemed to fit. Novara, a leading Platonist, had stirred in him the desire to conceive of the universe in terms of simple mathematical relationships. Arranging his celestial world according to his thesis, Copernicus gave a poetic description of the place given to the sun:

> But in the midst of all stands the sun. For who could in this
> most beautiful Temple place this lamp in another or better
> place than that from which it can at the same time
> illuminate the whole? Which some not unsuitably call the
> light of the world, others the soul or the ruler. Trismegistus
> calls it the visible God, the Electra of Sophocles the all-
> seeing. So indeed the sun, sitting on the royal throne, steers
> the revolving family of stars. (Crombie, 1952, p. 311)

He became diffident about his results, since those to whom he described them found them laughable; they were satirised on the stage in Frauenburg in 1531. To Martin Luther he was one of these cranks trying to upset the basis of astronomy, and anything that contradicted Holy Writ was clearly absurd. Everyone knew that Joshua had commanded the sun, not the earth, to stand still. 'Who will venture to place the authority of Copernicus above that of the Holy Spirit?' said Calvin. Neither of these pious clerics had much use for mathematics, or perhaps even for astronomy. The Catholics, more interested in theological discussion than the Bible narrative, at first

treated Copernicus's work as a piece of mathematical deduction, with no relevance to belief or terrestrial events. The pope
had knowledge of the work; consequently Cardinal Nicholas
von Schönberg asked Copernicus to make his views known to
the learned world. These were already fairly well known by
the time the book *De Revolutionibus Orbium Celestium*, dedicated to Pope Paul III, was published after Copernicus's death
in 1543.

The preface, which was by Osiander and not by Copernicus,
implied that the theory was merely a hypothesis. But it seems
that Copernicus himself did hold that he was dealing with
physical facts and not a mathematical design. Tycho Brahe
and Kepler took Copernicus's view seriously and worked upon
it. Tycho Brahe contributed much by his meticulous observations and the improved instruments which he used. Kepler's
calculation that the paths of the planets were ellipses and not
circles is well known, a conclusion distressing to the devotees
of orthodox Greek mathematics, which require perfect shapes
– circle, triangle, square and so forth.

The crucial importance of Copernicus was the response and
attitude to his theories of the minds of men of science, men of
the churches, men of the streets. It was a very long time, a
century or more, before the spinning globe could have much
meaning for the men of the streets; Galileo took the brunt of
the work that was necessary in science, as of the opprobrium
of ecclesiastical persecution. The figure of Galileo stands out,
in the record of history, as marking the point when human
consciousness moved into modern ways of thinking and, in
matters held to be of supreme significance, made its break
with the myths and superstitions of the past.

Why were Copernicus and his colleagues busy speculating
about the universe in this way? Surely the whole truth about
cosmogony had been settled long since by the interpretation
of the religion revealed by the coming of Christ. What need
was there for further enquiry?

Was it simply due to that restless, ceaseless activity of the
human brain, whose capacity had always exceeded its
biological requirements – to the insistent drive of the still-
expanding intellect? The movement of change was far more
complex. Part of the cause lay in the ever-widening dissemina-

tion of books of Greek literature, myths and poetry as well as science; in their stimulus to the imagination and a more sophisticated culture, as shown in the arts, painting, sculpture, poetry – Leonardo, Michelangelo, Shakespeare, and next, Milton. Multiple ideas and emotions were making their impact on the human spirit: concern with cosmogony revived not so much through the narrow striving of scientific intellect, as through pervasive religious and social unrest.

The great schism between Catholic and Protestant had tended to establish Catholic and Protestant nations, leading to wars waged for independence as well as religion, such as that between the Netherlands and Spain. Men were fighting also for liberty of conscience and personal liberty within the state. Power, whether royal or ecclesiastical, sought to maintain its dominance. Charles I in England ruled for eleven years without a Parliament, thus provoking the civil war which ended in his execution in 1649. In France, Louis XIV began, in 1643, his seventy-two years of absolute rule. Unlike Charles, whose official state religion was Protestant, Louis had official support from the papacy.

People were losing respect for the authority of kings as representatives of their god on earth, but still more for that of those more directly responsible, the bishops, the monks, the cardinals, the popes. The papacy was corrupt; princes and dukes in Italy did not neglect poison and dagger in their mutual warfare. Something had gone wrong with the Christendom so elaborately fashioned and imposed on the medieval world.

Smashing idols and the pomp of ornate churches, the English Puritans sought an immediate relation between the soul of each man and God his maker. They were often cruel and intolerant, as their opponents had been, but they were seeking in their religion and the relation of man to man, truths that had been corrupted and defiled. Maintaining their belief in the Christian God, they knew that he could not be ruling the world after the manner of these dishonest hirelings. 'Blind mouths that scarce know how to hold a sheep hook,' said Milton. He also spoke of the need to 'justify the ways of God to man'.

Man must find God and learn his ways. It must be possible

to apprehend God's laws – the 'laws of nature' which were not those of royal and papal charlatans. This concept of 'natural laws', of being able to find the will and purpose of God in the workings of the physical world, as distinct from the teaching of the spiritual authorities, was something quite new. It became influential and important. So in the end it was up to the scientists to redefine God in an image that would command man's reverence and worship.

The work and life of men and women, described as intellectuals, who become eminent, whether as poets, writers, artists, sculptors, architects, scientists, obviously shape but also mirror, the predominant climate and motives of their times. This was observable in Shakespeare, Elizabeth, Francis Bacon, now also in Milton; in Leonardo da Vinci, Galileo, Michelangelo; in the great French dramatists, Corneille, Racine and Molière, in thought, Blaise Pascal.

The conscious thought and emotions of such gifted people should be taken into account, for these offer a rich heritage to such people as are capable of understanding. Milton, so often presented in the schoolroom as the aged blind man dictating endless verse to his long-suffering daughters, actually lived in, was an integral part of, the pre-revolution, revolution, post-revolution of his epoch. The young Milton, at Cambridge University, bored with scholastic teaching, but not addicted to wenching and drinking, wrote those first poems 'L'Allegro', 'Il Penseroso', the masque *Comus*, all of them positively glowing with Greek myths and allusions. He travelled to visit the intellectuals of the Italian cities; enjoyed life, charmed his hosts. He was shocked at the effect of the Inquisition in stifling freedom of thought and enquiry among the Italian intellectuals, who envied the greater liberty of the English people. He told his fellow countrymen in *Areopagitica*:

> I could recount what I have seen and heard in other countries, where this kind of inquisition tyrannises, when I have sat among their learned men, for that honour I had, and been counted happy to be born in such a place of philosophic freedom, as they supposed England was, while themselves did nothing but bemoan the servile condition into which learning amongst them was brought; that this

was it which had damped the glory of Italian wits; that nothing had been there written now these many years but flattery and fustian. There it was that I found and visited the famous Galileo, grown old, a prisoner to the Inquisition, for thinking in astronomy otherwise than the Franciscan and Dominican licensers thought.

As a poet, he was, apparently, untouched by science, certainly not disposed to enter the lists in defence of the theories of Galileo and Copernicus, but stalwart in support of their right to hold them. Like his father, he was intensely a Protestant, sincere, forthright, courageous, convinced of and mainly concerned with the rights of the Parliament and people.

In his early thirties, politics bit deeply into his personal life. His wife, Mary Powell, of a somewhat profligate royalist family, left him within a month of marriage, ostensibly in fear of the imminent civil conflict. Milton had fallen in love, and no doubt had dreamed of much happiness. He wrote courageously in those far from tolerant times, a plea to change the law so that divorce for incompatibility might be possible. Ironically, after the civil war, defeated royalists sought shelter with Milton. His wife returned and bore him four children, but died soon after the last was born. It cannot have been a happy marriage.

In our own times, when the young with ideals take to violence in repudiation of an authority in whose dogmas they have lost confidence, it is not difficult to understand how the poet of cultured and flowery verses became a regicide. Nor is it surprising that orthodox believers continue to obscure Milton the pamphleteer by extolling *Paradise Lost* as the great epic of Christianity.

Milton believed that, in his time, God spoke through the common people. His magnificent defence of the freedom of speech, *Areopagitica, a speech for the liberty of unlicensed printing*, was addressed to Parliament.

I cannot praise a fugitive and cloistered virtue unexercised, unbreathed, that never sallies out and seeks her adversary, but slinks out of the race, where that immortal garland is to be run for, not without dust and heat.

When in 1651, Salmasius, a well-known scholar, expressed in the Latin *Defensio Regia pro Carlos I* the horror of enemies on the Continent at the execution of the king, Milton, though intensifying thereby the imminent threat of his blindness, wrote, in English, *Defence of the English People, by John Milton Englishman.*

> A most potent king, after he had trampled upon the laws of the nation, and given a shock to its religion and begun to rule at his own will and pleasure, was at last subdued in the field by his own subjects, who had undergone a long slavery under him. . . .

and of his fellow countrymen he wrote that posterity will accord them the name of 'deliverers':

> the body of the people having undertook and performed an enterprise which in other nations is thought to proceed from a magnanimity that is peculiar to heroes.

And in *Samson Agonistes*:

> How goodly a thing it is and how reviving
> To the spirits of just men long opprest
> When God into the hands of the deliverer
> Puts invincible might.

When the restoration of Charles II was imminent, Milton, whilst most other republicans were in flight, was making last appeals to his people not to betray the lives of those who had fought to give him freedom, in this a 'stupid reconcilement'.

Posterity did not forget Milton when it had need of him.

The Russian revolutionaries in 1905 sold translations of the *Areopagitica* to defy the censors; India too, was glad of its inspiration.

Mirabeau, in 1788, a year before the French Revolution, published a pamphlet *Sur la liberté de la presse, imité de l'anglais de Milton*, which sold out three editions.

Plunging deeply into Milton's thought through book after book of *Paradise Lost*, many have concluded that there is much in it which justifies not so much the ways of God to man, as of man towards his God. It cannot be a coincidence that, also in 1788, twenty-one editions of the great epic were published in France.*

So the English, then, ridding themselves first of the pope and next of the king, and therefore now without authority to guide them, still felt impelled to search for that God whom they had been taught to worship. They sought his will and purpose in the workings of 'natural laws' here on earth. They studied anatomy and chemistry, but no image of god himself, other than the accepted medieval figure, so far dawned on them.

The Christian schism, Reformation and Counter-reformation, continued to ravage Europe, where it produced greater turbulence and a more cynical frame of mind. In Renaissance Italy, despite the turmoil of corruption and murder by rulers of city states and popes alike, a great ferment of values, religious, political, aesthetic, scientific, issued in brilliant expressions of human imagination and intellect. For sensitive and creative spirits – as so often happens – to look upwards to the stars was a relief from earth's confusion. The life of Copernicus spanned this violent period. He visited universities in Italy, but that country suffered invasion from France, Spain and ultimately Germany. However, by 1543, when he died, papal authority had repented and reassumed religious aspect and direction.

Thus, by the time that Galileo (born 1564) was teaching at Padua University, the anarchic Renaissance type of free thinking was no longer likely to be tolerated.

William Harvey (1578–1657), the Englishman who discovered the circulation of the blood, and had also been physician to Francis Bacon, spent five years in Padua to study anatomy under Fabricio Aquapendente (1537–1619) while Galileo was there. He does not mention Galileo and there is no indication that he ever met him. Harvey himself lost much of his research into comparative anatomy during the English Civil War. These contacts and movements of scientists in troubled times indicate both the difficulties under which studious men laboured and their determination to overcome these in pursuit of their special scientific aims.

* For these references I am indebted to Dr Annette Rubinstein's book.

The aim of each scientist is the study of one special subject, whether astronomy, or anatomy. The method will largely be determined by the subject itself. The brilliant work of the universities of Oxford and Paris in the thirteenth century had brought about a distinction between experimental and mathematical methods, which themselves had arisen from the schoolmen's arguments on the philosophies of Plato and Aristotle. Experimental science, concentrating on the physical nature of the world, relying on induction, tended to move away from mathematics; on the other hand, an astronomer had need of mathematics, whilst medieval builders had readily understood the vital importance of geometry. English science, after Francis Bacon, leaned towards empiricism.

Copernicus was essentially a mathematician. Mathematics, a fascinating pastime for highly intelligent men, was in constant development. It had begun to simplify its works by inventing a language of its own, signs such as $= + - \div \times < > \sqrt{}$ instead of using ordinary words of speech, which made mathematical deduction and proof cumbersome. Galileo, who was familiar with the work of his medieval predecessors, became convinced that Copernicus was right. Till then Padua had been a leading centre in medical studies; it now began to attract the more mathematically minded. Ironically the renewal of the search for God in his heavens, occasioned, it may well be, by the chaos of his rule upon earth, brought the astronomers down with a bump into the very heart of that chaos – how to trace the path of a projectile issuing from the mouth of a gun.

Leonardo da Vinci had been faced with this problem; long before him, Archimedes, too, had been drawn into the service of war. It was in part due to the study of Archimedes' geometry that the seventeenth-century mathematicians began to work out the relations between moving bodies. They faced the old dilemma of mathematical deduction versus empirical observation. How real was mathematics? In the physical world a small atom – a point – could be subdivided, a mathematical point could not. What made things move? Already twelfth-century men had tried to make machines for perpetual motion and failed. They had also been fascinated by magnetic attraction between bodies.

Aristotle had defined a difference between the natural – physical – world and mathematics. The Greek word from which we derive 'physics' really involves a misunderstanding, since for Aristotle it meant what we call the world of 'nature', something very unlike the concepts with which modern physicists are concerned. If a thing moved by itself, said Aristotle, it had some inner life – the Greeks thought the stars and planets were living gods. A lifeless body could only be moved if pushed or pulled. The causes of what happened to substances in the world should be sought, but were not easily determined, like proofs in mathematics.

Galileo proceeded to make his well-known experiments in the physical world – with falling bodies, the pendulum, projectiles, applying mathematical calculation to his results. Objects fell faster as they approached the earth. What forces, other than firing the shot, operated on a projectile? It seems that the distance it would travel depended on the angle at which you fired it. If the earth were spinning, account must be taken of the fact that objects on the earth moved with its motion. By a mathematical hypothesis that a mythical physical object might move in empty infinite space, or down a plane that was entirely without friction, Galileo arrived at the notion of 'inertia', which apparently means that such an object will, on earth, continue to move in a horizontal line.

Again, invisible, intangible movements remained puzzling. Light moved faster than sound. What was light, waves, or particles? What really was magnetism? Instead of seeking to explain the causes of events in the physical world by the nature of substances themselves, the scientists found that their relation to one another and their movement could be defined in mathematical terms. Such mathematical terms appeared also to operate in relation to the movements of the planets in space.

Mathematics then was 'for real'. That structure of the physical world whose riddles man was bent on solving must rest upon that very mathematics by which events in space and time could so readily be explained. As the Dutch and Galileo continued their experiments with lenses, Galileo presently had his telescope with which to continue his viewing of the stars. The new image of God began to take shape. Some medieval artist, with prophetic insight, had already pictured god compass in hand; he was not only Architect, and Lawgiver of Natural Laws, but was to become the Supreme Clockmaker, who wound the clock and set the round world spinning, the earth and stars in their everlasting courses. Mathematics was the master of time and space; evidently God was also a mathematician.

By now the Copernican theory was no longer mere entertainment, but was seriously disturbing the minds of the men of religion. Many of these were themselves fully able to appreciate the reasoning of scientific truth; but could also perceive its challenge to their religious doctrines. In 1615 Cardinal Bellarmine wrote in a letter:

> If there were a real proof that the sun is the centre of the universe . . . that the sun does not go round the earth but the earth round the sun, then we should have to proceed with great circumspection in explaining passages in Scripture which appear to teach the contrary, and rather admit that we did not understand them, than declare an opinion to be false which is proved to be true.

He continues by saying that he does not believe such proof can be found, or that even appearances prove it. 'In case of doubt we ought not to abandon the interpretation of the sacred text as given by the Holy Fathers' (Crombie, 1952, pp. 325–6).

The Holy Office of the Inquisition considered the matter, and in 1616 Copernicus's book was placed on the index as not to be read without changes showing that it presented only a hypothesis. Galileo was not mentioned, but privately warned.

The Holy Office said the proposition that:

> 'the sun is the centre of the world and altogether devoid of local motion' was foolish and absurd philosophically, and formally heretical, inasmuch as it expressly contradicts the doctrines of Holy Scripture and according to the common exposition and meaning of the Holy Fathers and learned theologians; and that the proposition that 'the earth is not the centre of the world nor immoveable, but moves as a whole, and also with a diurnal motion' was also likewise

worthy of 'censure in philosophy' and 'at least erroneous in faith'.

Galileo held to the opinion which he honestly felt to be proven, thus, in 1633, he was brought before the Inquisition and forced to recant, solemnly on his knees, before the scarlet robed cardinals. His remark, muttered under his breath 'and yet it moves' is one of the pearls of the history of science.

Galileo was by then an old and distinguished man; he was spared burning at the stake. He lived on for nearly ten years, enjoying observing the stars, more especially his newly discovered moons of Jupiter. Newton was born in that same year 1642 and was 18 when Charles II founded the Royal Society, which stimulated the passion for studying the 'New Philosophy', as science was called. Charles II himself liked dissecting; Pepys had his 'little laboratory'. The long brilliant reign of Louis XIV began the following year, though the king himself was still a child.

In Italy, science had received a severe setback by the virtual suppression of Galileo. The new scientific star on the horizon was to come from France, René Descartes (1596–1650), was thirty years younger than Galileo, but his work coincided with Galileo's active years. These dates and places of work and origin are important in the resultant influences on contemporary thought.

René Descartes, in his time, was remarkable in that he was not a professional academician or teacher, astronomer, scientist, or even mathematician. He was a young man of bourgeois origin, who became fascinated by the theories of such men as Copernicus and Galileo. His father was a councillor in the Brittany Parlement. On his father's death he sold the property which he inherited, apparently to pursue a life of independence and some seclusion, in order to exercise his active mind on these new lines. From the Jesuits at La Flèche he had quite a good education.

Whether because social life was too distracting, or dull, or to supplement his income, for some years he kept on enlisting in mercenary armies. By his own account, while serving in the Bavarian army in 1619, he kept warm one winter by sitting all day meditating in a Bavarian stove, from which he emerged with the basic tenets of his own philosophy clearly defined.

Soon after this, he visited Italy and returned to Paris and, but for another brief period, gave up army life. In 1629, at the age of 33, he went to live in Holland, where he remained for twenty years, except for some visits to Paris and one to England. He had in mind a great book called *Le Monde*, which he decided not to publish. He agreed with Galileo's heresies and was probably aware of the private warning to Galileo in 1616. The mechanical ideas in this book were in *Principia Philosophiae*, which he did publish in 1644.

At this period the Protestant countries were more liberal, though independent thinkers everywhere had reason to fear persecution. Holland was outstanding in tolerance; it was then, and continued in the eighteenth century to be, the refuge of dissenters and free thinkers. Such men as the English Hobbes and Locke; Bayle of the famous dictionary, and Spinoza, found it wiser when they were out of step with the politics or faith of their own country to live and to publish in Holland. Even there Descartes did not escape persecution from Protestant bigots in the universities, accusing him of atheism.

The curious fact is that, while religious authority was active and menacing, secular authority, even royal, was anxious to become acquainted with the new philosophy. It was also customary, and even necessary, for writers on all kinds of topics to seek the support of wealthy and aristocratic patrons. In this way, Voltaire was, later on, at the Court of Frederick the Great. Descartes, unfortunately, accepted the invitation of Queen Christina of Sweden to come and teach her. Since affairs of state meant that the only time she would allocate was in the early morning, it seems that her philosopher contracted a chill, from which he died at the early age of 54. His famous *Discourse of Method* had been published in 1637, several other writings only appeared after his death, among them the book *De Homine* in which he attempts to deal with organic matter.

Isaac Newton was another isolated and introvert character, partly, in his case, because his father had died before he was born, and his mother remarried and left him to his grandmother. He went to Cambridge in 1662. His reputation as a mathematician was soon established, but he was secretive and slow in publication of his results. Some of his work is even now buried among the manuscripts left at Trinity College, Cambridge. He was, in my view, with the example of Galileo ahead of him, fearful of persecution. He practised alchemy; was heretical in that he did not believe in the Trinity, or the divinity of Christ. His *Principia* was not finally published until 1688, when William and Mary came to the throne. In the previous troubled years under James II, Newton had emerged into an extrovert career, becoming a Member of Parliament and Master of the Mint, and presently, the great prophetic, scientific figure acclaimed throughout Europe.

Newton had little use for Descartes; according to Voltaire, he looked at the first seven or eight pages of Descartes' work, wrote 'error' on each and read no more. He continued the work in the line from Copernicus and Kepler to Galileo.

None the less, it was Descartes, writing with the freshness, confidence and clarity of a young mind convinced of the originality of his ideas, who became the most influential populariser of the New Philosophy, and hence, at first, the most discussed and attacked.

These men, Copernicus, Kepler, Galileo, Descartes, Newton, who come down to us as famous in history – and many of their contemporaries less famous – were living in a time of great confusion of thought. Each one of them was still in the grip of an established religion, an image of God and the universe supported by authority and the faith of their fellow men and women. In spite of sectarian quarrels, that traditional flat earth of the Middle Ages had stability, a firm floor and walls, was secure like a comfortable, well-furnished dining room. This faith, images, certainties, were now dissolving about them. What was the God of this ball spinning in space? What were they, if no longer God's creatures on God's earth as the scriptures had taught them? Each one of them was in truth alone in the face of the universe. How could they come to terms with themselves? What should they say to their fellow human beings?

There were some things – one might say obsessions – that they had in common: a passionate desire to discover reality – the real world; an irresistible fascination (not, as might have been expected, with their own earth) with the starry heavens and the riddles of cosmology, time and space. And finally, a firm belief in the processes and fundamental certainties of mathematics. What then was the picture which they, jointly and severally, presented to posterity?

To enter into the calculations and conclusions of these brilliant men would clearly require the specialist mind of a scientist or mathematician. The lay mind can, however, by noting significant passages of their argument, attempt to understand the direction in which their thought was leading. All of them were concerned mainly with inorganic matter, and with the movement of such bodies in space and time. When they study cause and effect, they are not satisfied with the empirical evidence of their senses; they require mathematical proof.

There are many published translations of the works of Galileo. In representing a dialogue between two people about cause and effect, the one voicing Galileo's views says:

> As to what makes bodies fall, you should say that everyone knows that it is called Gravity; but I do not question you about the name, but the essence of the thing, of which essence you know not a tittle more than you know about the move of the stars in gyration: unless it be the name that hath been put to this, and made familiar and domestical, by the many experiences which we see thereof every hour in the day: but not as if we really understand anymore, what principle or virtue that is which moveth a stone downwards, than we know who moveth it upwards, when it is separated from the projicient; or who moveth the Moon around, except, as I said only the name, which more particularly and properly we have assigned to the motion of descent, namely Gravity . . . and to infinitely other motions we ascribe Nature for their cause. (Crombie, 1952, pp. 290–1)

He says further that if it be true that of one effect there is but one sole primary cause, and that between cause and effect there is a firm and constant connection, it is necessary that whensoever there is seen a firm and constant alteration in the effect, there be a firm and constant alteration in the cause.

Thus Galileo's conception of science was that it was a mathematical description of the relation of bodies in space.

As we know, he was the originator of the First Law of Motion.

Here is his definition of what he calls matter:

No sooner do I form a conception of a material or corporeal substance, than I feel the need of conceiving that it has boundaries and shape; that relative to others it is great or small; that it is in this or that place and in this or that time; that it is moving or still; that it touches or does not touch another body; that it is one, few or many; nor can I, by any effort of imagination, dissociate it from these qualities (condizioni). On the other hand, I find no need to apprehend it is accompanied by such conditions as to be white or red, bitter or sweet, sounding or silent, pleasant or evil smelling. Perhaps, if the senses had not informed us of these qualities, the reason and imagination alone would never have arrived at them. Therefore I hold these tastes, odours, colours, etc., on the part of the object in which they seem to reside, are nothing more than pure names, and exist only in the sensitive being; so that if the latter were removed these qualities would themselves vanish. But having given them special names different from those of the other primary and real qualities (accidenti), we would persuade ourselves that they also exist just as truly and really as the latter. . . . But I hold that there exists nothing in external bodies for exciting in us tastes, odours and sounds but size, shape, quantity and slow or swift motion. And I conclude that if the ears, tongue and nose were removed, shape, quantity and motion would remain but there would be no odours, tastes or sounds, which apart from living creatures, I believe to be mere words. (Crombie, 1952, pp. 392–3)

For Galileo it suffices that events, or action such as gravity whose cause we do not really understand, can be explained in mathematical terms.

Philosophy is written in that vast book which stands forever open before our eyes, I mean the universe; but it cannot be read until we have learned the language and become familiar with the characters in which it is written. It is written in mathematical language, and the letters are triangles, circles and other geometrical figures, without which means it is humanly impossible to comprehend a single word. (ibid., p. 295)

Such events may also be described in the words of ordinary language; if those words also describe the ultimate real world, such as the Copernican cosmology, so much the better.

Descartes, unlike Galileo, was not satisfied with the theory of action at a distance, such as gravity. He took the more Aristotelian view that bodies move because they are physically acted upon by other bodies.

The importance of Descartes' contribution lay rather in his method of personally coming to terms with the universe, out of which he evolved that separation of mind and matter which, ever since, has proved a bone of contention and source of distress to philosophers and ordinary human beings alike.

It was, moreover, also the primary cause of systems and institutions which still exist and relate to the way we now live.

Asking himself what was reality, what should he believe about himself and the world about him, Descartes reached his celebrated conclusion as to at least one certainty: here, sitting in the warmth of that stove, was a mind actually engaged in thinking. Therefore that mind, he himself, did exist: *cogito, ergo sum.* As to the rest of the world, perceived by the senses, imagined, or dreamed, there was no such certainty or clear definition. It could therefore be described in general terms as matter (*res extensa*) distinct from mind and occupying space. Movement came from God, who had set the universe in motion; it took place in the physical world of bodies pressing on one another in accordance with mechanical laws. Mind and matter were separate. The human body itself was a machine. Mind had no action on the body, except in one respect, that 'animal spirits' might pass into the blood from the pineal gland in the brain. The 'animal spirits' flowed along the nerves, which were tubes, to cause bodily action. The existence of a 'soul' inhabiting the body was not denied; but this was not the mind. Animals were pure automata and had no souls.

This is how Descartes, in *De Homine*, posthumously published in 1662, describes the human body:

> I assume that the body is nothing else than a statue or machine of clay. . . . I desire you to consider next that all the functions which I have attributed to this machine, such as the digestion of food, the beating of the heart and arteries, the nourishment and growth of the members, respiration, waking and sleeping; the impressions of light, sounds, odours, tastes, heat and other such qualities on the organs of the external senses; the impression of their ideas on the common sense and the imagination; the retention of imprinting of these ideas on the memory; the interior motions of the appetites and passions; and finally, the external movements of all members, which follow so suitably as well the actions of objects which present themselves to sense, as the passions and impressions which are formed in the memory, that they imitate in the most perfect manner possible those of a real man; I desire, I say, that you consider that all these functions follow naturally in this machine simply from the arrangement of its parts, no more nor less than do the movements of a clock, or other automata, from that of its weights and its wheels; so that it is not at all necessary for their explanation to conceive in it of any other soul, vegetative or sensitive, nor of any other principle of motion and life than its blood and its spirits, set in motion by the heat of the fire which burns continuously in its heart, and which is of a nature no different from all fires in inanimate bodies. (Crombie, 1952, p. 338)

When questioned as to what seemed to be mental activity in animals, Descartes even denied that their noises were an indication of a mind in control. In a letter to the Marquis of Newcastle (23 November 1646) he wrote:

> I know, indeed that brutes do many things better than we do, but I am not surprised at it, for that also goes to prove that they act in force of nature and by springs, like a clock which tells them better what the hour is than our judgment can inform us. And, doubtless, when swallows come in the

Spring, they act in that like clocks. All that honey bees do is of the same nature. (ibid., p. 341)

Descartes was interested in the work of the physiologist William Harvey, who had visited Padua and was influenced by the current mathematical and mechanical interpretation of all natural phenomena. Mathematical principles were applied to biology. The stomach was a retort, the veins and arteries hydraulic tubes, the heart a spring, the viscera sieves and filters, the lung a bellows and the muscles and bones a system of cords, struts, and pulleys. Such methods could be useful in the study of the skeleton and muscles, but not in other aspects of biology. The combined influence of Galileo, Descartes and Harvey did establish a tradition of mechanical approach to organic substances, which has been followed, many consider with disastrous results. The argument between vitalism, purposive behaviour, versus the physicists, continued. The theory of the atomic composition of matter has, up to the present time, led to the overall triumph of the physicists.

To explain the contribution of Isaac Newton in non-mathematical terms is not possible. He conceived of space as consisting of tiny points or specks, and time as instants, independent of the bodies contained in them. As to motion, the solar system, first set going by God, continued its own momentum by the force of gravitation. On earth dead matter, once set in motion (as it is by the earth's rotation) would continue in a straight line unless obstructed. Bodies attract one another according to their mass. 'Every body attracts every other with a force directly proportional to the product of their masses, and inversely proportional to the square on the distance between them.' (Russell, 1946, pp. 556–7)

Words such as mass, acceleration, dynamics, energy, come into common use. But more and more it is only possible to express cosmology, mechanics, and movement on earth, in mathematical equations. The language of mathematics continued to grow as new definitions, descriptions and calculations were required.

So there *were* laws governing the universe and nature. Man could decipher them, but not by means of the soul or religious doctrine. It was the intellect of man – his reason – which penetrated these mysteries and expounded their truths in this new language. Through Isaac Newton, their prophet, they had been brought to humanity.

> Nature and Nature's laws lay hid in night
> God said: Let Newton be and there was light.

Did Newton himself believe that he and his colleagues were finding truth, reaching out to the certainty of the real world? Surely they could not be living in a mathematician's dream, for the accuracy of mathematics could not be denied.

Probably Newton did believe that he had touched reality. None the less, he sounds a note of caution. At the end of Book 3 in *Principia Mathematica* in the General Scholium he writes: 'Hitherto we have explained the phenomena of the heavens and of our sea by the power of gravity, but have not yet assigned the cause of this power.' (Crombie, 1952, pp. 397–8)

He went on:

> I have not been able to discover the cause of those properties of gravity from phenomena, and I frame no hypotheses; for whatever is not deduced from phenomena is to be called an hypothesis; and hypotheses, whether metaphysical or physical, whether of occult qualities or mechanical, have no place in experimental philosophy. In this philosophy particular propositions are inferred from the phenomena, and afterwards rendered general by induction. Thus it was that the impenetrability, the mobility, and the impulsive force of bodies, and the laws of motion and of gravitation, were discovered.

Speaking of gravitational attraction, in The System of the World, section 2, he said:

> our purpose is only to trace out the quantity and properties of this force from the phenomena, and to apply what we discover in some single cases as principles, by which, in a mathematical way, we may estimate the effects thereof in more involved cases; for it would be endless and impossible to bring every particular to direct and immediate observation. We said, *in a mathematical way*, to avoid all questions about the nature or quality of this force, which

we would not be understood to determine by any hypothesis. (ibid.)

The Copernican universe presented by the trinity of rationalists Galileo, Descartes, Newton, which consisted simply of the mere movement, spinning or whirling of solid lumps of matter without colour, smell, taste or texture, was hardly attractive or appealing. Empirically minded philosophers and scientists, John Locke, Robert Boyle, John Ray, were bound to ask were not these qualities, now to be defined as secondary characteristics of matter, equally grounded in reality? Religious authorities and believers clearly perceived that there was now a fundamental threat to their whole way of life.

Robert Boyle (1627–91), a chemist of serious religious turn of mind, wrote an *Enquiry into the Vulgar Notion of Nature* and the *Christian Virtuoso* and founded a chair for lectures to demonstrate that the study of science would not run counter to, but reinforce, reverence for God and religion. He asserted (as did also Newton) that God was still there operative and intervening at every moment in the affairs of the world. Otherwise, in a mechanical universe, God had only to start things, by winding up the clock, or kicking off the football at the creation, since when everything had gone on cheerfully in its own way. Would not now those shocking atheists, adherents to Epicurus, assert that the universe was the product of the fortuitous association and disassociation of atoms, undirected or guided by any intelligence?

The Cartesian denial of purpose or final causes was seen as a further move towards Epicureanism. Is it by chance that we see with our eyes and hear with our ears, was there no divine purpose that ordered this so? Cudworth, the Master of Christ's College, Cambridge, one of the Cambridge Platonists, in his *True Intellectual System of the Universe* (1678) complains of these Cartesians or 'mechanick theists' for playing into the hands of atheism. John Ray (1627–1704), a botanist, author of the *Wisdom of God Manifested in the Works of the Creation* (1690), is sorely distressed at the prospect of not being able to praise God for his legs, if he does not know whether they were given him to walk with. He is in consternation at the destruction of the argument from design, which leaves him only the proof of the existence of the deity from 'innate ideas' – a proof, 'not easily', as he sadly remarks, 'understanded of the vulgar'.

> Wherefore these atomick theists [the Cartesians] utterly evacuate that grand argument for a god, taken from the Phaenomenon of the artificial frame of things, which hath been so much insisted upon in all ages, the atheists in the meantime laughing in their sleeves, and not a little triumphing to see the cause of Theism betrayed by its professed friends and asserters.

Moreover how can Descartes explain anything more than the planetary system by matter and motion, what of anatomy and generation? Both Boyle and Ray think they see their way out of the dilemma of the mechanical universe, by asserting that a law is a moral rather than a physical cause, which inanimate bodies are incapable of understanding. Hence the universe cannot continue to run itself according to laws laid down once and for all. Therefore matter is regulated by a power and not by laws. There is a confusion here between the 'laws of nature' frequently referred to as ordered by God, which nature obeys, but which are not 'moral' in the human sense. Boyle is of the opinion that the power regulating matter is God himself; Cudworth, on the other hand, suggests that it is some 'plastick nature', a kind of genie, or familiar spirit evidently, working under the direction of the deity.

John Ray inclines to agree with Cudworth, because he thinks that Boyle's hypothesis would 'render the Divine Providence operose, solicitous and distractious' and give a handle to atheism. God should not be performing the daily drudgery of the universe. Besides, if God's agent is omnipotent, then the process of generation is really rather clumsy. On the other hand, how to explain misshapen bodies and plants, if God makes them by direct action? In fact, for Ray, the plastick nature is a convenient hack employed by the deity and blamed for anything that goes wrong – a sort of whipping boy in chief to divine providence.

As professionals, Boyle was talking about chemical reactions and gases, in which he became distinguished: Ray's field was how plants and bodies reproduce themselves. Their preoccupation with the clash between the Father God, creator of Christendom, and this lonely, uncared for, spinning globe, is the more significant. Ray is one of the first examples of the famous argument from design, which proliferates in Christian apologetics all through the eighteenth century and into our times. Ray's book went into five editions between 1690 and 1709, and was followed by innumerable works presenting an almost identical argument. If Ray had been writing in mid-eighteenth century, one might consider that he had his tongue in his cheek. But his confused sincerity in the face of the extraordinary new notions he was being asked to accept is credible.

England was a Protestant country moving to greater tolerance in 1688, though pious dissenters could be as ruthless in persecution in the name of morality, as ever the Inquisition in the name of doctrine. Witches were still accused and burned even in the eighteenth century.

France was very different; a Catholic country under an absolute and vainglorious monarch, presiding over a sumptuous and extravagant court. At the same time, everything was tied up as tight as could be; discipline tended to increase under the King's latest mistress, Madame de Maintenon. Jansenist thought and Puritanical morality emanating from the famous Port Royal, defeated the more worldly Jesuits; for Protestants such as the Huguenots, there was cruel persecution or flight into exile.

One of the most tragic figures in the clash between these two epochs was Blaise Pascal, a man of brilliant talent in science, who, mortified in the cells of Port Royal not only his pride of intellect, but the gentle impulses of his natural affections.

He did pursue science; at the same time, in his famous jest 'le pari' he thought it safer to bet on belief in the existence of God. Pascal's inner conflict is recorded with eloquence and beauty of style in his famous *Pensées*.

'IF there is a god,' he wrote 'we must love him and not his creatures.' Yet, repudiating the intellect, he penned the words: 'Le coeur a ses raisons, que la raison ne connaît pas' (the heart has its reasons, that are unknown to reason), a phrase that became almost traditional in the mouths of the defenders of religion. Unlike Galileo, Pascal did not take pleasure in contemplating the starry heavens. 'Le silence de ces espaces infinies m'effraye.' This soul, very much alone in the universe, felt the need of a God.

The shock administered by the new cosmology was now intensely felt by all those minds which dealt with philosophy or religion. At this distance in time it may seem astonishing that what was merely an account of the way solid inorganic bodies move in space mattered so much; and was not only readily accepted, but presently acclaimed. Perhaps it was that human beings, their consciousness still not yet aware of the extreme complexity of themselves and their entire environment, were glad of some simple, clear-cut, proven answer to their contemporary riddles, till then unsolved.

Yet how did all this concern the 'average sensual man' as he went about his daily business? Well, somehow, at the end of the seventeenth century, it did concern him. As in the third century the desert fathers had laid the foundations of Christendom, so did Galileo, Descartes and Newton lay the foundations of the religion of the machine that was to come.

Perhaps a reproach may be addressed to Galileo and his colleagues, in that they despised and forgot those many colours of the rainbow which had so intrigued their predecessors, who had in consequence struggled with mathematics in order to explain its curve and invented the lenses that were to provide the star-watchers with their telescopes.

As for 'average sensual man', he had known from the beginning that God had set his bow in the clouds in earnest that he would not flood the earth again. So average man went cheerfully on to find the keenly sought pot of gold at the rainbow's end.

CHAPTER 8

You cannot stop progress!

To enter the eighteenth century is like opening the door on a room in which a Bloomsbury-type intellectual cocktail party is in full spate. A hubbub of voices, all talking at once, argue and acquaint you with every new notion or theory that has taken their fancy. It was an age when people had a lot to say and said it eagerly and abundantly.

Research into eighteenth-century thought, more especially in France, and the links and exchanges of thought in the period between France and England, was the reason for my postgraduate work, and my election to a Fellowship of Girton College, Cambridge. After some absence on war work in the United States, I returned to my studies and went to Paris in 1919. I do not now regret that events of my life prevented completion of my undertaking, because the book *European Thought in the Eighteenth Century* – almost the life work of Professor Paul Hazard of the Sorbonne – is the finest exposition of those important formative years in human history. His book was not published until 1946, two years after his death. Thus I did not read it until several years after the Second World War. Whoever really wants to understand what it is that makes our own modern world tick should read that book.

By the eighteenth century Newton's exposition of the Copernican cosmology had reached, if not the 'man in the street', at least all educated persons, that is, those who were interested, whether of the aristocracy, the upper bourgeoisie, or even the church. One might have thought – indeed Freud has advanced the theory – that when humanity lost its privileged position with a God as creator and special protector, people would feel humbled, powerless and afraid. Quite the reverse. The chief emotions felt appeared to be exhilaration and a sense of adventure. The new order of things belittled God rather than man. Instead of an immanent God at hand, within reach, through prayer, in time of trouble, a God far off, winding the clockwork, was not much use. What is more, the old dictator had been very severe with all his rules about sin and punishment, condemning man to be constantly penitent and miserable. Besides, since everything up there in his heavens was apparently going on all right according to Isaac Newton's laws, men turned their attention to their own society where the rise in the standard of living of the upper classes diverted them from godly thoughts to their own values and concerns. In England, with the polite literature of Addison and Steele and Pope's 'proper study of mankind is man', the mood of the eighteenth century really began earlier than in France, about ten years before, 1700, and did not express itself so much, as in France, in the sharp, intellectual discussion of ideas.

The first theme which I observed in early-eighteenth-century French thought was a general feeling that, instead of being humble and miserable, man both ought, and had a right, to be happy. (Later I found this also was the first point noted by Paul Hazard.) Inevitably this claim to happiness led to an attack upon Christian doctrines in terms of satire that was gentle or ironical, or – as in the infamous Pierre Bayle Dictionary in Holland – sarcastic and severe. Nor should one forget that, in his day, Jonathan Swift's *Gulliver's Travels* was a savage, satirical attack on the morals and customs of his time. Other trends that we shall find are the influence of the awe-struck reverence for mathematics on the taste for symmetry and order in literature as in architecture and gardening, as well as the quest for 'natural' law.

The eighteenth-century French hedonists were important because they discussed rules of conduct according to reason and man, rather than according to God. For let conduct once alter and society admit the change, and many a revolutionary theory may follow. In the elegant salons which were now usually conducted by women of social standing and enterprise, who vied with one another as hostesses, and earned themselves the title of 'femmes savantes' (blue stockings), the constant topics of conversation, mingled with compliments and witty badinage, were the fate and duties of man, the separation and relative importance of mind and body. The lay intellect ceased to be submissive and began openly to justify the lay mode of existence, and to wonder if men might not walk more satisfactorily by the light of reason than they appeared to do by the light of faith. Some of the more talkative committed their thoughts to paper in a succession of little brown leather bound volumes: *The Art of Knowing Oneself, Happiness, Dialogues on the Pleasures*, the *Art of not being bored, The Philosophy of Common Sense, The Theory of Pleasant Sensations*, and so forth.   .

An early sample of one of these books is the *Dialogue entre Messieurs Patru et D'Ablancourt sur les Plaisirs*, in which two friends express sarcasm at the violence of preachers, who seem to think that their best qualification is good lungs and their highest eloquence achieved if they descend from the pulpit sweating from head to foot. However little a man enjoys pleasure, it seems that he is a lost soul:

Upon my Word [says d'Ablancourt], I am sorry that some thousand worthy folk of my acquaintance who have much virtue and yet enjoy without demur the amenities which life sometimes offers, are therefore in peril of damnation. Is there no means of procuring indulgence for them? I tremble for myself at this very moment, I have just received in gift this day, two melons of fair aspect and some admirable strawberries. That is not sinful as you know, and there is pleasure in eating them, if then all pleasure is a crime, as your preacher assures us, I should not be very grateful to that person who, in sending me these fruits, either thought me wicked enough to taste of a forbidden thing, or has made me a gift which I cannot enjoy if I am a man of moral worth.

And yet it would be a great pity if strawberries and melons should be forbidden in commerce. If they carry it any further, figs, grapes and good Christian pears, won't have a better fate, and entremets and all confectioner's delights must be looked on with the same eye as arsenic.

Partridges will never stand their ground against this

severe morality. I do not even know if mutton can defend itself, and you will see that in the end these devout gentlemen will reduce us to the pease-porridge of our forefathers.

Patru, of course, upholds the church; d'Ablancourt challenges him on the utter impossibility of defending a morality that 'smacks so decidedly of the deserts of Thebes'. With sturdy Cartesianism at least, Patru maintains that reason is the enemy of the passions, and so argues that since pleasure means the satisfaction of the passions, then of pleasure also.

D'Ablancourt defends the senses, as also God given. This little book, which well shows how tentative was the challenge to the church, was, in 1700, condemned and publicly burnt.

These early treatises hark back in spirit to Greek ethics – to the ideal of the 'golden mean'. Fontenelle's *Thoughts on Happiness* counsels a sequence of gentle pleasures productive of a stable contentment, such that a man would not wish for change. Following his own recipe, Fontenelle himself attained a century of years. Common to all of them is the precept that the goal of human life is not virtue, but happiness. Christian asceticism is seen as virtual annihilation of self; the nature of man is conceived as if he did not have a fall. The exaltation of the intellect is evident in the definition of reason as the faculty that selects those pleasures which it is proper to enjoy. But how can we draw a line between higher and lower pleasures? Is it really the pleasure-pain principle that conditions happiness? In later treatises the Cartesian conflict between mind and body appears. Deslandes sees the 'art of not being bored' in giving way to the promptings of natural instinct, which do not include any necessity for thought. 'Though I shock the most superb of prejudices I maintain that reason is drab and useless when it seeks to place us above everything by the power of thought.' A few pages later, however, fearing that he may have overstated his case, he says: 'to feel properly we must cast aside all the passions that proceed from nature and make others according to their pattern which shall be less violent.'

Maupertuis goes further, in that he states that the criterion of pleasure is not whether it is high or low, but its intensity or duration. Epicurean and Stoic have distinguished between physical or mental pleasure, but all pleasure resides in the soul, whether derived from the bodily organs or no. 'Let us not fear to compare pleasures of the senses with the most intellectual pleasures, let us not cherish the illusion that there are some pleasures more noble than others; the most noble pleasures are those which are greatest.' This statement was criticised for its alarming implications. Followers of Epicurus had always made a point of the delicacy and civilised nature of their pleasures. Maupertuis, like Deslandes, stopped short. But Lamettrie, a medical man, immersed in the study of anatomy, boldly went forward and in *Man a Machine* he stated the case for nature and naturalism without humbug, ascribed his book to the more cautious Marquis d'Argens, heartily enjoying the scandal it provoked. He maintains that the scientist and physician know more about the 'labyrinth of man' than divines and moralists with their 'dark and idle studies'; he pleads for a scientific method in all branches of study, especially ethics. He insists that the human mind changes with the variations of the human body, and reverses Maupertuis's view that all sensations are of the mind because ultimately felt there. They are of the body, says Lamettrie, for thence they start. Virtue is a social and relative conception, rewarding only in the esteem of our social companions; like an old hag with a diamond ring on her finger, virtue is only wooed by those who covet the diamond. Another medical man, Louis De la Caze, has a more interesting approach. He saw primitive man as in need of security and the power to destroy anything that threatens him. If he cannot do so, his fear causes a contraction of the muscle of the diaphragm, and consequent physical distress. In civilised life cares and fears against which a man cannot take immediate action cause these contractions, which render him uneasy and miserable. Happiness depends on the free play of the diaphragm. 'A general who wins a battle, a woman who enjoys the triumph of her charms, an author who sees his fame growing, what do they feel in these agreeable moments? At bottom it is simply strong vibrations favourable to the play of the diaphragm.' The relation of man, mind and body to something set down under the general term of 'nature' pervades all this thought.

Voltaire was just 21 in 1715, when the Sun King's reign ended. The 'Age of Enlightenment', as it came to be called, or in England the 'Augustan Age' and in Germany 'Die Aufklärung', was spreading from country to country, gaining more and more recruits in the campaign for happiness and freedom of thought. In the field of ideas skirmishes were won, but in the sphere of power, there was little yielding by the repressive forces of church and state, more especially in France. Voltaire, a new recruit, was to shine out, for all time, as one of the greatest of them all. On a brief visit to England, he enjoyed the greater freedom of discussion and took a liking to the empirical philosophy of John Locke. He wrote the *Lettres Anglaises* in eulogy. Entering the lists in the battle in his own country, he took Blaise Pascal for his prime target. 'I dare to take the part of humanity', he cried, 'against this sublime misanthropist.'

If there is a God, wrote Pascal, we must love him and not his creatures.

> On the contrary [replied Voltaire], we must love and that very tenderly, human creatures, we must love our country, wife, father, children, so much so that God makes us love them in spite of ourselves. The opposite principle makes inhuman thinkers . . . if we were to act so, what would become of human society?

To Pascal's assertion of law and order, in that the public good should be placed above individual self-interest, Voltaire's blunt answer is that it would be as impossible to form and maintain a society without self-interest as to make children without concupiscence, or to think of feeding oneself without appetite. It was mutual need which led man to form a society and it is our own needs which make us tolerant of the needs of others. As the Christian divines and little Abbés replied by extolling the marvels of God's design and handiwork and purpose in nature, Voltaire's rapier wit flashed.

> od *might* have created us altruistic creatures, then merchants *might* go to India out of charity and the mason work his stone to give pleasure to his neighbours. But he made us otherwise; let us not question our instincts, but

employ them. You explain that God created moths to destroy cloth, and worms to destroy wood, in order to provide profit for the merchants of textiles and building materials. In vain, you tell me that my legs were made in order to wear boots, or my nose to carry spectacles.

Voltaire is thus in agreement with his enlightened fellow hedonists in a controversy which, though its aspects change, still continues.

Were these exchanges between men who rode about in horse carriages or were carried in sedan chairs, were lit by link men with torches, and dined by candlelight, and who, though they had cannons and muskets, still relied, in war as in peace, only on the horse for transport, relevant to the machine age? Certainly they were relevant. These eighteenth-century minds, who were accustomed to personal power in the form of God, church or state, were trying to make sense of a universe apparently created by an impersonal power which directed the movement of the planets by its causal laws and had, somehow, contrived that here, on this globe of apparently inanimate matter, were all these plants, trees, animals and, finally, beings capable of thought. Those beings – humans – could only begin by looking at themselves. How far could they follow their instincts, and how use reason? Discarding the father God, was man really so free? Was it any use to pray to this determinist power? It seemed that it could only be spoken to, or about, in the language of mathematics.

In the immediate world about them, male thinkers had given to everything which they had not made themselves, the comprehensive name of 'nature'. Only nature was there to answer men's queries. Seeking 'natural law', making clear that he did not mean the old God-given laws, Montesquieu wrote *The Spirit of Laws*. In the process it emerged that there was something not right in the attitude, even of Christians, to slaves, thus a candle was lit that later kindled the anti-slavery crusade. But however humanity might call out to nature to define her laws, the answer that came back was the echo of their own human voice.

Now began the passionate onslaught on the study of 'nature' which was to lead up to the Encyclopedias. The inquiring human mind seized above all with the desire to know, to find out, an obsession which, to this day, has never abated. The appetite for information at that date was insatiable. A work like that of the Abbé Pluche, *Le Spctacle de la Nature*, was designed to instruct and educate ladies and gentlemen and young people in a style which they could understand. His book appeared in a series of eight volumes from 1732 to 1751. By 1754 it had gone through twelve editions; each volume, as it appeared, was translated into Italian, Dutch, German, English and Spanish. Buffon's *Histoire Naturelle* is more famous, it was also sold out, translated and reprinted, up to and beyond the mid-century. This great number of books and editions prove that the desire for knowledge on serious topics extended to the literate of nearly all types and classes and does great credit to the intelligent among men – and women – of that place and period.

The living, rather than the inanimate world had begun to fascinate people. What was life? Experiments to try and see if life could be spontaneously generated were watched with excitement, but proved abortive in the absence of knowledge that was to come later. Maupertuis kept a kind of menagerie of animals in his house for observation and cross-breeding; Lamettrie saw the doctor of medicine as one of the saviours who could put right the mistakes of nature; he also came near to suggesting some kind of evolution. Buffon was strongly in favour of physical science in preference to mathematics. Mathematics existed on propositions devised by and resting in the mind of man, whereas physical science relied upon hard facts offering 'concrete certitude', 'quite independent of ourselves'. This observation was later to prove of very considerable importance.

Mathematics was not, however, so easily side-stepped. It had something to say about this 'nature': the natural world was deemed to be intolerably untidy and must be reduced to order, in which mathematics played no small part. Addison wrote in the *Spectator* in 1712, that gardeners 'instead of humouring nature, love to deviate from it as much as possible. Our trees rise in cones, globes and pyramids. We see the mark of the scissors on every plant and bush.' Some of the divines, believing that God would have a fine sense of order, were sure that the Garden of Eden was laid out to perfection like that of Versailles! Malebranche, who saw all things in God, once wrote: 'the visible world would be more perfect if the seas and lands had more regular features.'

Nature, under the guidance of man, would evidently not be allowed her great slopes and curves, except in geometric design. In a civilised society order was also requisite in literature: poetry was expressed in the Alexandrine of French plays, or the rhymed couplets of Pope. Shakespeare was untidy and barbaric. Architecture reverted from the gothic to the classical.

From all this ferment of discussion and thirst for knowledge emerges the conclusion that most of these thinkers had accepted as fact that some mechanistic power and not the old-style God was running the universe. But, feeling unable to discard the notion of the First Cause, very many of them became deists, though of a new type of deity, defined by each in his own terms. The First Cause was not exactly a god, but a sort of safety clause, or lifebelt against facing the prospect that it might all have come about by chance. This sense of security afforded by a sense of the mechanical universe has survived into our own time.

Resting on the security of these new beliefs, eighteenth-century man began to shape a new ideal of human nature and of man's purpose in the world. No one could deny that the new knowledge now flooding Europe had come about by means of man's intellect – his Reason. Reason had been demolishing the old authorities and superstitions; it was now time to build something constructive. The great Encyclopedia, undertaken by d'Ablancourt and Diderot, was going to record, for present and future generations, all the knowledge and skills acquired by mankind. Whatever there was of wisdom was not the prerogative of one nation or class, on the contrary, since man, by his own efforts, would devise it, it would be universal, acceptable, available to all. By his faculties of reason, memory and imagination, man would be the creator and arbiter in law, morality, education, science and the arts. Discarding sin, with confidence in his own creative power, his goal would be happiness for himself and his fellowmen, as well as the means to achieve it. Diderot made no apology for asserting that man was at the very centre of the universe:

If man, that thinking and contemplative being, were banished from the surface of the globe, the spectacle at once pathetic and sublime which Nature unfolds would become a silence and a desolation; the Universe is dumb, silence and weariness brood upon the scene, all has become one vast solitude, wherein phenomena now unobserved pass by us in a dim unheeding twilight. The presence of man it is that gives interest and meaning to the existence of living things, and how better could we record the history thereof than by taking this consideration for our guide? Why not give to man in this work the place which is allotted him in the universal scheme of things? Why not make him the centre round which everything revolves?

And the insertion of man in the Encyclopedia said:

Man: noun masc. A sentient, thinking, intelligent being, moving freely over the earth. He is above all other animals, and exercises dominion over them; gregarious in his habits, he has invented various arts and sciences, and has virtues and vices peculiar to his species. He has appointed rulers and made laws for himself etc. . . . (Hazard, 1965, pp. 227–8)

Diderot was by temperament a humanist, a man of many interests, sociable, affectionate, a lover of the beauty of the countryside. None the less, these passages reveal, towards the natural world, that arrogance of the superior being, characteristic of man ever since, after Babylonia, he ceased to regard nature as belonging to God, and next went on to condemn all her promptings as vile and sinful. The latter doctrine was now discarded in view of what man was learning about his own psychology, but still more because of his increasing knowledge of how nature could be used and exploited. Soon the phrase 'man's conquest of nature' became part of the new way of life. With it came the doctrine of steady progress in linear time, by means of scientific knowledge and invention – progress towards the perfecting of man's environment, indeed it might be, of man himself. Perfectibility and progress – these were the slogans.

It is not surprising that the teaching of Descartes and

Galileo as to the primary importance of the movement of inorganic matter in space prevailed over other considerations. After all this was in tune with the Cosmos. 'Give me matter and motion and I will construct the world' was ascribed to Descartes. Matter in motion, directed at a distance by mind: the alliance between the scientific intellect and the artisan – creators of the first machines – echoed down from the twelfth-century monasteries and universities of Oxford and Paris: the Encyclopedia spoke of the 'mechanical arts' with the voice of Francis Bacon. Disdain of the craftsman, said the Encyclopedia, had arisen from a mistaken view of things:

> It used to be thought that in practising or even in learning the mechanical arts, one lost caste, debasing oneself to the level of things toilsome to acquire, ignoble to dwell upon, difficult to explain, lowering to trade in, as infinite in numbers as they were negligible in value. . . . A prejudice which led to the filling of our cities with conceited intellectuals and unprofitable onlookers, and our countryside with petty, ignorant tyrants, idle and supercilious drones. . . . If it be true that the liberal arts are superior to the mechanical arts by reason of the greater intellectual effort that the former entail, and the difficulty in mastering them, it is no less true that the latter excel the former in usefulness. The man who invented the watchspring, the balance wheel, the repeater, is no less worthy of respect than those who invented and perfected the science of algebra.

Diderot and his colleagues take it even further:

> Put on one side of the scales the tangible fruit of the most exalted sciences and the most honoured of the fine arts, and then, on the other, put the solid advantages of the mechanical arts, and you will find that the esteem with which they are respectively regarded, bears no relation to the advantages derived from them. We shall find that we have praised those who tried to convince us that we were happy far more highly than those who took practical measures to make us so. (Hazard, 1965, p. 230)

The demand for happiness, here and now, on earth, recurs,

and the road to it is seen, more and more, to lie in material progress. While the intention may well have been to afford happiness to all, including women and children, man the male and his dominance through intellect is clearly the central theme.

The Encyclopedia did not make its appearance without surmounting difficulties. The first volume appeared on 1 July 1751. The opposing forces were active. Even a bookseller, it was found, was mutilating the text. It began to appear, ostensibly, from Samual Rauche of Neuchâtel. It was formally proscribed by the church in any shape or form. But it sold like wild fire all through Western Europe. The tale of the harassing of all men connected with this great new movement of ideas (Voltaire, Rousseau, Diderot, as the most eminent) needs no re-telling. Their support came to them increasingly from the mechanical arts themselves.

England was in the forefront of invention. In the textile industry, in 1733, John Kay invented the shuttle; in 1738 John Wyatt and Lewis Paul patented their weaving machine; thereby greatly increasing the speed, and hence quantity, of production of woven materials for furnishing and clothing. Machines were still driven by water power, but in England they were now more often sited in mills near rivers, tended by a work force and presently no longer in one-family concerns.

The smelting of iron, when done by charcoal and driven by water-powered trip-hammers, had conditioned the quantity produced and hence the maximum size of machinery and even of cannon. Wood was becoming very scarce, but now coal was increasingly mined, coke used for smelting and the blast furnace invented. By 1728 rolled sheet iron was produced and rolled rods and bars by 1783. In 1761 James Watt began his experiments with steam power; in 1768 he took out his patent. Work went on in other metals and substances. It was rumoured that Benjamin Franklin in Philadelphia had discovered the secret of lightning, i.e. electric power.

Matter was there for mind to manipulate, and nature offered new resources in energy and power. The industrial revolution was well under way before the end of the century.

Among those harassed for their opinions, Jean Jacques Rousseau has just been mentioned. He was the arch-heretic, dissenting from new as well as old beliefs and offering one of his own. Born to Calvinism in Geneva in 1712, after a life of constant moving about under threat, even changing from religion to religion in self-protection, for a time befriended by David Hume the philosopher in Scotland, Rousseau died in Paris, poor, insane from paranoia, in 1778. His life spanned, and, in a way, mirrored his century.

It is said that on one occasion when Rousseau visited Diderot, who was then in prison, Diderot suggested that Rousseau compete for a prize being offered by the Academy of Dijon, for an essay on the theme: 'Have the Arts and Sciences contributed to the benefit of Mankind?' Rousseau won the prize for his famous attack on the artificiality of contemporary manners and customs, the cult of luxury, extravagance, and consumer goods. He contrasted this with the simple life of native peoples, now becoming better known through men's travels, who lived on natural products and had no need of elaborate clothing.

He followed this up with many recommendations, urging women to breastfeed their babies; set forth his views on the education of Emile and Sophie – man and woman. In the latter he did not differ from the prejudices of his time, but was quite simply a male chauvinist, regarding woman, in all her functions, as designed for the service of man. Finally he outlined a concept of the government of a human society described as the 'Social contract'.

His works brought about a popular cult of feeling, which was bitterly opposed and condemned as 'sentimentality' by the apostles of reason, who saw it as the enemy of everything for which they had been striving. Inevitably there were quarrels between Rousseau and Voltaire. Yet these two apparent antagonists, taken together, represent the most precious gifts of the eighteenth century to human thought. There was reason: there were the passions – feeling.

After all Rousseau was the one who wrote: 'Man is born free, yet everywhere he is in chains.'

It is worth noting that those who prize man's intellect above all other faculties invariably condemn or misrepresent Rousseau. H. G. Wells sees him as anarchic and the source of the disorders of the French Revolution. Rousseau's work, he says, 'was essentially demoralising ... his tremendous vogue did much to swamp the harder, clearer thinkers of the time, and to prepare a sentimental, declamatory and insincere popular psychology for the great trials that were now coming upon France.' (Wells, 1920, p. 469)

The 'argument ad hominem' is generally regarded as ruled out in intellectual discussion. None the less, disapproval of Rousseau's personal life colours Wells's opinion of him, and even more so that of Bertrand Russell. Russell denigrates him utterly, seeing him as the forerunner of the philosophy of the German Nazis. Both these views are totally wrong and rest, first, on misunderstandings of what Rousseau meant by the 'general will' and second, on Russell's misinterpretation – as we shall see later – of the true sources of Nazi doctrines about race. Rousseau's 'general will' was more like the Quaker 'sense of the meeting' or consensus. Rousseau's influence on education has been widespread and profound; he has also something to say to the modern ecologists.

With the increase in literacy there was now also conventional education of women of the upper classes. This consisted chiefly in preparing them for entry into society, as regards manners, dress, elaborate toilet, intelligent conversation; possibly some drawing and painting in water colours and embroidery. Defoe, a man of progressive views and author of *Robinson Crusoe*, felt that there was a loss in not educating women, who obviously possessed ability. Women's influence in society was considerable, as also in politics. But this was by the feminine wiles and intrigues, considered to be natural and appropriate to her sex. Women's literary ability in correspondence was recognised, and presently also in the writing of novels, which were themselves eagerly consumed by domestically idle women.

Travelling in Europe, made swifter and more convenient by newly constructed and often luxurious coaches, became ever more frequent. Foreign travel was looked on as a part of a civilised man's education. Even those who could not afford to ride in coaches got about – as did Rousseau at times – on foot. Paris, very much a centre of Enlightenment views, attracted frequent and varied foreign visitors. Statesman like Horace Walpole came from London to court Madame du Deffand and frequent with her the salons; Milord Bolingbroke to discuss with its author, the Seigneur Louis Jean Levesque de Pouilly, vine-grower, the *Theory of Pleasant Sensations*, as also to foster the cause of the young Pretender, Bonnie Prince Charlie, and the 1745 rebellion in Scotland; Benjamin Franklin from Philadelphia, not only a potential statesman, but considerable in scientific knowledge. Even the very top level of Russian society, all of whom spoke French for preference, drawing wealth from their enslaved peasants – as did the men of other nations – came to Paris for enlightenment and pleasure. The Empress Catherine succeeded in enticing Diderot to leave his native soil; Frederick the Great wrote his own works in French and held court for men of learning. It was all most agreeable and innocuous at the level of intellectual conversation at the dinner table, or in the drawing room, but any practical outcome was barely envisaged.

The true centres of power in church and state were fully occupied in maintaining their grasp on affairs. England and France had been waging a series of wars to settle the possession of potentially rich colonies: in this England had been the more successful. Despite the plaintive plea of his devoted Scots, Bonnie Charlie did not 'come agen'. England held the power in Canada and in the American colonies.

She had her troubles with religious dissent at home, which led to the departure of the *Mayflower* and the founding of the settlement in New England. The hunger of the aristocracy and the wealthy for land had brought about the enclosure of the commons and hence the gradual transformation of the landless peasants into a new type of servile class to work in the machine-run mills of industry. The state was acquiring additional new power in the rising merchant class, who were not slow to imitate their bellicose predecessors, who had called inventive minds and their discoveries, into the service of war. Invention in the 'mechanical arts', it was now seen, could serve a vast extension of trading and profit for those in power.

Thus the use of machinery increased, and, with it, in the course of time, was also to grow the control of the machine over the minds and daily lives of many men, women, and even children.

The powers of church and state, however, had been unaware

of the deep discontent among sections of the populations they governed. In the American colonies there was unrest over taxation and lack of power; in France poverty-stricken classes, especially peasants, were the victims of the extravagance, and soon near bankruptcy, of the royal court; in England, as in Russia, resistance and revolt by the artisans and peasants was to come much later. Nevertheless all this incipient subversion was inspired and instigated by the mass of that pervasive and illuminating gossip, picked up in Paris, about a new version of humanity and human purpose.

The American colonies broke away in 1776; the great French Revolution for the rights of man: liberty, equality, fraternity, exploded in 1789, bringing with it celebrations and festivals of the sovereignty of reason. Closely following, in 1792, came the trumpet call of feminism, Mary Wollstonecraft's *Vindication of the Rights of Women*. In her dedication to Talleyrand she challenged: 'Who made man the exclusive judge, if women partake with him of the gift of Reason?' Her denunciation of Rousseau's male chauvinism, as indeed all of her fine book, might well have been penned by advocates of women's liberation today.

Significantly, whereas the English, when executing their king in 1649, had taken no note of Copernican cosmology and science, the French Revolution, by contrast, was impregnated through and through with habits of thought scientifically inspired.

Men of the eighteenth century had come to differ from their predecessors as to the nature of the power directing the universe, yet both groups of revolutionaries believed that they were acting in accordance with that power – 'the ways of god to men'.

Characteristic of eighteenth-century consciousness was a search primarily for truth, and a refusal of ambiguity. It did not conceive of retaining faith in the Christian Father God, side by side with the great clockmaker or first cause.

It is an amazing and glorious spectacle to see unfolding, as the century unfolds, all the flowers of thought, all the spreading trees of social and political reform, that sprang from that one seed, the little statement: 'Man has a right to self-interest, man has a right to be happy.' Turning uneasily in her slumber, seventeenth-century France murmured it, and it became a flame, and then a consuming fire, fierce in destruction, that transformed first the face of France herself, and then leapt forth to kindle the world.

For there can be little doubt that the ideals of human brotherhood and democracy which ultimately brought about the Revolution, and which are moving humanity so profoundly today, had their roots in the theories of the early eighteenth-century hedonists; and they again owed everything to the gentleman who so resolutely refused to be damned for eating strawberries and melons. The cloud no bigger than a man's hand is herald of a deluge; from such concealed and negligible sources do the relentless streams of progress rise.

CHAPTER 9

Machine power

The French Revolution had immense influence and repercussions in its own time and in all future history. It seemed as if the Utopian dream of the Enlightenment for human destiny had proved, like mathematics, to be 'for real'; something that could be realised in social relations, not only in books and armchair discussion. Man *could* free himself from those chains that Rousseau deplored; those three magic words, liberty, equality, fraternity, powerful in their day, took possession of human consciousness and henceforward proved indestructible.

When the Americans came to make their constitution, its words, 'life, liberty and the pursuit of happiness' echoed what they had learned from exciting pre-revolutionary Paris. They continued to keep in touch. Imlay, an American, who became Mary Wollstonecraft's lover, met her in Paris, when he came to try and interest the newly formed revolutionary government in some enterprise. The young English poet Wordsworth found, in revolutionary France, political inspiration and a personal first love.

> Bliss was it in that dawn to be alive
> And to be young was very Heaven.

Though Edmund Burke might defend hereditary and traditional power and the Church of England, and express chivalry towards Marie Antoinette, England was seething with political and religious dissent. Dr Price, a dissenter, and advocate of parliamentary reform, in 1789 preached a sermon 'On the Love of Country', celebrating the hope of political and religious liberty in France, to which Burke replied in 1790 with his *Reflections*.

Mary Wollstonecraft, who knew and admired Dr Price, gave battle with a *Vindication of the Rights of Man* two years before her defence of the rights of women. As a true revolutionary, Mary saw Marie Antoinette as a spoiled, decadent aristocrat; she castigated Burke for neglecting the distress of poverty-stricken mothers and the 'hungry cry of their helpless babes'. Together with Thomas Paine, who wrote the *Rights of Man*, Mary frequented the circle of intellectuals around Joseph Johnson the publisher. William Blake the poet was among these and, in 1791, helped to save the life of Thomas Paine, by warning him, after being given an account of a speech by Tom which Blake thought seditious, not to sleep at home that night. Next day Paine was on ship for France just before officials came to arrest him.

William Blake is now greatly honoured for his marvellous poetry, possibly, just as with Milton, to evade noting his support both for the American and French Revolutions, as also his early hostility to the industrial processes which were destroying the work of craftsmen. Blake was by profession an engraver, and his work suffered neglect, like that of the fine silk weavers and watchmakers, and other craftsmen in metal and wood.

Poets, writers, historians, critics, philosophers, artists, the cream of what might be called culture or the liberal arts, hardly one among the great names of the period, Wordsworth, Coleridge, Cowper, Robbie Burns, Byron, Shelley, Hazlitt, Paine, Wollstonecraft, William Godwin, Carlyle, Ruskin, was untouched by the fervour of that dream of progress and perfectibility that they felt to be made manifest in revolutionary France. There came the romantic dream of the love that justifies all, rejects even marriage, and all quest for property rights; there were actual plans to go away and create Utopias, based on new kinds of men and women. These people did not notice, or did not even know of, the shrewd warning of Diderot that in enthusiastic praise of those who extol or enjoy the right to be happy, they should not forget and undervalue 'those who took practical measures to make them so'. In other words the 'mechanical arts' and their artisans, now vested in the industrial machine. This whole phase of development in Britain is a tragic confusion of contradictory ideas, beliefs, and strenuous, often violent action, with results whose values, good or bad, could not easily be foreseen.

Human nature, and its instrument reason, unhappily did not as yet show itself sufficiently perfectible as to overcome the age-long struggle for personal aggrandisement and power. Disillusion began with conflict between sections and personalities, mainly in Paris, which reached England in exaggerated reports of the extent of the Terror. For the French, as their critics abroad failed to understand, the issue was clear-cut, but involved more varied and more powerful elements than the seventeenth-century English Revolution had faced. A pervasive, dominant church not split by dissensions, and headed by an infallible pope; the divine right of the king; the entrenched landed and wealthy nobility; centuries-old customs and beliefs, had to be overcome at one fell swoop and replaced by a republic of free and equal citizens, in whose principles the revolutionaries devotedly believed. They were prepared to defend their republic against violence from their class enemies, who would assuredly otherwise have destroyed them and their revolution. Nor were they unaware that enemies were gathering outside their borders.

After their early failures, when there arose among them a leader of exceptional courage, force and skill, Napoleon Bonaparte, they were prepared to crusade for, and, if need be, impose by force, the conversion of their neighbours to the republican cause.

Tragically the peoples of Europe, who could have been united by the vision of a new way of life and human purpose, instead found themselves at war with one another, each proclaiming that very cause. In 1812 the French met the agony of the repulse outside snow-bound Moscow, and thereafter military defeat at Waterloo – by the very neighbours who had been learning from them this new great ideal of human progress, embattled in alliance against them. But wherever the revolutionary armies went, they left behind them that assertion of the inalienable rights of man: to be a citizen, free to live, to travel, to work, to earn, to use and speak his mind, to be governed only by consent. Words had been spoken that were now imprinted in human consciousness and could not be bypassed or erased. Serfs began to be liberated, the Americans set free their black slaves.

In England the landed proprietors had not lost their heads, in either sense. They were pleasantly occupied in opening up, on their estates, what were to be profitable coal-fields. The merchant and manufacturing classes were building more factories and adjacent unattractive terraced housing for their workers. They were, as Napoleon rightly said, a nation of shopkeepers.

The English scene differed greatly from the republican democracy which was, later on, to be established in France. Having accepted the return of the monarchy, England had settled down into a state composed of classes, which, though not consciously defined, were, none the less, distinct: a constitutional monarch, the Lords, the Commons, clergy, gentry, the army, and navy, professional classes, business men, artisans, agricultural labourers. Jane Austen's novels give a picture of the social scene in her contemporary world, just as Dickens was later to portray what that contemporary world became. Power over government rested with the Lords and such gentry as could get themselves elected to the Commons. Power over morals and beliefs rested with the Established Church, which, though Protestant, was harried by dissenting sects and presently also by rationalists. No great wind of change, like that in France, came to sweep away all this smugness, prejudice, élitism, inequality. Temperamentally empirical, the English did not plan this society; it just grew, and went on, each superior class despising the one below and each inferior class aspiring to climb into the one above. The churches continued to teach the doctrine of the soul and the body and God as defined in the scriptures; the state, unwittingly Cartesian, upheld the supremacy of the men who manipulated ideas with their mind, over the men who manipulated matter with their hands. The gap between the cultures, art and literature and the sciences widened. Neither culture at first took much account of those 'mechanical arts' and the clockwinder God.

Church and state had good reason to fear the effect on their people and their own power of this French crusade against the 'aristos', coupled with the insolence of the 'sans culottes', the chanting of the Marseillaise, and the dancing of the Carmagnole. The army, directed and officered by the upper class, was sent to make an end of Napoleon; whilst naughty young English children were scared into goodness by nurses and Grandmammas with the threat that 'Boney' would come and get them. And providing wherewithal for the army and waging war meant more work and employment for the factories. After 1815, many of the returning soldiers went into weaving.

The mercantile and business element had been active. Canals had been dug, roads surfaced and improved by private enterprise, charging tolls. This meant easier ways of moving merchandise than on earth tracks by mule and horsepower. But now steam, which had powered many types of machines, including pumping water from the mines, was applied to transport and thus began to overtake the use of the canals.

By 1821 the first haulage by steam engine began; by 1826 the railways were carrying passengers. Then dawned the great epoch of England as the 'workshop of the world'. Building the first English railways was epic; the workers who undertook it seemed to be a special new type and class of men. Increasing numbers of the population were now engaged in industry, indeed the population itself seemed to respond, by increasing itself in order to supply 'hands' for the machines.

Machine civilisation, with its inventors, engineers, technologists, rose, as if by the touch of Aladdin on the lamp of the genie, in regions of the country where coal and iron were handy. Then came the iron ships, exports and imports, railroads, steam engines, built by England almost all over the globe; iron ships of increasing size that expanded world trade. Presently followed all those triumphs of nineteenth-century discovery, invention and science – coal gas, many chemicals, electric light and power, the telegraph, telephone, wireless. Of all these Europeans, as the innovators and prime movers, can justly be proud. Progress, that eighteenth-century vision originally inspired by belief in the clockwinding architect of the universe, was well under way. What became of its boon companion, comrade and instrument – the perfectible man?

In Britain sections of the population became prosperous. To start with only those who had a certain amount of money – or credit – were able to build a factory or business. But, as manufactures and trade brought prosperity, middle and upper class people could afford to make use of existing schools, or establish new ones for their children. Many of these were able to go on to universities, and from there into the professions, the law, the church, the army and navy, or Parliament, or, as it came into existence, the civil service. For the most part, those belonging to this social world and culture knew next to nothing about the industrial machine and those within it, on which their comfort and affluence were based.

Industrialism and its attendant machinery was left to the devices of those who were occupied with it, which meant the employers with the power of capital and hope of profit, and the workers, who needed to earn a wage in order to live. Many new processes were evolved, many new skills had to be found and learned. The very first canal, in 1761, was, oddly enough, the enterprise of the Duke of Bridgwater, who needed to link his colliery at Chat Moss (Worsley) with Manchester. The Duke's foreman, Brindley, trained as a millwright, on a wage of £1.1s. a week, had to work out for himself how to dig a canal, including how to render it watertight. He had to act as surveyor, contractor, engineer, foreman of the works and inventor of the necessary appliances. So new and untried was the project, that the Duke was not able to even raise £500 up north and had to come to London for the £25,000 needed to complete the Manchester–Liverpool canal. That these early developments took place during the war with Napoleon is some tribute to the birth pangs of nascent industrial Britain.

The story of hostility to the coming of the machine is well known. It did not only come from the workers; people of taste and culture were not slow to see that mass production could destroy the creative inspiration and art of individual craftsmen. Poets and artists were distressed at the ugliness, dirt and squalor attendant on mining and the growing industrial towns; at the ravages of the railways as they cut through the beauty and charm of the countryside. Those who did not choose, or were not obliged by necessity, to work in factory or mine, tended to regard both with annoyance or dismay. But since shareholders also began to receive profits, there was little that anyone could do about what soon came to be regarded as the onward march of progress.

Some curious facts emerge from the reaction of Britain to the impact of industrialism. When the ruling classes had succeeded in fighting off the threat of extremism and feared invasion from the Continent, came a period of recovery from the economic cost of the war, followed by expansion and hope, but considerable hard work. A reaction from extravagant aristocratic manners and morals set in. And, as Milton's England, absorbed in its own political crisis over the divine right of the king, barely noticed what was going on about Galileo and Copernicus, so mid-century England did not relate the mechanism spreading over her own soil to any clockwinding deity up above. The Christian churches and sects saw no incompatibility between their religion and mechanical civilisation. Unlike Diderot and his colleagues of the Encyclopedia, they did not envisage a choice between God the father and God the clockwinder, nor perceive, in the new proletarian class, those practitioners of the 'mechanical arts' which had been hailed as the foundation of human welfare and happiness (including that of the clergy!) On the contrary, when religious and well-to-do people involved themselves in measures to relieve the misery and suffering caused by industrial exploitation, they treated this as charity done to the poor.

An illustrious example of nineteenth-century benevolence is the 'great Lord Shaftesbury', the most compassionate philanthropist and social reformer of the period, both in and out of Parliament. He owed the inspiration of his life's work to Anna Maria Millis, an evangelical Christian, a housekeeper, whose love and care during his childhood compensated for the indifference and cruelty of his parents. Champion of the cause of all the exploited and oppressed, women and children in mines and factories, chimney sweeps, 'ragged school' boys, lunatics, he espoused laws for factory reform, and the ten-hour day; every kind of work, in his view, should stop at six p.m. It was written of him that he did for the slave children of Britain what Wilberforce did for the black American slaves. He sided with the North in the American Civil War.

Though he supported the emancipation of the Roman Catholics, in his own church he was less tolerant, opposed to the High Church Oxford movement, as also to Dean Stanley and any attempt to water down Christianity, by evading the doctrine of the atonement, through Christ, for sin. Again, though he was more anxious to see the humblest educated rather than the middle class, he was not in favour of much extension of the parliamentary franchise.

On science he did not oppose 'humble and reverent research into the secrets of Nature', because he felt sure that any discoveries would rebound to the glory of God. When young, he had even thought of devoting his time to science and was more especially interested in astronomy; he interested Peel, then Home Secretary, in the building by James South of a great telescope in the Observatory at Campden Hill. But he did not associate the study of the heavens with any notion of a clockwinding God.

Not long before his death, Shaftesbury wrote in a letter (to Frances Power Cobbe): 'When I feel old age creeping upon me and know that I must soon die – I hope it is not wrong to say it – I cannot bear to leave this world with all the misery in it,' words that might well be echoed by all do-gooders in any place and time. It may not nowadays be known that the memorial to Shaftesbury is the statue of Eros in Piccadilly Circus, on which is inscribed a glowing tribute from another great old man of the century – Prime Minister Gladstone.

There were indeed many more do-gooders of varied temperaments and views, mostly Christians. Notable among them were the constructive work of Robert Owen; the birth of the idea of co-operatives; social work to improve the health and sanitation in the towns. Shaftesbury had no illusions as to the limitations to what a peer, or the upper class, could do to help those people who were described – though never by him – as inferiors. As the workers organised into what became the trade unions, in joint attempts with them at improvements by legislation, he suffered the bitterness of the usual distrust of the go-between negotiator. Among the working class, striving both for the full right of one-man one-vote, for parliamentary candidates, as well as for the improvement of their conditions, the teachings of Tom Paine, and the ideals of the French Revolution, the vision of a better world and better people in it, survived. In 1835 the word Socialism was first spoken. For some, Christian teaching also survived, as a source of compassionate inspiration, but others had begun to see purely in mass production by the machine a way to relieve men of heavy labour and increase their prosperity. Thus materialism and self-interest became more closely associated with the dream of happiness and implicit in benefits for a class, rather than for all. Conflict and division once more overcame the chance of unity of the whole in pursuit of an ideal.

The intellectuals, in philosophy and science, were far from idle, but, except in technology, they, like the poets and artists, did not have a great effect upon practical life. Locke's psychology, the gradual creation of individual conscious thought by means of sense impressions, had much impressed Voltaire, but English education, ignoring also Rousseau, continued to teach on the religious basis of soul and body. Jeremy Bentham's extension of hedonism to the 'greatest happiness of the greatest number' was hardly the gospel of the mill and mineowners. Bentham and John Stuart Mill, interested in economics, which was regarded as a developing science, were very much of the middle class and not much concerned with the idea of socialism. Mill, however, was one of the first to take up the cause of women's rights. The women's movement of the period, influenced by Christian and Victorian prudery, neglected Wollstonecraft's brilliant manifesto, on account of her unorthodox sex life. An attempt to raise the sex question, and birth control, by Bradlaugh and Annie Besant, was suppressed by church and state, as Bradlaugh's refusal to swear the Christian oath was used to exclude him from taking his seat in Parliament. The Secular Society and its members, founded in England just a hundred years ago, was constantly under threat from the blasphemy laws.

In respect of freedom of thought in morals and economics, church and state kept their hold upon human consciousness. However, due to an increasing, and perhaps peculiarly English, practice of separating thought into various pigeonholed compartments, scientific research, in the industrial world and in the universities, did increase in volume and influence. Chemistry advanced with the atomic theory, the classification of elements, the analysis and study of the reactions of various substances. Chemicals and dyes were evolved for industrial use, fertilisers for agriculture. The constant instinctive drive of curiosity – of the intellect – was, as ever, to find out how things were made by taking them to pieces. Applied in biology or medicine, it spelt the dissection of dead or living bodies. But the notion of splitting the atoms themselves fired the ambition of some men of science. Others, seeking new energy to drive machines, had by the end of the century invented the petrol-driven motor.

As science revealed so great a potential for powering the machines which were creating prosperity, religion, provided that it could maintain its hold upon morals, accepted cosmology as defined by Isaac Newton. The rapier-like eighteenth-century quest for naked truth was somehow blunted.

But let Darwin appear with the theory of evolution and immediately war was once more declared. This was not really a new quarrel: fundamentally it rested upon man's age-long refusal to accept his animal origin and inheritance, his ambition for the status of a god and power over everything in the world.

To the religious, who believed in the special creation of man by God, the theory of evolution was blasphemy. Might not the philosophers and scientists, in their zeal and pride at man's superiority and growing power over nature, have also been inclined to reject the suggestion of their own animal origin? Not at all: for them Darwin's work demonstrated first of all, the ability of the human intellect to probe ever further into the 'secrets of nature', and second, what was probably more important, it confirmed the new faith in the continued progress of humanity through centuries of time.

Since Descartes and Newton the goal had become knowledge, and hence power, by means of the intellect, and was already proving itself in prosperity brought by the industrial machine. The philosophy put forward by Bergson of the *élan vital* – a driving force within organic nature – was frowned upon and rejected, as savouring too much of divine purpose, by minds already conditioned by mathematics and mechanism. A new concept of the functioning of the intellect had begun to appeal to empiricists. Buffon, we saw, had preferred the empirical method to mathematics, because, in his view, its conclusions rested upon brute facts, which were outside of, and indifferent to, the opinion or desires of the investigator. In science man's intellect should, above all, be cool and impartial in assessing and dealing with its conclusions. The findings of science would command greater credence and respect when extricated from the irrational influence of human feelings. Of such impartiality there was no better example than the machine.

I have been attempting to convey the general outline of the way of life and thought in the English society in which my generation grew up – the last two decades of the nineteenth century, when Edwardian relaxation began to replace Victorian restraint. It was a society that looked forward to years of some pleasure, growing prosperity and peace, a society that believed that the international interlocking of industry and trade would prevent what Norman Angell's book described as the 'Great Illusion' – the outbreak of war. A world which, in our time, has been regretted in Peter Laslett's penetrating analysis, as *The World We Have Lost*.

Authority was vested in the patriarchal family, the church, and a state of imperial power, all three supported by the Christian religion as by Parliament established. Industrialism was already making its inroads into family life and the health of working people, but it affected the upper ranks of society but little, except in so far as to contribute to their wealth and comfort. The three strands of authority were fused into a coherent whole to which the majority gave allegiance, only slowly becoming aware of the challenges which were to come from the women, the workers, the scientists and the freethinkers.

Education, as I experienced it, and much as it still is today, was pigeon-holed into separate subjects and compartments. I was urged by my religious mentors to be good that I might please God the Father and go to Heaven when I died. Where or what was this Father God or this Heaven was left to the imagination. True, he was supposed to be somewhere 'up there'; I was invited by Pascal to gaze into and be affrighted by the silence of those infinite spaces; Kant exhorted me to see in the starry heavens the sanction of the moral law. Perhaps it is significant that this advice came from the French and then a German thinker, both of peoples who had been more addicted to stargazing than the British. So, like many other simple people and the artists, I peopled the skies with robed and bearded prophets riding with dignity on the clouds, and the blue vault of heaven with guardian angels. But there was more fun and friendliness in my childish fantasy world of elves and fairies.

Meantime my school atlas told of the round world, its journey, with that of the planets, round the sun. I learned, too, something of the chemistry that underlay its surface, though not, of course, at that date, about the human body and sex. Except that I was told that God had made all things both great and small, all this was just school knowledge that bore no relation to everyday life and the thought and habits of ordinary people. I do, however, remember vividly how the scientific approach to thought began to dawn on my young mind.

One incident is worth recording, because it illustrated that there were some efforts to reconcile science and religion in the minds of the young. The vicar of my church, striding up and down the aisle as he conducted Sunday school, suddenly put the question: 'What is colour?' Putting up my hand with what came to me as a sudden inspiration, I called out: 'It is something which light makes.' I received a moment of surprised congratulation. Until I reached university I met no one who did not fully, some even devoutly, accept Christianity. No one had attempted to piece together the many diverse facts discovered by science, into a general concept or philosophy of man in relation to the universe. So completely did the concepts of medieval religion dominate the average mind.

But science and technology, by themselves, increased their influence on economics, daily life and the imagination. H. G. Wells was to become one of the prophets of the New Age; his science fiction stories, in the *Strand Magazine*, were avidly read by many people. Then came the shattering of the *real* Great Illusion by the outbreak of war.

CHAPTER 10

Full speed ahead

The outbreak of war in 1914 administered a shock to the consciousness of the peoples of Europe from which they have not yet fully recovered. One of the major causes of the war was the phenomenal development of the machine, instrument of industrial expansion.

In 1780–90 Great Britain had still been mainly agricultural, with a population of about 8 million. Scarcity of labour for industry had played its part in hastening the invention and introduction of the machine. By 1914, due to scientific research and mass production, not only Britain but the countries of Europe were all relatively prosperous industrial and colonial powers; Britain, indeed, laid claim to imperial status; Queen Victoria became Empress of India in 1877.

The foundation of industrial prosperity had been laid on European railroads by British engineers; steam engines puffed their way across Europe, Canada, North and South America, carrying merchandise and, above all, passengers; people for whom new and rapid transport offered fresh aspects of personal 'liberty and equality' – to travel, to work, to trade, to acquire knowledge and riches. But mechanism and invention knew no limits. The British 'world workshop' now had its competitors, of whom the chief was Germany. What is more, the machine was voracious. It needed to be fed with new types of materials from all lands; expansion, too, was a condition of its existence, its wheels must turn, now night as well as day, to ensure – in those words that were to become sacred – productivity, profit, competition.

To protect themselves from exploitation, the American

colonies established the Monroe doctrine, which excluded European enterprise from the Western hemisphere. In consequence, Europe turned upon Africa. In the mid-nineteenth century only the barest fringe of the dark continent had been touched by white European exploration and incursion; by 1914 England, France, Belgium, Germany, Portugal, Spain had carved up the whole map of Africa between them. Rivalry between the British and Dutch settlers had brought about the savagery of the Boer war, as well as sharp dissension on the home front as to that war's morality and justice. Among products needed by industry, rubber was the cause of colonial brutality in the Congo, in which King Leopold of Belgium was implicated.

Industrial Britain had become very dependent on the import of food. Now German invention and industry, less handicapped than Britain by class snobbery, increased in quantity and quality, alarming the British capitalists and government. Both nations prepared for war by rivalry in building battleships to protect overseas trade, and ruthlessly sought whatever money and materials might be needed to promote arms manufacture.

Such were some of the first fruits of the civilisation which the machine, while its wheels revolved at the behest of the captains of industry and the – as ever – power-drunk governments, brought to mankind. Intoxicated with their success and prosperity, Europeans, of *all* classes, were convinced of their superiority over all other races, in their capacity for science and invention, by means of which they would exemplify man's 'conquest of nature' and presently dominate and civilise the rest of the world. Such civilisation, now bringing with it the great boon of material progress, would inevitably, as we have seen, be accompanied, or even preceded, by conversion of the heathen and savages to the morality and faith of Christianity. Funds for this purpose were easily raised from the charitable at home, where the teaching of orthodox Christianity, supported by states and churches, continued, as it still does today, in Europe and the Western hemisphere.

The machine, now an instrument in the hands of wealth and power, rolled on; but with it came a rising tide of that rational creative thought to which it owed its origin. To cover all such trends of thought and currents of feeling is impossible, and not always relevant to our theme. Two innovations appear with increasing frequency: new types of social association and new types of men and women who initiate and organise.

The old physical empathy, brotherhood and sisterhood, did survive and even used those very words, but coming together for a common purpose now had a far more rational and intellectual basis. Unlike the peasants, the workers in industry, the proletariat, as they came to be called, adapted to regularity and fast-moving machines, measuring and assessing size, quantities, number. Of necessity they adopted the habit of suppressing emotion; so also did the engineers, designers and planners, who caused machines, bridges, steam engines and railroads to be built. Industrial man, emerging as the mechanic, technician, chemist, research scientist, was carrying forward the eighteenth-century insistence on the divisive clarity of thought. Even women, following men's type of organisation, in efforts to achieve the vote, revealed to what an extent that right was seen as a symbol of rational, intellectual, legal, rather than instinctive organic social cohesion.

Very many of the leaders and thinkers of the future were to come from the industrial world, workers and intellectuals often self-educated, whose origins were working class. As in the twelfth century, men of science, intellectuals and innovators of no matter what social class, felt a natural affinity with the artisans. Political and social life of the pre-1914 years is illumined and starred by a galaxy of names too numerous to mention: such as Keir Hardie and John Burns, George Lansbury, Dr Richard Pankhurst (one of the founders of the Indpendent Labour Party); his wife Emmeline Pankhurst, his daughters Christabel and Sylvia; Lloyd George, who gave a new life and new meaning to liberalism; the Fabians, among whom presently Bernard Shaw and Beatrice and Sydney Webb were active. All of these people, watching the effects of machine production, were disturbed to see it affording great profit for the few, when, while indeed lightening men's labour, it might be providing comfort and leisure for all.

Already in 1848, the workers of Europe had achieved sufficient unity to make a first attempt, inspired by French republicanism, to throw off their chains. One result of this was the arrival in England of a refugee, Karl Marx, who was in close association with Engels, a business man in Manchester, a town which above all others at that time teemed with new movements and ideas. Of those who were thinking beyond practical politics, in terms of a philosophy that was definitely opposed to religion, Marx is important because of his long and far-reaching influence. Like most of them, he derived from the Cartesian split between mind and matter, coming down heavily on the side of matter, on which however, he was to exercise a very vast extent of mind. His immediate predecessors were the German philosophers Kant and Hegel who, in the tradition of those whom we have styled the 'stargazers', were of a metaphysical and idealistic school. For all his elaborate analytic reasoning, Kant was primarily an ethical and religious figure. Hegel too, started out with a mystical vision, which, after being subjected to all the mysteries of dialectic dissection, emerged as an Absolute, universal unity of reason, somewhat reminiscent of the notion of Averroes the Arab of Cordova University.

In that period of emancipation from Victorian doctrines and morals, two names stand out because they relate science to ordinary life, and both to the universe. Neither politicians nor religious teachers, they none the less had very great influence in both those fields. They were Thomas Huxley and H. G. Wells.

Thomas Huxley, about forty years older than Wells, belonged more to the nineteenth century, in that he was one of the very courageous free-thinkers of that period. He was the opponent of Wilberforce in the famous debate about Darwin's *Origin of Species*. He was mainly self-educated, but managed to achieve a place in the medical profession by getting a scholarship as intern at Charing Cross Hospital. From there he learned about the privations of the London poor and, as an assistant surgeon on a ship of the British navy, he saw something of the treatment of black slaves and the impact of Western culture on primitive peoples. He was convinced that the 'blessings of civilisation' brought them disease, drunkenness, corruption and subjection. His concern was not that of the Christian missions; on the contrary, he believed profoundly in what scientific research might achieve for humanity, once liberated from false beliefs. At home he gave very much of his time to lectures for working men. There is an echo of the intransigent clarity of the eighteenth century in the prophetic words of his letter to his wife in 1873:

> We are in the midst of a gigantic movement greater than that which preceded and produced the Reformation . . . nor is any reconcilement possible between free thought and traditional authority. One or other will have to succumb after a struggle of unknown duration, which will have as its side issues vast political and social troubles. I have no more doubt that free thought will win in the long run than I have that I sit here writing to you, or that this free thought will organise itself into a coherent system, embracing human life and the world as one harmonious whole. But this organisation will be the work of generations of men, and those who further it most will be those who teach men to rest in no lie, and to rest in no verbal delusions. I may be able to help a little in that direction – perhaps I may have helped already. (Rubinstein, 1953, p. 811)

Thomas Huxley's grandson Julian, who became distinguished as a biologist, thought that the battle for Darwin was as vital as that of Galileo for Copernicus. In his work Julian wrote of evolution as imparting an encouraging sense of change and human progress.

H. G. Wells struggled out of poverty and a lack of education, and, threatened with tuberculosis, took to writing as sedentary work, was enamoured of science and began to make it come real for my generation. Now it meant something more than those school-book maps, or geography lessons. He took us to the moon, from which we learned the meaning of the loss of gravity; he brought those dreadful Martians from their red planet to invade us, with graphic descriptions of the conflict. We travelled with him in space and time, beyond our revolving planet, and soon beyond the limiting barriers of national geography and politics into our own whole world.

Meantime our parents chuckled at the adventures of Mr Polly and Kipps, whilst shocked publishers rejected the novel *Ann Veronica* which actually dealt with adultery and implied free love. At last, in 1912, that book was published by the enterprise of the young Stanley Unwin, who was also to become the publishing ally of Bertrand Russell. Thus, at Girton, in Cambridge, on the eve of the war, we young women were reading *Ann Veronica*. Some of us were disappointed that, on the outbreak of war, H.G., our revered storytelling companion, and already a champion of causes, gave the war full support and was critical of conscientious objection.

But the war did change him. The post-war H.G., losing none of his wit and delighted impertinence in challenging orthodoxy, assumed the mantle of the prophet. Undaunted by the spectacle of savagery, carnage and destruction, he saw, as had Huxley, that the struggle for better human life and progress was going to be a long job. He set about telling people the history of their world and species, with volumes on the science of life, helped by Gip Wells, his son, and Julian Huxley, as well as a number of willing colleagues. These books, which did not deny the follies and cruelties of which man is capable, set forth how far, none the less, he had advanced, and what great hopes there were for the future. As I sat in Paris early in 1920, returned to my eighteenth-century research after my experience of the power of the machine and technology in the West, now in war as in peace, wondering what the revolution in Russia would bring forth, the first edition of that great world history was published. Here was a book which broke through the pigeon-holes of education. In the schools, and for most adults, history was the nationalist story of kings and queens and their wars and alliances. In most countries people did not look beyond their own political and social life, whilst, in their colonies, they taught the subject peoples the history of the colonial power, ignoring, or seeking to eradicate, inherent local traditions and beliefs. How the world began was still told in the book of Genesis; fossils and prehistoric monsters were a matter for specialists.

H.G. tried to place ordinary adults and children within the picture of what was known about their universe, and to tell the story of mankind, developing, through science and knowledge, a gradual discipline and self-government. Showing how those who sought a life of civilised thought and scientific truth were, at all times, more important than the warmongers, he looked forward to the time when such reasonable and cultured men and women would assert themselves with greater insistence and vigour.

In the history is this paragraph:

Hitherto in all countries this has been the characteristic attitude of science and literature. The intellectual man has been loth to come to grips with the forcible man. He has generally been something of a courtier and time-saver. Possibly he has never yet been quite sure of himself. Hitherto men of reason and knowledge have never had the assurance and courage of the religious fanatic. But there can be little doubt that they have accumulated settled convictions and gathered confidence during the last centuries: they have slowly found a means to power through the development of popular education and popular literature, and today they are far more disposed to say things plainly and to claim a dominating voice in the organisation of human affairs than they have ever been before in the world's history. (Wells, 1920, p. 337)

H.G. continued on his mission, with books and novels – the *World set Free*, the *New Utopia* – ideas about devoted bands of Apostles or Samurai, who would put the world to rights. Ultimately he gave us the *Shape of Things to Come*, which made a superb film, that prophesied the next war almost to the very day, and, moreover, foretold and pictured the first journey round the moon. H.G. was indeed the heir to that eighteenth-century dream of perfectibility and progress, a man – not of his own back yard, but of the whole planet and the universe.

As I knew him well (we were colleagues in political battles for women's liberation), H.G. represents for me very vividly the hopes and fears of that period between the wars. I shared his fury and impatience at the stupidity, short-sightedness and intolerance of statesmen, educators, fanatical politicians and priests. Conscious as he was of his powerful scientific and human imagination, he did see himself as something like an Old Testament prophet. I was aware of this gift of insight in him. I believed, as did my then husband, Bertrand Russell, in the power of science and knowledge to improve human life, but I did not share H.G.'s enthusiastic welcome for all the products of industrial technology, nor the faith cherished by both men in the dominance of the intellect.

H.G. remains for me the great prophet and evangelist of the Religion of the Machine Age. In those campaigning years his attitude was one of confidence in Newtonian cosmology, and, one might say, of that clockwinding God – perhaps the first cause. During the war, when he wrote *Mr Britling*, he – who was otherwise very much of an environmentalist – felt conscious of a driving force *within* him, which led him to write *God the Invisible King*. But he was no believer in the orthodox religious sense. He might, as it were, touch his cap at that Fate, or someone above whom he jokingly called Mr G. One of his characters, at point of death after an accident, was heard to remark, incomprehensibly 'neat o u, Mr G.' What H.G. himself thought about Mr G, when he himself was dying, we shall come to later.

There were plenty of sensitive and intelligent people in those inter-war years of the twentieth century, who strove with heart and mind for peace, co-operation and tolerance in human affairs, both nationally, and internationally. H.G.'s importance is his attempt to promote a comprehensive human world history.

Revealed religions, of course, continued to expound their own world historical views. Among the thoughtful section of the industrial proletariat were those who had emerged from nonconformist religious dissent into a socialism which aimed ultimately at universal brotherhood, based on the contribution of the machine to prosperity, and the lightening of labour. On the other hand, there were the followers of Marx. If Marx had not pursued his work in such a class-ridden society as that in England, possibly the class war might not have been so dominant in his theorising. However that may be, he and his followers had evolved what they held to be a scientific appraisal of the inevitable accession to power of the class concerned with the current means of production of economic goods and prosperity. This economic basis would, equally inevitably, determine the nature of any cultural superstructure. This 'materialist' (or economic) determinism of history' was tantamount to a religion based upon the machine. Marxists resolutely opposed any revealed religions, which they stigmatised as the 'opium of the people'. Marxism was already widespread internationally before 1914; its adherents had a wild hope that the intervention of the proletariat internationally, by a strike, might stop the outbreak of war. One revolutionary socialist, Jaurès, in France, was shot by an opponent. The failure of international action by the workers was a bitter disappointment, but led to the calling of the Second International, after the war, in revolutionary Moscow of 1920.

Yet Marxism itself was extremely parochial. It was concerned only with organised workers in industry, who were, however, said to be destined to dominate the world. Yet, in vast regions of the world, no industrial production, and consequently no proletariat, as yet existed. Marxism took no account of the rest of the universe, by stargazing. Yet it owed its existence to those machine-making mathematical minds who were inspired by that divine clockwinder.

Men engaged in scientific research, in the post-war period, whether they were concerned with applied science (technology), or the so-called 'pure' science of the universities, began to seek a unity among themselves, based on the fact that science had a language of its own that could be understood and truths that were accepted by all. Some of these, who were Marxist, saw science as a consensus, that might prove as uniting as the Catholic religion had been in Europe of the Middle Ages.

Among these trends of human consciousness, there were also, of course, the philosophers. They continued divided by the Cartesian split between mind and matter. Contemplative and imaginative spirits tended towards metaphysical and ethical discussion, idealism; admirers of science opposed such woolliness and mysticism, preferring to discipline their minds to the very utmost impartial non-emotional thought, in order to analyse and interpret scientific truths. The Bergsonian theory of the 'life force' seemed like an attempt to interpret organic life. This philosophy did appeal to some ordinary persons, who were encouraged by the idea of evolution. On the other hand, profit-seekers put forward the 'survival of the fittest' as an argument for cut-throat industrial competition, while the mechanically minded dismissed the life force as a type of religion.

After the Armistice of 1918, as the angry passions of the war abated, all these creative forces began to strive for peace, co-operation, educational and sex reform, any measures that might contribute to the improvement of the human condition and to human happiness. There were great hopes, among the intellectuals and industrial workers, of the inspiration of the Soviet Revolution, some of whose leaders, in exile before the war, had been known to their colleagues in Europe and America. But almost all the potential leaders of the war gener-ation in Europe had been lost on the battlefields of Flanders. The older generation, still holding power, saw Russia as the new enemy. In England the rising Labour Party in 1924 succeeded in making Ramsay MacDonald, a war-time conscientious objector, their first Prime Minister. He was brought down by propaganda which asserted that he was being manipulated from Moscow. Industrial economics had become the key to politics. Men of the machine, capitalists supported by government and the proletariat of the new fairly powerful trade unions clashed in 1926 in a strike conflict verging on revolution, for control of the machine on which both sides depended. Though no one was aware of it, in Europe and America and presently in Russia, the religion of the machine had taken over.

CHAPTER 11

The machine: God visible and manifest

The Labour Government of 1924 and the General Strike of 1926 had not even seemed possible when, just after the armistice, I returned to my research into pre-revolutionary French thought. This had begun as a literary, somewhat academic exercise on the opposition of the rational hedonists to ascetic Christianity, a process in which I had found much affinity with my own personal emancipation from that faith.

Contemporary politics had not, so far, appeared relevant to my work, or assumed much importance in my own mind. Inevitably the war changed the outlook of all affected by it. My experience of a year in New York in the British War Mission to the American government, revealed to me the nature of a highly industrialised nation, as also the power of the huge corporations that were in control. As I now sat, postwar, in the Bibliothèque Nationale in Paris, the question of the rise of industrial civilisation began to take precedence over the hedonists. I began to wonder what really did happen to the mind and imagination of man, as the walls of the smug medieval world ruled by a father God broke apart and vanished, and man found himself whirling through space on his tiny ball at the mercy of forces as yet unknown and uncomprehended.

My close association with Bertrand Russell had begun: he was urging me to go with him to visit the Soviet Union whose revolution was inspiring universal enthusiasm and hope or, on the contrary, furious opposition and hate. Russia was reckoned to be a backward nation of illiterate peasants, only recently freed from serfdom, who, moreover, were steeped in a medieval type of the Christian religion. What would the Russians make of God the mathematician, clockwinder, master of time and space, and dynamic power, ruler of the galaxies, who did indeed set the planets in their courses, and hold them there with mathematical precision? In the summer of 1920 I went to Russia to find out.

At the very outbreak of the revolution in 1917, although England was still at war with Germany, Churchill had sent Josiah Wedgwood, MP, out, via Manchuria and Eastern Siberia, to find out how best to oppose it. Wedgwood's entertaining and friendly report on his encounter with the Bolsheviks is little known, nor did it prevent Churchill and other enemies from persisting in their armed attacks. In 1918 the British dockers had tried to support their Soviet comrades by refusing to load ammunitions for a British expeditionary force against Russia, which did, however, set forth and make landings in the north at Murmansk.

Visits by civilians were opposed and obstructed by the British government and were only achieved secretly by individuals. But in 1920 a group of trade unionists and members of the Labour Party, in which was Bertrand Russell, achieved an orthodox visit with official sanction. I also succeeded in entering the country on my own, but by the secret route. I was not a party politician, I knew very little about party policies or strife, but the war had made me a pacifist. Consequently, I probably approached the Russians with a more open mind than many visitors at that time. I observed, asked questions, listened to the answers, began, almost half-consciously, to assess their historical development.

Here was a people still for the most part immersed in medieval Christianity, who had not passed through anything like the Protestant Reformation, still less the sceptical more rational period of the Enlightenment: this last had only touched the very top level of their society. There was not, in Russia, a great deal of industrial development. Now the people were being led by a party inspired by modern industrialism, that very 'proletariat' which, according to Marxist doctrine, was, for the sake of the revolution, to impose a dictatorship, though it was insisted that this would be merely temporary. As the comrades explained to me how everything in the social system would carry on harmoniously, virtually regulating itself, once the communist order had been set in motion, I suddenly perceived an affinity between this ideal and the dream of Descartes and his followers, by which the intellect of man, making machines and commanding matter, could shape the destiny of the world. They seemed to me more like Cartesians than Marxists. In fact, in their assertion of the spirit of man taking control over matter, I described them as splendid heretics to the Marxist materialist determination of history, and to the empirical viewpoint of the West. Indeed, reflecting on the unhappy state of industrial relations in the West, I thought it possible that this 'a priori' ideal might hold the key to the taming of industrial society.

But I also saw in the leaders of the revolution, many of whom had in exile worked in factories in the United States, an enthusiasm for Western technology, almost a fanatical faith in the power of the machine, which they would communicate to a religious-minded people. And this was a new concept. They believed in the power of the machine not simply to lighten the burden of labour and speed up production, but, what was more important, to organise and regulate the very structure of the social system itself.

Could man remain master of the machine he was creating? I became convinced that the machine would threaten liberty, and make an end of democracy as we then understood it; that it would be run by an élite of oligarchs or a dictator at the top, holding the key to the clockwork, like the new God of the universe, dealing in power and calculation, and with human beings the mass, indifferent to the individual, except as a statistical work unit. I had a vision of the machine invading ever more territory of individual labour, running the full twenty-four hours, setting times and hours of shifts, impinge-ing on every detail of personal lives. Mankind would live by the clock, in a clockwork world, in a system which could not run without the co-operation of the units within it, but which, by its very indifference to the individual, would destroy the only source of such co-operation – the human heart. I saw industrialism as a persecuting religion (in which capitalism and communism were merely two contending sects) spreading and establishing itself all over the earth, absorbing ever more converts in its steely bosom. It offered some reward in prosperity, it was true, but at the price of almost every other cherished value in life. In the sacred cause of progress, for three centuries, men had been worshipping and obeying the god of mechanism. The dream of Descartes, fulfilling itself in our times, was transformed into a nightmare.

Would man or the machine conquer? I raised this issue as regards the modernisation of Russia, in the chapter which I contributed to Bertrand Russell's *Practice and Theory of Bolshevism* as also in a long letter to the *Liberator* in New York, which they refused to print. On my return from Russia, I had been anxious to write a book attempting a reconciliation between Soviet communism and the West, by means of what I felt was Russian renaissance idealism uniting with the more sophisticated empiricism of the West. At this stage Russell and I went to China, and I could not proceed with a book which it seemed would not be accepted or understood. No one was studying or thinking about the possible effects of industrialism in itself, isolated from contending ideologies. On board ship, on our way to China, Russell and I disagreed very seriously about Bolshevik Russia, to a degree which seems to have hurt him far more than I realised at the time. The issue was personal freedom, which had first priority for him. I was convinced that it would inevitably be destroyed by the system which the machine would impose.

The typescript of my letter to the *Liberator*, dated 20 October 1920, and sent as from the Government University, Peking, is beside me as I write. Some extracts from this letter were quoted by me in my book *Tamarisk Tree*, Vol. 1. Although it puts forward ideas with which the reader of this book will already be familiar, it seems correct to record some part of the argument in its historical context. In this letter lies the true origin of this present book.

Russell's book on Bolshevism had angered his left-wing supporters. I was defending him against the characteristic Marxist accusation that his views were conditioned by his class origin. Besides this, I insisted that Marxism was not, as Marxists contended, a scientific interpretation of history; on the contrary, it was not even politics, but rather a new religion associated with Newtonian cosmology. I suggested that even

Newtonian cosmology was now questioned by Einstein, and the supremacy of the human intellect by Freud's theories of the unconscious. Following Russell, I was then still intensely partisan of the impartial scientific method. At the same time, unlike him, I greatly admired the essence of what the Bolsheviks were trying to tell the world and the heroism of their stand against their enemies. So also did Arthur Ransome, who was there at that date, sending home to his paper, the *Manchester Guardian*, reports that they would not credit or print.

As for the supporters of the Russian Revolution in the West, I said that they persisted in regarding Russia

> as a dream country, with an ideal state and ideal superhuman citizens and rulers, and in not recognising the immense differences between conditions there and conditions and temperament in the West. Facts should be faced by those people who sincerely desire to better the structure of society according to *scientific* principles, and the *fact* about Russia is, that ... the Bolshevik leaders, having introduced communism before the country was industrially ripe for it ... with an ignorant and unwilling population, cannot help resembling European governments in backward countries. That being so, their procedure must not be crystallised into a criterion for permanent communist government all over the world. I believe that the dangers of holding communism as a persecuting religion cannot be too much emphasised.

Drawing an analogy with the contest between the dogmatism of religion and the habit of free thought, which had now become almost instinctive in all people liberated from religion, I continued:

> I believe the communist ideal to be as clear and fiery as free thought, just as invincible and unanswerable, and just as likely to receive joyful acceptance. It will pass, too, from the sphere of reason to the sphere of instinct, and the time will come when it is universally recognised that oppression in the interest of economic inequality is as absurd as oppression in the interest of some particular belief about

God and the future life. But this will happen more surely and permanently by propagating disbelief in the importance of property than by disciplinary redistribution of it. Because that redistribution must depend, in the last resort, on the general will of the community to accept it. It is capitalist industry that is the persecuting religion and its central dogma, the importance of private property and wealth. Communism should aim at creating a society of men and women to whom that doctrine is merely laughable. To them economic justice will be instinctive, they will desire economic justice, as they will desire developed industry, not as an end in itself, nor as a means to communal luxury, but as a means to the higher development of the community. If communism concentrates only on goods and the mechanisation of life, and if it attempts to establish itself by dragooning majorities with fire and the sword, it thereby submits to the machine and adopts the capitalist dogma and the capitalist method, and proves itself to be no advance of science, but merely a further phase of this persecuting religion of industrialism, from which we hoped it would free us, and from which free thinkers will have to liberate the world some hundreds, perhaps thousands, of years hence.

As to dogmatic belief I wrote:

Since Newton, religious thought has tended to take refuge in the notion of the First Cause; God becomes merely a clock-maker or cinematograph operator turning a handle, no longer closely concerned in individual lives, or with individual desires. He is the impersonal origin of the laws by which the Universe is regulated, laws which are strictly impartial and no more favourable to man than the rest of creation. I believe this to be the instinctive religion of the average modern mind; though not formulated as a dogma, it dominates the imagination. With it goes a passionate belief in the solidity and importance of matter, likewise derived ultimately from the Newtonian gravitation theory. Good, or rather goods, come to that man who sufficiently understands the working of natural laws to achieve material prosperity by their means.

The modern theory of the State derives, like the old one, from the current religious conception. It envisages the ruler, or group of rulers, as scientific winders of the clock, who construct society according to certain fixed laws regulating the distribution of matter, in complete disregard of ranks and classes, prayers of individuals, or received moral standards. This, I think, is what is meant by the exclusion of the 'ethico-deific argument'.

Instead therefore, of a 'divine right' of kings, we have, as it were, a 'mechanical right' of kings and opposition to the mechanism is an abominable heresy. Criticism of men like Lenin is as absurd as criticism of the impartial First Cause, since they are no more responsible for the social upheavals involved in their clock winding, than God for the earthquakes occurring in His well regulated universe. Further, to object that the State was made for man and not man for the State, is as antiquated a superstition as the pretension that the Universe was made by God as a comfortable dwelling place for humanity. All that we can do, in both cases, is to sigh and wish that the Creator had spent His time in anything but creating.

I went so far as to suggest that the upsetting of Newtonian cosmology by Einstein might well have the result on the human imagination of destroying the mechanical religion's concept of dynamic whirling lumps of matter.

I can imagine that future generations may make a similar imaginative translation, and may evolve complicated, irrational, non-materialistic, yet thoroughly scientific theories of the State, beside which Marxism may look like Christian theology.

And with a shaft aimed at the noble would-be 'proletarian dictators':

I suggest that what we are all after is to become the super moral First Cause and push everybody else into the mechanical society we create. And not a soul among us individually desires this mechanical society. We know it already under capitalism. What we seek is freedom and green fields, dominion over our mechanical life, not further subjection to it.

At no point did I ever suggest that it was communism, or Bolshevism, that invented totalitarian control by the machine. This tendency had already begun in the West, and was inherent in the structure of industrialism. Argument on all aspects of the subject continued between Russell and myself in Peking, my letters to my mother and to Ogden convey echoes of the debate. We decided that the lectures Russell was to deliver later in Japan, would elaborate this theme. Our joint book, *The Prospects of Industrial Civilisation* resulted and was published in 1923. Russell's serious illness, our return home, the birth of my son, politics and elections intervened.

I began my book on the Machine Age religion, whose first chapter 'The Soul of Russia and the Body of America' still exists. But it was impossible to get time and quiet to concentrate on a difficult theme which apparently did not make sense to anyone but myself. Politics at home were lively and challenging – with the rise and fall of a Labour government; women achieving the vote at long last; the agitation for birth control; the General Strike in which I played my part. In those twenty years between the wars there was in England – and also elsewhere in Europe – a creative spirit of belief and hope, a drive towards a better world, which could have responded to the inspiration of the Bolsheviks had it not been frustrated by the power and profit-seekers on the one hand, and the dogmas of the machine worshippers on the other. The Russians, as I knew them then, were truly heretics to Marx, temperamentally not at all Marxist-Leninist: a warm, outgoing, emotional people, with their own special style of wit and humour. Tragically no attempt has ever yet been made by the West to understand them. My romantic vision of a great translucent wave uniting East and West, washing away dissension, and subsiding to reveal a new and smiling world, would not, in those years, have been an idle dream.

As Russell and I turned towards education, I renewed my challenge to asceticism and Descartes in my book *The Right to be Happy* (1927) in which I asserted that the organic, biological instincts of human beings ought to be the basic foundation of the state.

CHAPTER 12

The machine makes war

War had not yet been mechanised in 1914/18. At the outset there was still the cavalry; cannon and vehicles were still horse-drawn. Soldiers faced long-range artillery, machine guns, the horrors of those trenches, water filled, sodden with mud; the bayonet charge. Armoured vehicles, tanks and aeroplanes came late on the scene.* But the greater involvement of the civilian population became apparent as men were conscripted to fight and men and women to make munitions in the factories. Aerial bombardment had begun; it was evident that people and property anywhere might be exposed to this threat.

The peoples who had experienced war now sought a peaceful existence: new methods of education, more equal economy and relations between men and women, marriage and sex reforms. The destruction of the war in Europe, coupled with the ruthless economic exploitation of the industrial machine, had brought about a financial crisis and severe unemployment. In Spain civil war broke out to gain power for the élite classes.

In science and philosophy brilliant minds in Europe pursued truth with the intellectual impartiality traditional ever since Descartes, allied with an even older tradition of enquiry – taking things to pieces. Psychologists and philosophers were analysing mind, physicists analysing matter. Matter, inorganic, as defined by Galileo, was now equated by Einstein with energy. Could energy be released by splitting atoms of matter?

* It is interesting that the story by H. G. Wells, 'The Land Ironclads' in which he invented the tanker, was first published in December 1903 in the *Strand Magazine*.

The German physicist Jungk, in his book *Brighter than a Thousand Suns*, has described how the physicists of Europe came together at Göttingen in Germany, intent on solving the splitting of the atom, all of them oblivious, at that time, of the remotest possibility of the use of atom fission for war. Since some of these scientists were Jewish, Hitler's rise to power scattered them back to their national laboratories. In England, notably at the Cavendish at Cambridge, Rutherford was at work, as also for a time was Capitza, the Russian.

The Nazis, who supported what they maintained was the blond Nordic, superior race of Herrenvolk, combined with the persecution of the Jews, have constantly been described as revealing the brutal, animal savagery latent in man. The reverse is the truth. The Germans, living among post-war ruins, poverty, hunger, unemployment, needed just what Hitler – with some help from industrialists – gave them, a programme of reconstruction, the building of roads, factories, tanks, battleships, weapons of war. To believe themselves supermen roused them from despair to action; to despise, as inferior, the race who had an intricate hold on their financial structure, was likewise a powerful incentive. Totalitarian war did not take its rise from instinctive, animal savagery; it was a calculated, unemotional, intellectual product of the machine. Highly gifted minds find it impossible to believe that the intellect may make mistakes. When things go wrong, they throw the blame on instinct, on the emotions. H. G. Wells, as we saw, dismissed Rousseau as an emotional, anarchic, disturbing force in the rationality of the French Revolution. Similarly, Russell condemns Rousseau outright as the true basis of the ideology of the Nazis. One may argue the point with him; suffice it here to say that his main reason is that the conclusions of the intellect convince by their truth, while emotions are individual and variable.

To my mind the lesson of that second war with the Germans was a vindication of my thesis as to how the take-over of a people by the machine can be total, mind, body and soul. Hitler's legacy to mankind (culminating in the surrender of the scientists to the atom bomb) is that all future wars will be totalitarian, a total war machine involving the entire population from which there can be no escape.

The explosion at Hiroshima made plain to any person of intelligence how great is the power of the modern industrial state and those at its head, when supported by the discoveries of men of science. Recognising the war-like element in the consensus, Eisenhower referred to the 'military industrial complex'. With the aim of attempting to preserve peace, the United Nations organisation was set up. This was, however, a coming together of heads of state, directing from the top downwards, with no democratic basis other than fringe access by the non-governmental associations.

Agonies of conscience began to afflict the scientists. They had now for a long time had a dream of how the scientific pursuit of truth would result in bringing together men of different races and nations. Science spoke a common language, using terms that scientists, in their own fields, could understand. Somehow they failed to note that their assistance, at all stages of history, had always been called in by the war-maker, great or small. But now they had become involved in a most terrible and spectacular act of war, which was also a fantastic scientific discovery, for which the utmost secrecy had been imposed. Scientific knowledge should be free and open to all men. Such had been the creed of the Royal Society in England. Sir Henry Dale, its then President, just after the war, declared that there should be no more secrecy. This ideal was soon forgotten in the vain endeavour to prevent the secrets of the bomb from reaching the Russians. Some scientists did try, with only small success, to uphold the internationalism of science. Others, like Sir Edward Appleton FRS, concerned with national research, maintained that the politicians and general public, not the scientists, were responsible for the results, outside the laboratories, of the discoveries made by the scientists within them. Among young people there was a considerable revulsion against the study of science, in view of the abominable uses to which it was now put.

It might have been expected that the statesmen who had used the nuclear bomb, as they insisted, to bring about an early end to the war, would, none the less, have shared the public distress and resolved to try to end the prostitution of science to destruction. On the contrary, their propaganda services put out one story after another, boasting of the splendid contribution made by the scientists and their devices to victory.

Before long, although the distaste for science among university students did not cease, fear and distress among the general public abated, when it appeared that nuclear power might be used in the service of peace, to supply the energy needed for industrial production. Next came the bonanza of the new consumer goods supplied by science: inexpensive small radio sets, tape recorders, electric cleaners, washing machines, television, small-size calculating machines, finally computers. Whereas, before 1945, most information about science had to be sought in technical journals, extensive exposition of its benefits and methods flooded into popular journals and radio, and on to the television screens. On all sides was heard the cry 'You can't stop progess, science must go on.' At the same time young people, looking for the human element in social life, either 'dropped out' of the machine world, or studied sociology.

The mass of the population, on the other hand, were very soon reassured by the rising standard of living – fitted carpets, a multitude of new gadgets, and even new substances, created by technological skill and invention. All kinds of plastics began to be used in place of china and glass; nylon and other chemically made threads to supersede natural products, silk, cotton, and wool. The crowning gift of scientific progress was the cherished personal motor car, which every family, unless very poor, and soon every individual, was proud to possess. And the aircraft which had brought death and destruction, were now the instruments of package holidays into the sunshine and, as Anthony Crosland MP, put it, of the pleasure of eating fish and chips on the Costa Brava.

To defeat Hitler's bid for hegemony had demanded desperate means and effort, but it had to be done. In the process the victorious allies acquired not only the techniques of mechanised and scientific war, but, in addition, the technical and psychological devices for instilling into the masses such emotions as were necessary to ensure appropriate behaviour and loyalty under totalitarian control. Statesmen and the mass of the population in America, Europe and Russia, were well satisfied with their machine god. Unlike Russell and myself in

1920, they were not dubious about the prospects of industrial civilisation. Professor J. H. Plumb, a historian at Cambridge, published a book, *Death of the Past*, in which he wrote:

Industrial society, unlike the commercial, craft and agrarian societies which it replaces, does not need the past. Its intellectual and emotional orientation is towards change rather than conservation, towards exploitation and consumption. The new methods, new processes, new forms of living, of scientific and industrial society have no sanction in the past and no roots in it. The past becomes, therefore, a matter of curiosity, of nostalgia, of sentimentality. Of course, vestiges of its strength remain, particularly in religion and politics, which are still in conflict and in crises within the new advanced industrial societies.

One may note that Professor Plumb has found very ample 'vestiges of the strength' of the past and outlets for his own nostalgia, in his collaboration with the BBC's fine television programme on our National Heritage of works of art and historical records.

Ernest Gellner's book, *Thought and Change* (1964) nearly twenty years after the war, is a carefully reasoned advocacy of industrialism as the next necessary stage in social and economic progress. He sees the world as now divided into those parts already industrialised and those undeveloped, in the process of industrialisation:

in the twentieth century the essence of man is not that he is a rational, or a political, or a sinful, or a thinking animal, but that he is an industrial animal. It is not his moral or intellectual or social attributes which make man what he is; his essence resides in his capacity to contribute to and to profit from industrial society. The emergence of industrial society is the prime concern of sociology. (p. 36)

This definition of the present human condition must be accepted because:

Industrialism is good and industrialism must happen.

Industrialism is good on independent grounds, but is also good in virtue of being inevitable.

What is more:

It is implicitly recognised that the basis of power, the criterion of social institutions and arrangements of policies, is the establishment and the running of an industrial system.

Only those who possess the knowledge appropriate to industrial organisation and processes should be permitted to rule society:

Power rightly belongs to the possessors of the new wisdom, and the new wisdom is the gateway to the emergence of a rightly ordered soul and a rightly ordered state.

The recipe for educating such exalted persons is as follows:

Village size social units are no longer competent to produce fully life-sized human beings. . . . Villages in general do not have the resources to produce anything but second class, merely potential citizens. The *manufacture* (his word) of a human being requires more than the resources of family and village, it requires the resources of an educational system. The fragment of an educational system that is present in the village cannot be sustained by the village. At a pinch, villages can bear the cost of erecting and maintaining school buildings, and they could even pay the schoolmaster's wages; but they could not conceivably train him or bear the cost of the whole machinery required to produce and reproduce the teacher in turn.

   The minimal requirement for full citizenship is literacy. This is the minimum; a certain level of technical competence is probably also required. Only a person possessing these can really claim and exercise his rights, can attain a level of affluence and style of life compatible with current notions of human dignity and so forth. (p. 158)

Gellner admires Sir Charles Snow's critique of the split between the two cultures, literary and scientific, and, while stressing the importance of literacy, he shares Sir Charles's mockery of the humanist who is ignorant of and hostile to science, while accepting all the benefits of technology for his comfort and well-being.

The relation of the search for God to faith in science is more apparent in Professor Christopher Hill's book *God's Englishman*, in which he contrasts the stability and spiritual strength of the medieval village within the widespread acceptance of the Roman Catholic church and its reassuring ritual of confession and absolution with the solitary Protestant conscience perforce seeking alone to read God's purposes and laws. He sees the scientific 'consensus' as a substitute for a powerful religious orthodoxy. In a world of 'scientific certainties'

the desperate search for god has ended by squeezing him right out of the universe. And science is a collective activity. Knowledge is pooled. Man can again share his certainties with a community and he is no longer passively at the mercy of a hostile, material and social environment, he can control them both within extensible limits. The individual need no longer bear the sky on a single pair of shoulders. An approach to the world which in the [seventeenth century] period produced a Luther, a Descartes, a Milton, a Bunyan, today produces psychiatric cases.

But, if you are neither a Roman Catholic, nor a believer in the Marxist scientific consensus, you will still have to take the sky on your shoulders and hope to escape insanity.

Ernest Gellner's book is dedicated to Bertrand Russell. Perhaps this is the point at which to examine the significance of what all these devotees of the intellect in relation to science, truth, god and the universe, are, in effect saying.

> O what a dusty answer gets the soul
> When hot for certainties in this our life.

wrote George Meredith.

Russell of course also doubted whether such abilities as man possesses can enable him to attain certainties. But to him man's intellect was the faculty best adapted to this search and the results achieved by the methods of science were the best proof of their importance. In a letter to Lady Ottoline Morrell he wrote:

> I have a perfectly cold intellect which insists upon its rights and rejects nothing. It will sometimes hurt you, sometimes seem cynical, sometimes heartless . . . you won't much like it. But it belongs with my work – I have deliberately cultivated it and it is really the main thing that I have put discipline into . . . the sudden absolute cessation of feeling when I think must be trying at first. And nothing is sacred to it – it looks at everything quite impartially. . . . (Clark, 1975, p. 139)

In the many discussions which we had in Peking and later, he always insisted that mysticism and psychic insights were self-delusion – the product of imagination or emotions and desires. Philosophy and logic could teach us how to keep various forms of knowledge in correct departments, but did not pretend to teach us how to live or organise our practical affairs.

When in 1946, Russell published his splendid *History of Western Philosophy* with its sub-title 'and its connection with Political and Social Circumstances from the earliest times to the Present Day', I wrote to congratulate him on the book, adding that I felt that I had perhaps had some part in the reflections that prompted him to write it. However that may be, I presently found in a report of the Science and Freedom Congress in Hamburg in 1953, once more his uncompromising assertion: 'the belief that metaphysics has any bearing on practical affairs is a proof of logical incapacity.' Religion surely belongs in the category of metaphysics. One might then say that all religious beliefs from the superstitions and myths of primitive man onwards derive from logical incapacity. No doubt they do. But they have had an enormous bearing on man's conduct of practical affairs.

Hence from Copernicus, Galileo, Newton, Descartes, Voltaire, Gellner, Professor Hill, even Marx, H. G. Wells and Russell himself we are being told that the true and proper guide to life is this faculty of intellect developed by man. None of these people really lived by the intellect, and nor do any of us. This is not to say that the intellect is not a powerful faculty when judiciously used and applied.

Russell, for instance, sees Rousseau's theories as implicit in Nazism because he interprets Rousseau's 'general will' as a dogmatic assertion of an intellectual consensus, admitting no dissent. On the contrary (Rousseau, it must be noted, also insisted that social communities should *not* be large) the 'general will' was more like what the Quakers conceive as the 'sense of the meeting', based upon conclusions reached by a group of people – in them a combination of reasoned and emotional experience. Nor is it impossible in a state, under the 'general will', for dissent to exist. The way that our democracy at present operates is by argument between powerful bodies like the trade unions and associations of the employers. This is by general assent and by no means dictated by totalitarian rule from above. And Rousseau has been acclaimed as the pioneer of the reverse of authoritarian rule in education. Nor did Russell live by reason alone when he and Einstein issued their plea to the world: 'Remember your humanity and forget the rest.'

Rule from the top down by the wisdom of the scientific planning élite is quite definitely the doctrine of the machine religion and its correlative industrial expansion. Even in the Reith lectures by the eminent African Ali Mazrui is found the suggestion that the organisation of social systems based upon work and planning is rightly taking the place of tribal association. Gellner, too, definitely has little use for rural customs, asserting that not to achieve literacy is a *moral* defect, and discarding all previous definitions of the nature of man for that of man the 'industrial animal'. Industrial man is *not* an animal. He long since forfeited the right to that dignity when he turned his back on the natural world to become an automatom, cog in a machine, or digit in a computer.

In 1962 Professor Raymond Aron published his study of industrialism *in itself* based on eighteen lectures delivered by him at the Sorbonne. This is the first study of industrialism in itself, since Russell's and my book in 1923, that I have been able to locate. Aron states bluntly that with the decay of traditional religions there is no true consensus binding society together. We find ourselves, he says, in a system which is essentially economic, but lacks any religious foundation. It is for us to discover whence will arise the new order to direct the functioning of this economic society. He proceeds to contrast in detail the capitalist direction of industry in the United States with communist direction in the Soviet Union. Setting aside any political affiliation, he tries to show the effects of each ideology on the direction of the industrial machine. Every problem or crisis, in both systems, can be found thoroughly investigated in this book. He notes how the inherent nature of industrialism tends to cause the systems to learn from and approximate to one another. But he observes drily that this will not diminish their mutual hostility. So many are the possibilities that must be taken into account by anyone seeking solutions that he himself declines to prophesy and concludes with the reflection that it may be for the benefit of man that he cannot predict the future.

Professor Peter Laslett, and his colleagues in Cambridge University, in his book *The World We Have Lost* (1965) offer another interesting perspective on changing values and customs as industrialism increasingly affects the way that people live. What was the past really like? Is the present really any better? And, in 1967, Lewis Mumford published his fine book the *Myth of the Machine*. This was by no means his first assault on mechanism or on the theory of tool-making as the prime instrument of human progress.

A curious feature of the writings of the supporters and advocates of civilisation according to the industrial plan, is that none, even those with some misgivings, seem to admit, or face, the possibility of the machine breaking down. Nor do we find any real consideration of the cost of competitiveness, armaments and war. Not even, after Hiroshima, the likely culmination of all their efforts in global suicide.

Perhaps H. G. Wells, who had hoped so much from man's application of his mind to science, and had, rightly, boasted of man's achievements, was, in his disillusion, the most honest of the devotees of the intellect. I wonder if, when, knowing that he would soon die, he wrote his last prophecy *Mind at the End of Its Tether* (1945), he recalled the hopes he had expressed in 1920 that the men who cared for science and knew its value would have more influence.

The intellectual has been loth to come to grips with the forcible man. He has generally been something of a courtier and time server. . . . Hitherto men of reason and knowledge have lacked the assurance and courage of the religious fanatics. (1920, p. 337)

Now, as the familiar Newtonian cosmology of our geography books gave way, like its predecessor's medieval walls, to a universe defined in events in Einstein's space-time, it seemed that the human mind would never be adequate to understand and tune in to the universe.

Man's mind accepted the secular process as rational and it could not do otherwise, because he was evolved as part and parcel of it . . . congruence with mind, which man has attributed to the secular process, is not really there at all . . . the cosmic movement of events is increasingly adverse to the mental make-up of our everyday life.

The human mind works by retrospection: for man there is really no 'shape of things to come' (1945, pp. 2–3).

Cocking a final snook at old 'Mr G' – now styled the 'Antagonist' – in protest at the untrustworthiness of His Universe, Wells complains:

Hitherto events have been held together by a certain logical consistency as the heavenly bodies, as we know them, have been held together by the pull of the golden cord of gravitation. Now it is as if that cord had vanished and everything was driving anyhow to anywhere at a steadily increasing velocity . . . events now follow one another in an entirely untrustworthy sequence. But no one but a modern scientific philosopher can accept this untrustworthyness fully.

Of man himself he says:

Man must go steeply up or down and the odds seem to be in favour of his going down and out. If he goes up, so great is the adaptation demanded of him that he must cease to be a man. Ordinary man is at the end of his tether. Only a small highly adaptable minority of the species can possibly survive. The rest will not trouble about it, finding such opiates and consolations as they have a mind for.

CHAPTER 13

Humanity: eclipse or deliverance?

If Wells had lived to see his space fiction journeys to the moon turn real as man stepped from the first spaceship on to the moon's surface, he might have been comforted at the proof that, after all, the mind of man was neither so limited, nor the universe so untrustworthy as, in his last days, he had feared. These astronauts, in their spaceship and their suits adapted for travel beyond gravitation and the atmosphere, daring, and successfully overcoming, the dangers of weight-lessness, might they not be the pioneers of a new species of man moving upwards to fresh discovery and conquest? Already man could do all and more than other creatures on the earth; he had finally achieved aerial flight; his ships moved with speed on the surface and in the depths of the seas; tunnelling into the very substance of his planet he found, and used, its treasures, lavishly and wastefully for his own ends.

Mathematicians were not dismayed at the untrustworthy universe. On the contrary, they were delighted as observations proved that gravitation could bend the path of light and thus demonstrated how Einstein had upset the calculations of Newton. I had been, in fact, with two eminent mathematicians from Trinity College Cambridge, Russell and Littlewood, on their joint holiday, when the news of this observation was received. Both were intensely excited. They were, of course, devotees of research in pure science, not what might be its consequences outside their special field. At that date, 1919, it was, in any case, too early to perceive what might result, in imagination or practice, from Einstein's thought. But it was to have a determining influence on Russell's philosophical interpretation of the world.

As the astronomers from their Observatories continued their heavenward gaze, in the workshops and laboratories of the advanced industrial peoples science achieved more triumphs. Transistors were invented; the age of electronics, computers, and microchips began.

If it had not been for the computer and countless other inventions and experiments, and tests to which brave would-be space men voluntarily submitted themselves, the exploration of space could not have been undertaken. Amid the maze of probabilities, man, indeed, may not be able to *predict* the future. But what his imagination dreams of can come to pass. As Bernard Shaw wrote in *Back to Methuselah*: 'You see things and you ask why? But I dream things that never were, and ask why not?'

Around 1931, the author of the novel *Hunger and Love*, Lionel Britton, wrote also a play which was highly praised by Shaw. This was *BRAIN: A Play of the Whole Earth*, in which there was a super-brain, which finally dominated the world. As I recollect, neither the author nor Shaw thought this a Good Thing. Nearly fifty years later, it seems as if the computer, with its manifold uses, has become central to machine society. Although 'programmed' by man, its pervasive use can act as an instrument of a superbrain – in the way that Christians imagine the Holy Spirit acts – through inspiring matter to direct events. Or, to follow the Cartesian dream, mind, through matter and energy, deliberately creating man's world.

The computer can do man's sums for him, however complex. It can think much faster than man and of more things at once; almost instantaneously it can buy stocks and shares, move currencies and thus rule the financial market. It can virtually run an office; be programmed to run a whole factory, to build cars and other machines. The planes of air travel are piloted, except on take-off and landing, by computer, as are, of course, space vehicles, manned or unmanned. Finally, war can now be fought almost without armies: nuclear weapons, deadly accurate through computerised triggering and targeting, will rise from sea and land and fly through space. A very modest number of men, in comparison with the size of the world's population of men, women and children, are needed, in war or in peace, to direct this Super Brain of the Almighty Machine.

It is scarcely necessary to add that such oligarchs have the power and wealth to control a technological society, as also the instruments of information and education. A considerable number of trained men and women, with highly disciplined and accurate minds, are needed for administration, as also to service such parts of the machine as require it.

Accordingly education is increasingly directed to producing such an élite of faithful believers in the scientific system, while discouraging those studies which are irrelevant, or likely to be subversive. Secrecy is already demanded of all public servants, although it might be supposed that the public should be allowed to know what its servants are up to. Secrecy also obtains in the private sector, for the protection of processes that make for profits. The morals of the system are not at the moment in question; let us first look at the system itself as it exists in advanced technological societies.

As things are, the advanced industrial, technological planned economic system is like nothing so much as a great joy-wheel at a fair, of vast size, spinning at high speed, with power at the centre; those skilful enough to stay furthest from the edge are least likely to be hurled off.

Whether public or private, the basis is intellectual, economic planning, which views people quantitively in the mass. Trade is not by barter or gold, but on paper or even by electronic exchanges of credit; life is conducted strictly according to time by the clock! Work is done, by those for whom work exists, by persons of either sex, according to and rewarded for appropriate ability and training, without regard to their sexual life or family. Just how children born are provided for, or cared for when young, remains a bit problematical, but must, it would seem, fall back on the spare resources of the machine.

The actual rights and status of children in machine civilisation are much in question. To whom do children belong? Are they, as according to tradition, the property of their parents? Or do they belong to the state, which now takes so great a part in their support, education and training? Or do they belong to themselves? What are their rights? When their behaviour is questioned, parents and teachers are at loggerheads as to who is to blame. As far as finance is concerned, possibly the simplest solution might be to ensure to each child at birth, not to either of the parents, an income for subsistence and education. Such incomes, equal for all, might be augmented by the individual's own efforts in study, necessary work, or other contribution to the community.

Let us say here and now that a mechanism or instrument invented, devised or guided by man is something to marvel at and a source of immense pride. It is only necessary to think of the nerve and skill of a man, at risk of his life and machine, manoeuvring a helicopter to save others at sea, or fallen on a cliff or mountain; or to consider even the strict accuracy required in keeping such machines, or planes, or parachutes in full repair and readiness. In every scientific profession, whether chemistry, biology, medicine, surgery, engineering, such accuracy of measurement, observation and responsibility are required.

We are surrounded by this mass of external gadgets in and by which we live. And science has offered us, through these, knowledge and power beyond the limitation of our senses. We can magnify, see far; observe the infinitely small; hear beyond our auditory powers; speed up and slow down images of objects in motion, and thereby watch the actual growing of plants and flowers.

Surely the people who have achieved all these wonders must possess not only ingenuity and skill, but goodness, dignity and wisdom? We can ask therefore, not only 'Why not?' but, in addition, 'Why?' and 'What for?'

Clearly they embarked on industrialism, in the first place, for the purpose of increasing production, while easing the burden of labour, and to obtain all the good things and advantages described by such advocates as Ernest Gellner. One might add that the use of the computer eases the burden of calculation on the mind: its almost incredible, multiple other achievements must also be recognised. What man apparently did not foresee were the immediate results of the shift from an agricultural to an industrial economy, and further, the ultimate consequences of the spread of the industrial system to the greater part of the world.

While engaged in industrialising, a people must either possess a food surplus, or obtain a loan. The loan, with interest, cannot be repaid except by the profitable sale of manufactured goods, abroad as well as at home. As people leave the land for the cities, food production diminishes, and food must be bought from undeveloped countries, or agriculture itself be industrialised. As we have noted, industrialism, as operated within nations, is the source of competition between private enterprise and also between employers and workers. On a larger scale, when directed by governments, it reinforces a similar rivalry between nations, constantly fostered by statesmen and constantly bordering on war. Competitiveness rather than co-operation becomes the driving principle and the slogan most heard. Men of science, courtiers and time-servers, as Wells truly said, are obliged to turn their energies to the invention of more and still more ingenious and powerful weapons of war and destruction. In the end, the great industrial empires, mind and body in service to the Great God Machine, stand embattled, armed as we used to say, cap à pie, poised ready to destroy their misguided worshippers and with them every particle of organic life and beauty on earth.

Ingenuity and skill, indeed, but where are goodness and wisdom?

Have not the high priests of the people, in pursuit of the truths of science, falsely identified goodness with knowledge, abandoning not only the wisdom of foresight, but, in addition, altruism, compassion, mutual aid? Perhaps they were only repeating their early error, of confusing the infinity of the mathematician with the eternity of the mystic. There are some who still fondly imagine that knowledge, casting the clear light of awareness, inspires and contains goodness within itself. But others, and they are the majority, have continually proclaimed, with Francis Bacon, that knowledge means power.

The mind of industrial man, well trained and disciplined, cannot be a respecter of persons, but must operate with steely indifference to all considerations but the purpose of the machine which he serves! A machine, which, its purpose bereft of every other emotion, is driven solely by the lust for power and its hyena accomplice, greed.

Accepting the idiotic 'balance of terror' which the brilliance of the male intellect has imposed, can humanity, preserving a precarious peace, continue to enjoy all the obvious and desirable benefits which industry can bestow? It began to dawn on a few intelligent people that, unhappily, there were flaws in the grand design. At first it had not been noticed that the increase of automation would leave a very large number of unemployed men and women, whom it would not be easy to support in the style to which they had become accustomed. But before the problem of surplus labour came the unsolved problem of surplus manufactured goods, and, what was more serious, the shortage of materials required by industry for production, or to provide energy to drive the machines: kinds of metals, some rare and scarce, coal, gas and oil. How could any machine, large or small, function without driving power? How could households manage without the amenities now demanded of gas and electricity for domestic use and every comfort and pleasure? Men of power began to wonder how those tanks would roll, bomber planes fly, how even would the computers be able to spark off those deadly missiles? What is more, how would the shop assistants and others do their money sums, if they had not bothered to learn their tables?

Here then are urban populations relying more and more on an artificial environment, in towns often called 'jungles' of concrete, steel and glass; going to work in train or car, often warmed; protected against daily awareness and experience of wind and weather; with, for most people, only a very moderate amount of garden, open space, or parkland available. Continuing to expect farming and agriculture to supply their food, the urban population requires it suitably cleaned, prepared, almost manufactured; but, if put to it, how many of them would really know how to set about its production? Dependent on the machine for almost every activity, how would such a population survive, if forced back on its own initiative and inner ability? They are faced with even further anxieties, as they realise that the materials used up by industry are not renewable, like things that grow; that moreover, land and water to provide foodstuffs and sustain healthy life are being swallowed up by buildings and polluted by the poisonous wastes created by industrial man.

These are the agonising problems that industrial man has

brought upon himself, as indeed on the whole of life on his planet.

Let us turn from him and look at some other aspects of human aspirations.

> The world is so full of a number of things
> I am sure we should all be as happy as kings

so wrote no less a person than Robert Louis Stevenson in the mood of the Victorians.

The odd thing about the male person is that he did not care much about that 'number of things' and was only happy if he could be king himself. All around him were what he liked to call the 'wonders' or 'mysteries' of nature, plants, animals, insects, all organic species, sharing with him the instinct to survive. Lewis Mumford indicates that human intelligence was such that survival by no means claimed man's full attention, and that the source of his inventions lies in his play impulses. Certainly man seems to take a greater delight in what he himself makes, or what his cleverness achieves, than in whatever the natural environment, in great profusion, has been able to offer him. We have noticed how, when he had finally imagined and placed a supreme god 'up there' outside of but governing his own planet, he rejected his natural habitat and split himself in half so that he might emulate the concept and ultimate power of that deity.

The taboo placed by religion on animal nature was severe: it hindered anatomy, and misled medicine and also biology along the path of mechanism and dissection, from which they will take some time to recover fully. But, from the classification and study of the propagation of plants, and such necessary study of farm animals, began to develop the exploration of how living organisms were born, grew, lived and died. The vast expanse and scope of these interests and studies in our century needs no emphasis. The care and affection for pet birds and animals; assembling them in zoos for pleasure and study; sallying forth with binoculars for bird-watching; crouching uncomfortably concealed in hide-outs for observation by night; campaigns against cruelty to animals and for the saving of endangered species; all these speak of a remarkable turning of man's mind from mechanism and the inorganic to sympathy and concern for organic life.

Associated with a growing interest in the nature of organisms, prompted by the study in physiology of how the nerves and muscles in the body actually work, was the philosophy of Bergson. As for Bernard Shaw, it provided the sceptic with a faith-in-life substitute for revealed religion. I remember the most intellectual of my uncles, Uncle Troopy, who was not, like two of the others, a clergyman, discussing Bergson with me when I was in my teens. I had not read Bergson; I accepted the popular account of him as the proponent of the élan vital, or life force, quite recently described by Lord Brockway as a definitely non-Christian belief that he had derived from Bergson via Shaw. Similarly Bergson may have penetrated my own consciousness.

Russell was already critically examining Bergson before ever I was an undergraduate. His famous colleague on the work of *Principia Mathematica*, Alfred North Whitehead, accepted Einstein's cosmology with acclaim, and regarded the results for science and human enlightenment of the controversy over Galileo as of equal importance with the birth of Christ. Yet he differed from Russell in his estimate of Bergson; he saw in Bergson's theories the means of resolving the Cartesian mind/matter split and of providing the groundwork for his own philosophy of 'organism'. Whitehead left Cambridge in 1924 to take up a lectureship at Harvard University. When, in 1926, I was writing *The Right to be Happy*, I knew nothing of the lectures that Whitehead then began to deliver. What concerned me then was my eighteenth-century researches: man versus the machine in relation to Descartes and ascetic Christianity. I was asserting man as an animal whose biological values were thus the natural foundation for human society. I repudiated Descartes in my quest for the 'wholeness' of personality. Neither then or *ever* could I regard myself, or any other human being, as anything but 'whole'. In this I seem to have been at that time on a wavelength with Whitehead, though I would not have agreed with all his conclusions. Incidentally, though he was, as a philosopher, very greatly honoured in the United States, his views did not carry weight. As is usual, the possible value of the human vision of an intellectual to influence practice did not avail in that country to shake the iron grip of the machine.

In assessing Bergson, Russell was in a dilemma quite common to philosophers. There is *technical* philosophy, which tries to explain man in himself and his relation to the external world and, nowadays, to interpret the findings of science; there is also the popular notion of philosophy as a guide to values for action in life. Russell himself points to this distinction, when he describes the effect of philosophy upon politics. He sees Bergson, like Rousseau, as a symptom of a revolt against reason, beginning to dominate ever larger areas of world thought. Again, he admits that a philosophy is dominated by whatever it is that leads the philosopher to philosophise. Philosophies of feeling love happiness; theoretical philosophies love knowledge, whilst the practical love action (Russell, 1946, p. 819). Russell's aim is quite obviously truth; as a real professional, he insists upon logic, proofs, ability to handle abstractions.

Bergson describes the intellect as divisive; Russell argues that Bergson's 'intuition' is emotional and not clear. He complains that Bergson does not understand mathematics, not realising that numbers are, in themselves, abstract entities, not merely a means of enumerating events or things. The true rationalist and sceptic cannot accept an explanation of the movement and growth of things in terms of the life force, since this would admit a purpose in nature and hence could imply the existence of God. Russell followed the modern physicists in explaining phenomena, as far as possible, in mathematical terms. He even disliked the expression 'force of gravity': 'force was the faint ghost of the vitalist view of the causes of motions, and gradually the ghost has been exorcised.' (ibid., p. 561)

Bergson is writing of the constant moving flow of life, Russell of the mind in a more static state, at rest in contemplation. Lack of space forbids discussion of their fascinating differences on time and memory. The biochemist, Dr Rupert Sheldrake, has an interesting reappraisal of Bergson in his *New Science of Life* (1981). He would find Russell over-rational and would not agree with him. But it *is* also arguable that Bergson opens the door to mysticism. What we are concerned with here is the relation of the intellect to organic life, whose relevance, as Joad might have said, 'depends on what you mean'.

On this question I think that Bergson was right in his contention that the intellect is divisive, and that it had – at least up to the time when he wrote – mainly concerned itself with, and discussed, a concept of matter as inorganic. This is the Cartesian position and even harks back to Galileo. I do not think that Russell escapes the Cartesian split, in that he does see the intellect as something superior and apart from man's animal life, rather than an intimate part and faculty of a 'whole' man. He was, in his philosophic thought, though he did not perhaps realise it, in line with those who turned their backs on man's animal nature.

This is a crucial point, as appears in the brilliant book by the philosopher Mary Midgley, *Beast and Man: The Roots of Human Nature.* The first sentence of her introduction reads:

> We are not just rather like animals, we are animals. Our difference from other species may be striking, but comparisons with them have always been, and must be, crucial to our view of ourselves. (p. xiv)

Human beings apparently belong to and have evolved on this planet; if then there is not some trace of evolving rationality in animal life, then 'the human intellect is still left as an alien intrusion in the world'. She rejects the Christian solution of the 'soul': every religion in fact demands that far more should survive than the intellect.

> The chief difficulty about accepting continuity between man and other species, or between the human intellect and the rest of man, now comes not from traditional religion, but from those who do amputate the soul. It stems from the deep reverence people now feel for human success, and particularly for success in science. People . . . revere what they take to be the highest human capacities, particularly the speculative intellect, so deeply that they are inclined to find natural explanations for them quite as blasphemous as religious people used to find natural explanations of the religious faculties. Reverence for humanity, which at first

is a most respectable tendency, often slips across into an overtly religious form. (ibid., p. 254)

She continues by objecting to men's aspirations to be like gods, as in the Utopian dreams of Wells and others. The objection is also to the adulation of the machine, and to what Russell once called 'cosmic impiety'. I use Russell in this context because he was one of the finest examples of intellect that affected my generation.

What is the purpose of human life? This is the issue. Russell is often quoted as defining the good life as one 'inspired by love and guided by knowledge'.

When he writes of 'loving' happiness, knowledge, or action, clearly he means what, temperamentally, you may like doing. All of these, even knowledge, take their rise from impulses of the body.

> Tell me where is fancy bred
> Or in the heart or in the head?
> How begot, how nourished?
> It is engendered in the eyes
> With gazing fed; and fancy dies
> In the cradle where it lies.

So this is not love. What is this love that inspires goodness? In a revealing passage in his autobiography Russell says:

To follow scientific intelligence wherever it may lead me, had always seemed to me the most imperative of *moral* precepts [my italics] for me, and I have followed this precept even when it has involved a loss of what I myself have taken for deep spiritual insight.

Russell must have seen that there he was confusing goodness with knowledge, just like Gellner calling literacy a moral quality. Scientific intelligence, though bestowing goodies, had also created the machine and poised mankind on the brink of nuclear war – that very threat against which Russell himself was campaigning. The spiritual insight and morality to which he reverts seems to have been love as it had been defined for him in his lonely Christian upbringing. And for him, as for so very many others, this itself was the source of inner conflict.

What was it that drove this lonely and divided spirit to his tempestuous and desperate campaigns, pleading with and exhorting his fellow men? Was it the ancestral voices of the prophets calling for repentance of sin, or the love and compassion that embraces all humanity, or a wise man vainly seeking sanity? It was all of these, and it was more – the cry from a whole man of an endangered species about to destroy itself by its own brilliance and folly. 'Remember your humanity and forget the rest'?

This famous manifesto received extra publicity from the fact that Einstein had signed it, only just in time, before he died. It was, in historical context, the first real effort to call in scientists to warn the public of nuclear war dangers. And that one sentence, so often quoted, was not as it might appear exclusive to humanity. The document contained the statement that animals, 'who could not be accused of communism or anti-communism', would also perish in the nuclear blast. The risk was, it concluded: 'universal death'.

With that document Russell was making an almost super-human effort to bridge the cold war by the intervention of scientists. What it does, undoubtedly, by identifying man with all life on the planet, is to break down the religious taboo on organic life with all its connotations of the 'sinful lusts of the flesh'.

The study of animal life by observation rather than by analysis grew in quantity and variety. The works of Lorenz and others are well known. Surveying all these extensively, Mary Midgley concludes that the human species has evolved an inherent emotional and social disposition to which she relates, and discusses, the usual and current problems of philosophy. Edward Wilson's book, with its views on 'sociobiology', came in for sharp criticism from American scientists and also from Mary Midgley, though for different reasons.

The scientists, obsessed with the mechanical outlook, and consequent reliance on the external equipment, apparatus and gadgets with which they can extend the capacities of the senses, did, in fact, react to Edward Wilson's views as blasphemy. To the environmentalist and behaviourist the idea of a human being 'programmed' from within was anathema. Humans had many animal instincts, of course, most of which were deplorable, but human nature was malleable and could be conditioned by religion, and social and cultural education. They proclaimed belief in inborn or inherited tendencies to be Fascist and racist and a denial of equality between human beings. The extremists held that comprehensive education would show that there were no inherent differences of ability.

Mary Midgley answered their challenge in a BBC radio broadcast (1978). Agreeing with her, I came to her support in a letter (*Listener*, 28.9.78) with my argument, as already outlined, that to describe a belief in inborn tendencies as Fascist or racist was ludicrous; that Nazi racism was not born of instinct but a myth invented and used by Hitler to control and power the technological machine for war. I added:

> Those who believe that human beings are, or can be, manufactured by environmental methods, are in danger of falling into the same error.

No one denies that human beings are educable, but what comes from within reacts and combines with what comes from without.

The whole human being is an organism, containing a great variety of faculties interacting with the environment. This surely is life? To isolate the intellect, as modern man has done, into complete absence of feeling and a deliberate, cold impartiality, and then give it sovereign power to plan, direct and manufacture the appropriate human complement lies at the heart of the appalling danger facing the so-called civilisation of the advanced industrial world.

How mankind got into this terrifying predicament is one question which this book has been seeking to explore.

CHAPTER 14

Liberty and love

As we contemplate that world of today built by human intellect and the expansion of science: massive tall buildings, swift transport by land, sea and air, extensive factories equipped for automation; these many signs of human power and ingenuity obscure the tiny primitive beings created, by stages, through evolution, whom we considered in our first chapter.

The human species arrived on the planet to witness a profusion of living organisms, in great variety, which had already been evolving and changing over vast periods of time. But, from the advent of human beings, it was their interaction with the environment which would determine the shape of things to come. Solid and permanent as our concrete jungles and mechanical transport appear, they rest on the shoulders of two small living organisms, the male and female of the human species.

Now, after centuries of overpopulating the planet, and genius in manufacture and construction, the human race finds itself on the edge of mutual annihilation by war. Since it would seem obvious that social cohesion and mutual help were essential to survival, why in our earliest recorded history has it been taken for granted that there will be wars, that the strong will oppress the weak, and that to be a soldier is man's finest profession? Only in recent times has there been any serious attempt to change these values, or to alter what we call human nature in the slender hope of bringing peace to the world.

The first and obvious question perpetually asked is why do men fight and what for – food and survival or power? At a very early stage of their existence human beings needed to defend themselves in order to survive. Like any other animal they had to eat and protect themselves against predators. The phrase 'nature red in tooth and claw', so often used, carries a moral implication of savage cruelty inherent to the instincts of all animals, not excluding man. This is just not true. We do not blame our cats for catching mice, we merely try to persuade them to spare fledgling birds. The life impulse, which we understand no more than we understand gravity, drives even the very tiniest particles of living matter towards expansion, whether by joining, absorbing or growing and giving birth. Even crystals grow. Almost everything, plants, animals, will expand in height and width just as far as environmental circumstances permit.

Primitive humans, in early times, cannot have lacked food, once they discovered what suited them. Nor can we really determine just when or why they ceased to be vegetarian.

The real riddle of the Sphinx, as far as the human species is concerned, is why, with a creative life instinct common to all species, the human male has been so neglectful and destructive of his own.

Much publicity has recently been given to the many studies of the social life of animals. Ironically, such studies have been made possible by our advanced technology which provides means of observation, photography and reports. Animals such as wolves and jackals are seen to show not only parental nurture, but even extended family life, in the care of their young. Nor shall I ever forget a television programme of Jane Goodall's, in which a mother ape carried an injured small ape on her back just as long as he could manage to hold on. As the group moved she did not abandon and leave him. Feeding the young is naturally the main occupation; habits vary, sometimes one parent, sometimes both play their part. Among active mammals such as lions it seems to be the females who hunt to provide meals for their cubs and protect them to make sure that they get their share. Aggression among males in various species revealed the technique of graceful withdrawal after a trial of strength. A destructive fight to a finish within a species is rare.

In the human family food must have been shared under the

guidance of both parents. It is unlikely that the mothers, who took part in food gathering and cultivation, failed to see that there were fair shares. Tribal life brought the emergence of males superior in strength and seniority to leadership, but there is no reason to suppose that bloodshed was incurred over the leadership succession in early stages. To lead was not to dictate.

Communal taking of decisions by palaver has been recorded and observed in Africa, as among the American Indian tribes. Reports by explorers arriving on the shores of America or the West Indies told of the gentle friendliness of the natives, who would bring food and fish. There was evidently a deep-seated understanding among humans that the species must eat to live. Something of this survives in the long-honoured custom of hospitality to a travelling stranger. It has been lost now except as a part of commercial company deals. Over the centuries there have also been remnants of the withdrawal technique to avoid, or arrest, combat.

The knightly code accepted that honour could be satisfied without death by a fair and courageous jousting; duelling among gentlemen had a similar code. In the conduct of wars between national armies, codes also existed and these, as regards the treatment of prisoners and the wounded, even improved. But as men, by means of mechanical warfare, were removed more and more from close personal combat, the fight to the finish, by any means, overrode compassion. Had the British, for instance, in 1917, when the armies of both sides were stuck fast in the Flanders mud, called for a truce instead of calling for the Americans, there might well have been agreement for a united Europe, no cold war against the Soviet revolution, a reasonable peace and no Second World War. This is not the same thing as appeasement; it is common humanity and sanity after a trial of strength. The size of the embattled empires and the deadly nature of weapons of today are outside the human dimension of control. Mankind would seem to have forgotten how to make a gesture of friendship and reconciliation. Without this and scrapping the machines, the computers will make war.

In the first chapters of this book I indicated how the desire for power over other men and armies developed alongside the growth of urban and social living. Defence of foodstore or territory cannot have had a high priority when groups were small, food not hard to get, and there was plenty of room. Did men become war-like when they and their neighbours had acquired possessions? There is something that goes deeper than all this. Koestler, in a recent book, suggests that there was some unhappy mutation in man's evolution. Otherwise how could we account for these defects in so beautiful a species, so richly endowed? Original sin is the answer of the priestly mentors. Is it possible that the sin lay with them rather than in the nature of their flocks? Mistakes, wrong choices perhaps, but not sin, or even mutation.

In the book *Social Biology*, which provoked such controversy, Edward Wilson likewise attributed human family behaviour to hereditary genes, similar to those of animals, who are observed to bring and share food. He accepts the males as defenders of territory, and the strongest as tribal leader. But, in his theory, the preservation of a given species takes no account of the individual but is purely directed by the genes. This offers no real explanation of the effects of the rise and development of human consciousness nor of how man's unquenchable thirst for power, as social life increased, made him a predator on his own species; nor the disharmony that developed between the sexes.

When looking into human characteristics it is often useful to notice the meaning of the words in which they are first described. The word for power which comes to us from Latin carries the sense of 'potential', to be able; in French it becomes pouvoir – Je peux, I can. In German it is Macht – from machen, to make. Did the word originally describe man's struggle with nature rather than with his own kind? And has it deteriorated from describing evil practices?

In one respect this power impulse has mattered most vitally to the male, has been, and still is, held by him in the highest esteem; this is his sexual drive, his power in relation to women. Not to be potent, lacking sexual power and prowess, failure to beget and reproduce himself, offends male pride and dignity and has subtle effects upon the whole of his conduct in life. For women, too, to be barren carries a similar feeling of inferiority and inadequacy. But in their case, under patriarchal custom and law, it can mean contempt and divorce from husbands.

Intense intellectual concentration on their work by scientific or literary men can often so inhibit the sexual impulse as to render them impotent. By continued abstinence women may become frigid. Some women, when breast feeding a baby, have found that intellectual work inhibits the flow of milk.

Because the sex impulse is as unconscious and compelling as the impulse to eat – or run for cover when afraid – the way it has been handled in human history is quite as significant and important as the long-winded boastful recording of conscious heroism in wars. Both sexes may well have been afraid of one another because of this inexplicable, irresistible impulse which drove them into physical contact and union. To primitive peoples there was 'mana' in all things – in a sense it was their definition of the life force – a magic within a tree, a stone, a person, which had an inner power to do you good or harm. The 'magic' by which a woman gave birth to a new human being can have seemed a terrifying power. A man could only extricate himself from the mana of a woman at such times as he did not feel, or could inhibit, his desire. The first thing needful was to keep under control this dangerous fellow-traveller and unpredictable bedfellow; and of this Adam's God gave him fair warning. Thus, from the start, men drew apart into their own secret counsels. As time went on we have seen this male flight from the body assume an immense variety of aspects: superstitious rituals, religious asceticism, chastity, the enclosure and subjection of women; marriage customs; the power to make all laws. My argument here is neither frivolous, nor in jest. To liberate himself from biological bondage and to establish his own individual identity, became a vital ambition for the male. We saw that it did not occur to him that any such similar aspiration might exist in woman.

The belief that there is a personal God who judges between good and evil was invented by the male when he began to exercise conscious thought, in order to express such values in human terms. Through conscious thought, human actions acquired purpose; they were no longer inevitably guided by spontaneous desires; these came to be called animal impulses. So reason was born. Since humans communicated by gestures and, as yet, *without words*, were thinking in pictures, imagination, possibly the most powerful of human faculties, was already there. It is manifest in the cave paintings. Reality was vested in sense perception. Rhythm to inspire dancing was also in the body and, with the beating of drums and making simple instruments and coherent sounds, came music. But most of all speech and language. All these gifts are there and derive from every cell of the body. Love was born of those first fumbling sex couplings: there was brotherhood and sisterhood of a sexual and physical empathy, all presently supported by common purposes and aims, as social life formed and grew.

Sex is the attractive bait; awareness of parenthood, though slower to reach consciousness, is the vital fundamental drive and feeling. I cannot elaborate here on what I wrote on these matters in the *Right to be Happy* and *In Defence of Children*. But in attempting some conclusions I must sum up what seems to me to emerge from the enquiry in this book.

When the male of the species, enamoured of his stargazing, set up a God outside this planet as arbiter of all events upon it, and repudiated nature, together with sex, for a promised dream of a future life, he turned his back on that creative life and inspiration that lay within himself and his partnership with woman. In very truth he sold his birthright for a mess of pottage. True, he believed that creative life and inspiration came from his God, but this 'soul' is defined as a spiritual force outside the body, the very reverse of the earthiness which characterises his own bodily life and woman.

When a woman experienced sex, which may or may not have been pleasurable, she soon knew that this act was almost certainly the prelude to pregnancy, and to all the care and nurture of infant life entailed by maternity. Whatever burdens these imposed, there was, for woman, a certain biological wholeness and harmony. Only when means of birth control were devised, could women separate sex from parenthood. This is no more than a truism now, but its consequences were not foreseen and are not yet fully understood. It may well be that this separation, enabling women to 'use' sex like men, together with our mechanical way of life, could create disharmony and conflict in the psyche of modern women.

The male, establishing for himself a superior identity by

attempting to live in his mind and soul above animal life, identified, and tended to define procreation simply as the act of sexual intercourse in which he took part. It is quite clear that ascetic religious doctrines even deplored that sex was necessary to beget children. This flight from the body, as we have seen, set up in the male an inner conflict by which he is at war with himself and his own species – an error not committed by the more instinctive creatures sharing his planet. What is more, he comes to differ from them also in that the early creative care of his offspring ceases to be his main concern. Yet that very care of children, small, vulnerable, fragile, separate from, and yet a part of, the self, is the seed of altruism and the source of the deepest life-giving feeling – human love.

From the possibility of that family love and partnership the male need not have been excluded; he withdrew in favour of his own chosen identity to dominate and rule those 'animal' origins from which he had risen. So doing, he attained a liberty of thought and action and the release of his energies for those almost incredible achievements which are his glory. At the same time he extended and implanted in the course of human history, and stamped upon human institutions, the tragic inner conflict which never ceased to rage within his divided self.

What, for man, became of love? Religion ordained that his love – in effect the expression of his aspirations – should be given above all to his God. His earthly love he entwined about sex, the delights of seeking a mate, of courtship, anticipation, adulation of the beauty of youthful bodies, joy in the fulfilment of desire. To all these pleasures and pains of love, poetry, the arts, dreams of romance, have been dedicated. Nor do I disparage all that the union of two personalities in sexual love means for men and for women. But, when it comes to parenthood woman has been no more than a breeding machine; she and her children are property, enslaved and exploited. So long as women have gone on producing children, nothing has been so cheap as human life. The history of the treatment of young children and even young adolescents, continues to this very day to disgrace the reputation of the fathers who begat them.

A history of childhood from the earliest periods recorded shows that at all times unwanted babies were exposed to die. Children were also sacrificed to the gods, consistently 'broken in' to obedience in learning, and exploited in work, by regular bullying and beating. The idea of nurturing and educating children as whole human beings has only very recently occurred to their elders.

Lacking the generous altruism that accompanies involved parenthood, fatherhood as protection was soon transformed into patriarchal power. With a powerful male élite, because of the way the male psyche developed, war was inevitable. Men became cannon-fodder, and ill-paid labour; women likewise the drudges in home, factory and farm, deprived of education and advance. At least, in past times, men apparently did not dragoon women into becoming soldiers. Nowadays, on account of the absurd way that we equate the meaning of the word equality with identity, it is argued that for women to be equal with men implies that women should serve in the armed forces. Women have fallen for this bait, instead of demanding that the pursuit of war should cease to be a career for men.

Our very institutions, such as Parliament and the law courts, are in fact founded on this conflict within man himself. Parliament, a substitute for civil war and duelling, proceeds not so much by the search for a solution in just laws, as by scoring off the other fellow as an individual or party. The fate of a prisoner up for trial may well rest on the logical or rhetorical skill with which his or her legal champion can floor the prosecutor presenting the case.

For many men the first lesson for their sons is how to box, while our educational system is riddled with rivalry and competition, as is our commercial life at home and abroad. How weary one grows of that perpetual slogan 'our competitors', of the accepted notion that co-operation and fellowship are dirty words.

More than once in my life I have written that our concept of the state, which rests upon force and repression at home and armaments and hatred abroad, could equally well have been a vision of the state as the father and mother of the people, with hands stretched out to offer friendly partnership to fellow citizens beyond the frontiers. An absurdly emotional ideal? Yet if we do not achieve something like this now, we are all likely to die, or, in correct machine parlance, to self-destruct.

It is not only from my conviction of our need for the voice of woman that I stress the importance of the relations of men and women and the animal origins of human beings. It is because the state of our world is desperate, and on all sides neither statesmen nor scientists offer any help or solution of our dilemmas. Nor can I claim to find any answer, but I can at least point to some things that seem to me fundamental and that have been overlooked.

In all the histories of the rise of civilisation that I have found the story is of wars and conquests, of advances of knowledge, of the Ascent of Man, what the male of the species did in evolution (rightly countered by Elaine Morgan, when she called her book of suggestions about evolution, the *Descent of Woman*). Nowhere, even by very conscientious male writers, is there, except when agriculture begins, mention of any special contribution by hand or brain made by women; even that they were deemed capable of such a contribution, or surprise at its absence. Women, in any real sense, do not appear even in H. G. Wells's *History*, or Russell's *Western Philosophy*. Women, of course could not do philosophy, though the Greeks did accord them the magic voice of the oracles! The first attempt at a real history of the status of women I found in the book by John Langdon-Davies, published in 1928 by Jonathan Cape.

The colossal error in human history was the relegation of woman to the animal kingdom and the denial to her of a soul and mind and thus of a share in the purposes of man.

Robert Graves expressed a profound truth, though some thought that he was joking, when he wrote:

In my view the political and social confusion of these last three thousand years has been entirely due to man's revolt against woman as a priestess of natural magic and his defeat of her wisdom by the use of intellect.

We have seen how consciousness, expressed in terms of the impartial intellect, has moved further and further into the cold atmosphere of concepts, abstractions, mathematics, planning; science the only criterion of truth. This industrial machine

system was to bring prosperity and happiness to all, democratic citizens to vote rationally, without regard to sex (which
had long been an outlaw), work to be done for payment by
individuals without sex differentiation or regard to family
responsibilities. Paradoxically, with all our modern sexual
permissiveness, the entire basis of our advanced industrial
system is a flight from sex. Since to suppress emotion and
reach out for impartiality and accuracy in thought and daily
work imposes too severe a discipline, rage and violence inevitably underlie our social structure.

We forget that intellect itself is part of the body, serviced
and driven by the feelings of men and also of women. We have
our choice as to the wind or current by which we steer our ship.
It is a common assumption that men, especially statesmen and
scientists, are rational and women emotional. What of the rage
and hatred directed and inspired against those whose religion
or ideology are disliked? Are they not felt and inspired by the
irrational impulses that drive men? Only very recently in a
Party Conference a woman who argued against nuclear
weapons was greeted by a man with the remark 'that is just
an emotional spasm', to which she replied that she preferred
it to a spasm of death.

As we have become aware of feelings, we have given names
to them as we do to almost everything which we try to understand. We all start from fear. Bravery, audacity, rage, anger,
severity, authority, all these tend to be regarded as feelings
of the male; altruism, sympathy, tenderness, self-sacrifice as
female. Of course these emotions can arise in both sexes. What
I am saying, with all earnestness, is that the heart of the
problem as between individuals, and society as a whole, is that
civilisation is not built upon motor cars, washing machines
and nuclear power, but upon the creative drive of two sexes,
men and women, who have never yet learned fully to understand, to love one another and act together in harmony. Not
only that, but the first responsibility of that partnership is the
care and nurture of their children, from whom alone will come
social living, knowledge, the arts, inventions, love and liberty
in harmony, peace or war.

Love and physical sex between human beings, without children, can mean much when it contributes to insight into person-

ality; merely to use it for fun to appease appetite, or as a technique, seems to me to degrade both liberty and love. Childless sex, in the sense of homosexual relations or lesbianism – sexual partnership with one's own sex – has always been an aspect of human love, though condemned by religions. Preference for such departure from heterosexual union appears to be on the increase in our times. In part it is yet another expression of that divisiveness imposed by the classifications inherent in mechanical society, but more so of a refusal, by both sexes, of the responsibility of parenthood.

For some feminist women lesbian relations enable them to enjoy sex while offering a way of defying men's misuse of their offspring by a virtual birth strike; whilst for both men and women, unisex is a step towards diminishing excessive population. Not to have a child is clearly an individual right and choice.

In spite of over-population, teaching about sexual technique without clearly associating it with love and parenthood is to evade the essence and meaning of being human. Technological societies may well cease to breed, because it is too much trouble, and the impulse to love children has got lost.

Was the machine then another human mistake, another aspect of the absence of the female hand on the tiller? Conservatism is said to be characteristic of females. Significantly it was a woman, whose book *Silent Spring*, first drew attention to disappearing butterflies and insect life. Women have been foremost in deploring the devouring of the countryside by urban development. But the reality of pollution and the depletion of non-renewable resources have now aroused widespread anxiety. When cosmonauts were able to reveal the desolation of the moon, men and women began to understand their good fortune in living on a still-productive planet. Would life on earth be tolerable, lived in a succession of cities of concrete towers, airports, asphalt motorways, filthy rivers and sea, acres of poisonous or unsafely buried poisonous waste? No animals, few plants or trees, possibly artificially manufactured food? Life in herds moved about by machine, according to clockwork time, measured down to the last second, in large schools, factories, offices, even hospitals, has somehow become meaningless. Sport, run by great organisations, buys players without the old regard of their loyalty to their origin; yells of applause burst from thousands when a mere fragment of a second is cut from a foot race that was originally run for fun, just to see who came in first. Babies due for birth are induced in hospitals to accord with the timetable of doctors; surgeons replace parts of bodies with those taken from the dead. There is something humanly wrong with all this. What is it all for? It provides in some measure, for comfort and prosperity, though unevenly distributed and for human health and welfare, but it seems not to cater for very deep-seated creative needs.

Young people have been opting out of it all, first because the ultimate triumph of science seemed to be the hydrogen bomb, but afterwards because they could see no sign that those in power are even attempting to change their course. They see young men and women either being trained for the machine, or thrown on the scrap heap. So they take to astrology, magic or meditation, to the search for a god in religions, old and new, or to violence in the streets. If we escape annihilation, are we destined for a new dark ages? There are times for building, and times also for destruction. Are we moving towards a return to a near animal life?

There is no longer much room for civilisation to die in one region and be re-born in another. We are all together in what we now like to call our space ship. Some have their eyes on the stars and actually envisage emigration to other planets and settling on them to reproduce, not trying to return. If earth survives perhaps it may evolve creatures who do not need to breathe oxygen. Life was able to carry on when it came out of the sea.

Let the astronomers continue their observations, but there is still so much to explore on our earth; so much that we do not yet know about living things and natural forces, much, too, that we instinctively knew before we took to relying mainly on conscious thought. We have learned about the intelligence of dolphins, of which the myths of the ancient world told us, but we did not believe them. Would we ever have believed that whales sing to one another across the deep of the great oceans? Here we have a positive creative use made by one of the instruments of modern science.

It would seem that there is also much to learn about

magnetic fields. They have been used lately to heal broken bones. In the field of human relations, what did we mean by the old term animal magnetism? Something about personalities that attract or repel? Why does the mere touch of hands between two people stir a passion that becomes love, whereas dozens of other handshakes leave them unmoved? Or have we, by cheapening sex, lost that sensitivity in our hurried busy lives?

Is this clockwork world that we have built on Newtonian cosmology and mathematics – solid inorganic matter, dynamic force, measured linear time; work by night and day; travel by mechanised clockwork; fire and explosions the main energy that drives our machines – really the habitat suited to human beings?

Scientists themselves, Einstein and the physicists, already present a new cosmic vision – relativity, uncertainty, time combined with space, solid matter atomised into particles so minute as to become part of the atmosphere. In the natural world creatures seem to have their own time-clocks, do birds travel by space-time and/or by some magnetism in their bones? Going uphill is really further in space-time than going down.

Do we really need to go so fast? We can no longer see the landscape from trains as we pass. Were not the early scientists, who were interested in sunlight, the rainbow, magnetism, before the invention of gunpowder, mechanism, nuclear fission, better advised? Taking matter to pieces, our chemists reassemble it into new substances that do not belong and are a danger to the natural world. What shall we do with all those indestructible poisons stored for use in war, not to mention the nuclear waste? These are very confused times. Even in regard to the sciences, the way we use our imagination depends on what is our main interest, whether physics, biology, medicine, psychology, engineering, or whatever. Almost every profession or occupation has its own language and vocabulary, that must be learned to understand what it is about. In actual fact, our world now provides more information than our minds can digest, or our hearts, as yet, employ creatively to advantage.

The physicist tends to see all substances as dancing atoms like the dance of Shiva, or the disintegration of the space travellers, in TV *Star Trek*, descending on a planet. The biologist sees life starting from bacteria, forming ever larger and more capable organisms. Joseph Needham suggests that individual human organisms can gradually come together and so create a unity of a people or a nation. He has hopes for this in China. The biologists Julian Huxley and Jonas Salk both suggest ways by which humanity should, and could, contribute to the further evolution of our species. In the famous institution which he founded, Dr Salk's idea was to bring together science, humanitarian studies, and literature, to act as a creative stimulus working against impulses for destruction. Eminent men like Bronowski and Lord Ritchie-Calder were among those who joined him.

In an interview with Bernard Levin (*Listener*, 17 June 1982) Dr Salk suggests that humanity, now conscious of the extreme danger to survival, is also becoming aware of increasing interdependence. In a world divided between collective or individualist social systems (the USSR versus the USA) he hopes that there may be a coming together which he defines as 'mutualism'. New words are constantly required in order to induce changes of attitude in people! I am reminded of my dream of the 1920s – the soul of Russia and the body of America united in the humane direction of the industrial machine.

As E. W. Nesbit once told us in a fairy tale,* the machine does not, like the horses that it replaces, die a natural death. Once there, it is still with us, aided and abetted by its manifold worshippers and by science. And the pursuit of science by the intellect may well continue as long as man survives.

The machine was not an inevitable stage in human biological evolution; it has, in fact, created a clockwork time prison unsuited to human life, in which we have immured ourselves.

In theory we saw the machine as a means of lightening labour, in addition bringing prosperity by the more rapid manufacture of goods required. There were some people though unhappily not the majority, who saw in it a means to leisure in which civilised and cultural aims might be pursued. The spirit of peoples thus released might express itself, giving

* *The Magic City*, *see* Dyson, 1979, p. 3.

rein to imagination in literature, poetry, music, the manifold arts, all our dreams of perfection in beauty of form, colour, line, in what we choose to grow, or to make, even new machines. In such a mood of inspiration, scientific research would no longer be prostituted to war. Now that some countries have, by means of technology, reached that stage of leisured liberation, what has in fact happened? We are even more afraid than in our very first beginnings, terrified of those monstrous engines of destruction devised by the so-called brilliance of our intellects. Have we then evolved a religion of industrial mankind – the lack of which Raymond Aron hinted at – that might supersede or surpass the 'liberty, equality, fraternity' of one previous revolution? To destroy the machine is not simple, nor might it be desirable. It may well run down through lack of materials, through riots; through dearth of interested skills. But it can be tamed to serve and provide the basis of human existence, clothing, shelter, amenities, food. To do this will require revolutionary changes in our mode of thought and values. We have seen that the industrial urban way of life in fact requires toleration and co-operation both within and between nations. These do not and cannot come into play because they reside in certain primary instincts that have been lost or obscured by the dominance of computerised minds, as by our habit of living through externalised aids and gadgets, rather than from inherent personal initiatives – that is from within ourselves.

I actually heard a man recently say on television that we do not need to think for ourselves, because the thinking has already been done for us. It comes from the planners who direct the economy and send the electronic information that goes into empty but receptive minds. Indications of the future are that we will no longer need to go into libraries seeking books, burdening our memories with information thus derived. It will all be there, computerised and available in flickering type on the screens, at the touch of the appropriate buttons and knobs. In primary schools and the home adults and children are becoming familiarised with the use of computers. And computer technique has its own jargon, which seems already to be causing some dismay even in the legal profession. What happens if you press the wrong buttons, or the energy fails that can put those momentary, eyestraining flickers on the screens? Book scholars, it is true, suffer eye strain, but their minds can acquire well-informed, reflective, lasting memories, conducive to forming judgments.

Stress is laid on the fact that an individual can learn from machines without need of a teacher, as, in effect, also on the concept that every individual is a special person, apart and separate from family relations, since these belong with tribal instincts now deemed obsolete. Individuals learn roles, according to which they may play their parts and earn their keep in the social and economic system. The character of their learned role may also affect their personal relations, whether as males or females. It would seem that such extreme individualism must rest only on the basis of one individual *vis-à-vis* the state. In the economics of such a system, therefore, the state should provide for all individuals, from birth, sufficient income for their needs, but may expect, in return, to receive whatever services they can render to the community as a whole. From each according to his or her ability, to each according to his or her need. In a mechanised society, thus defined, as consisting of individuals, the individual, perforce, becomes a mere unit or cog who must fit into the right place at the right time, within what, also perforce, becomes a totalitarian organisation. Hence there is, in a mechanised industrial society, no real difference between the one that emphasises the individual, and the other that bases itself on collectivist mass action. And, in both, the individual will be considered to have been manufactured rather than born.

Bemused by what may be done with computers, the devotees of the machine, as we saw, continue to tell us that it obliterates the past, and opens the road to ever new achievements in the future. All that I can discover about the forecasts of our experts is that they envisage nothing but 'more of the same' – preoccupation with numbers and maths, with information stored and communicated electronically, and ingenious mechanisms that leave less and less to be done by the human body and brain.

Those who direct the state and industrial economy inevitably become cold hearted and dictatorial, because the very definition by which the state exists rules out the deepest human needs: the feelings of lovers, the relation of wives to husbands, husbands to wives, parents to children, and children to parents and their brothers and sisters, and teacher to pupil, all those human bonds, those very tribal instincts, from which, in the first instance, sharing, comradeship, co-operation and toleration were born.

Instead of entering into the paradise of our dreams, we stand poised and trembling on the edge of Armageddon.

So far from obliterating the past, we need the past in order to set ourselves free. We need to go back to and look at ourselves, review our history with its tales of human endeavour, its myths and timelessness, in order that we may understand the nature and depth of human passions that underlie our frail reason, as well as those desperate human aspirations that reach out beyond mere survival.

How in these days do we define a human being? Do we have instincts, or is everything learned? Few would deny now that we are an organic animal species which has developed remarkable capacities, over and above that of other species in respect of intelligence. Some would add to that other faculties 'god-given' by an external spiritual force. Others deny this and maintain that such a spirit is self-created and only exists in the human imagination.

However that may be, such differences in belief result in rules of custom and conduct that are a constant source of conflict between peoples and nations. Our own society in Britain, formerly directed by customs and laws based on Christian precepts, now contains very many people whose views of the universe and God, with consequent habits and conduct, are in total opposition to our traditions.

We endure also the conflict of those ideologies that arise out of the economic and industrial structure that we have created. All these may be called civilisation's wars, and they are world-wide.

But the *uralt*, ancient, and – I insist – instinctive male, plus his subservient female, are still within us, clinging to the dreams and myths of ages past. Not long ago an Israeli declared in discussion with Americans that, if it be denied that Jerusalem is the capital of the Jewish people, then the Bible must be rewritten. Yet, by reading that very text of Holy Writ, we could have known what the Israelites would do to regain the whole of Canaan, once they set foot again on its soil. Nor do they differ from others in this.* Mindful of Mahomet, the Arabs do not forget. Whilst many other peoples, having tied their Christianity forever to Jewish history and myth, are entangled in these ancient quarrels. 'To build the New Jerusalem', 'Jerusalem the Golden, with milk and honey blest', inspires their songs, pervades their dreams. And we have seen, in very recent times, a similar outburst of passionate defence of territorial rights to a small strip of barren soil, in the Falklands war. Once more Shakespeare has the words for it. Seeking permission to cross Danish soil to attack Poland, Fortinbras's Captain tells Hamlet:

> We go to gain a little patch of ground
> That hath in it no profit but the name
> To pay five ducats – five, I would not farm it. . . .

Learning that the land will be defended, Hamlet reflects:

> Two thousand souls and twenty thousand ducats
> This is the imposthume of much wealth and power
> That inward breaks, and shows no cause without
> Why the man dies. . . .
> I see
> The imminent death of twenty thousand men
> That for a fantasy and trick of fame
> Go to their graves like beds, fight for a plot
> Whereon the numbers cannot try the cause
> Which is not tomb enough and continent
> To hide the slain?

Or, if we turn to another poet, speaking, not of distant colonies, but the homeland:

> Breathes there the man with soul so dead
> That never to himself hath said
>   This is my own, my native land?

The intellect will not get us out of this dilemma.

Ample actual experience shows how political party allegiances, economic considerations, even ideologies, are swept away by the force of primitive tribal impulse. Nor can we avoid

* This was written a year before the recent happenings in Lebanon.

being aware of how cunning and skilful political manipulators may stimulate and use this force for destructive purposes.

None the less, the contention throughout this book has been that human fellowship and peace on earth must be sought in empathy and not in abstractions, dogmas, and obsession with man's 'higher faculties'. We may dream of world government, world laws, world language, but without solving this primal basis of our being, we are what Ilya Ehrenburg once so aptly described as 'passportless loafers'. One might at this very moment point to the millions of refugees fleeing from religions or ideologies that they cannot accept, seeking a home of their own.

The time has come when we must face the reality that, however accomplished, we are animals living on and by the resources of our small planet. We must come to terms with this anarchic force, the ultimate surge of life within us that holds the seed of creation or destruction. Our task is so to civilise it that the whole planet will become 'our native land'.

We have spent centuries educating and admiring the intellect. Let us turn our attention to educating what we feel. I believe that three aspects contribute to creating a human personality: first, his or her relation to the self; second, to the 'culture' or 'consensus' in which he or she has been reared; and third, to what each person finds or accepts as a satisfactory relation to the universe. This probably sounds a mere platitude, but when one thinks about it, the road to peace lies through harmony between the three aspects of the person. Conflict within the self gets transposed to the environment. The natural environment should be preserved and safeguarded, and the urban environment we manufacture should be sufficiently free to enable persons to have confidence in realising their own creative powers. As for the universe, each of us is alone in face of it, and we should be left free to come to terms with it in our own way. We perceive the surge of life in nature all around us, creatures born, following their inner drive, then declining till death. Never mind how it all came about, or what life is, perhaps in time we shall find out. What matters is how we use this power that is also within us, to make something of our heritage and our future.

I am aware that to lay emphasis upon instincts, or upon

differences between the nature of men and women, is by many considered reactionary. The obsession with numbers, percentages, technologies, the disparaging and trivialising of the emotions, are so effective that most people do not trouble, or are afraid, to look deeper into themselves. We all play many roles; you can train animals to do most of the tricks that you want them to perform. The point is, does performing the tricks make them happy, or serve a good purpose for their future? Because emotional drives and instincts have been misused and distorted to serve reactionary laws and customs, is no reason to run away from them and deny that they exist. Family life does not have to be patriarchal; the patriot's love of his native land does not have to be conditioned into war against his neighbour. The best way to defend our native land is to learn how to make friends, not enemies. And to encourage, as widely as possible, the pride and privilege of living on this bountiful planet; how, too, to maintain a balance between what we may still need to use for production and preserving the rest of the natural world. We need an entirely fresh start. Not one of the world's statesmen really knows what to do next. These oligarchs have neither compassion nor common sense.

There is a way of living a human life on earth that has, I feel, been more characteristic of women than of men. It has a sense of kinship, of belonging with the rest of nature, an intelligence applied to the necessities of daily living, grace and harmony in friendships and social relations. In part it is described in the words of Joseph Conrad which I put on the first page of this book: 'The trick of the thing, the readiness of mind and the turn of the hand that come without reflection and lead ... to excellence in life, in art, in virtue, in crime, and, for a matter of that, even in love.' 'Thinking', he continues, 'is the enemy of perfection.' Possibly not many of my readers will agree with him there. Nor do I remotely suggest that women do not think. Conrad, in fact, is here speaking of what is desirable in men. He would agree with most of what I have been saying in this book about the intellect. And, oddly enough, only a few days ago, Alistair Cooke described those men now at Geneva, deliberating about their nuclear weapons, as somehow 'educated above their intelligence'. Do some people then begin to understand?

It is difficult to write temperately and persuasively, as I have sought to do in this book, in the face of the evils that are being planned and accepted in nearly every corner of the world. I am convinced that it is the voice of women, proclaiming what their hearts say, crying aloud in defence of life on earth, that is the one last hope of our deliverance. 'Breathes there the woman with soul so dead' that she can tamely sit watching the bulldozers of the machine shovelling up the corpses of innocent children, women and men, along with the rubbish and rubble from their shattered homes?

This is but one crime among many that illustrate the prevalent utter contempt for human life. What is it all for? What has become the purpose of human life? Is there no better use for all these inventions of men's brilliant minds?

We are made aware of these wars and repressions by the remarkable invention of television and radio, both powerful instruments in forming and controlling public opinion. Then why are they being used to inflame us with emotions of fear, violence and hate? They poison the minds of our children, destroy that eager sense of liberty and love that they already long for in their cradle. It is not impossible to use these media to make our new beginning, to create the atmosphere of equality, liberty, fraternity; of life, liberty and the pursuit of happiness. Above all, to inspire that individual trust in your fellow man or woman, that you would feel in the joint effort of a common task, or in the risk and courage of an attempt to save human life. The rift between the sexes, between male and female consciousness, can be healed, the various gifts understood, to help the common endeavour. Why did Adam not listen to Eve – she may well have had some knowledge of good and evil that he ought to have shared?

All men and women have indeed shared in the great discoveries and findings of what has, so far, been male science. The intention of this book was never to denigrate or hold in contempt all that skill and patient endeavour in the quest for knowledge and truth. It was to expose the dangerous error of reverencing in worship only one aspect of human achievement, and, what is more, of letting it be prostituted to the service of the destructive elements in the human psyche.

Unless violence brings about the collapse of our society, it would seem that, for the present, certain main sources of energy and social services will need a considerable scale of industrial mechanism. Enthusiasm for ever more technology shows no signs of abating. We cannot escape the argument as to what persons or morals should be in control. The knowledge of good and evil remains the fundamental question.

Dr Salk's 'mutualism', a merger or partnership between the individualist and collectivist systems, would not, in the existing political climate, alter the essential character of the machine itself. Created by the intellect, it lends itself as a powerful instrument in the hands of those who seek liberty for profit and exploitation. For the less selfish and compassionate, who seek liberty from the machine, or to control technology for human health, happiness and welfare, it is not so easy.

As I write these words, plans are being revealed to throw open to the methods of the market place the whole of our new telecommunications technology, by cable and satellite. Their great power will be outside the control of Parliament or people. It is not likely that they will be used, as I have suggested, to promote human understanding and unity. On the contrary, this is a liberty that may well create aesthetic, cultural and ethical chaos. The crisis of our society, already, is not economic, but moral.

With traditional authorities discredited, by what standards shall we live? No matter what their race, colour or creed, all men and women who now think themselves helpless and insignificant, should begin to shape a human way of life, seeking to discover, not their differences, but on what they are agreed about the human condition and its needs. Their unity in thinking and feeling can pervade and influence telecommunications and lead on to the direction or dismantling of the machine.

The quest for liberty and love is never ending. It will not be served by those who rule by power, but only by the acts and decisions of ordinary men and women. Why should we not live more by space-time than by the clock; simplify our lives; do away with the fetish of money; give more opportunity to the arts; have festivals with dancing and music, in the place of military parades to celebrate what may well prove to be empty victories? Nor is all this so difficult as it might appear. The number of people in the world who now begin to believe that humanity can both change its destiny and change itself is growing. The masses who openly declare their suspicion of technology and nuclear power are beginning to give pause to governments.

The human race, as it now is, can achieve the birth of individuals of great beauty, stamina, intelligence and dignity. If we believe in ourselves and assume responsibility for the planet to which we belong, we still have a great destiny.

Let us put an end to persecutions. Let us accept the freedom of each to think and believe as he or she wishes. By that we live and love.

Humanity will ever seek, but never attain perfection. Let us at least survive and go on trying.

Epilogue

As this book was going to press, my son Roderick suddenly died. He was still young. Because we will not now be able any more to talk about its contents, I want to explain just why this book was specially for him.

In almost all respects we shared views of life and politics, passionately felt. There was no generation gap. In our many discussions, when I spoke of the machine age, he insisted that this was my own special original idea and that the book must be written. Later he became more insistent, after he was himself a victim of machine civilisation. He was ceaselessly active in his angry opposition to reaction and hopes for socialism and international understanding. In 1954 when he became liable for military service, he lodged and obtained a conscientious objection, in terms of what was his own original idea. He was not a pacifist, he would defend his country, but would not take service in an army that proposed to use nuclear weapons. It had been announced that the British Army would do so. Russell and Einstein had then just issued their joint declaration against nuclear war. Roddy and friends tried in vain to obtain publicity for the fact that genocide was a ground for conscientious objection. Now, thirty years later, this argument, that a true patriot must refuse 'nuclear service', is gaining ground.

Roddy felt great affinity with the workers. He deliberately chose to do his years of service in the mines. While helping to pull out pit props where the roof was unsafe, a fall of rock put him, age 23, in a wheelchair for life. As all who knew him are aware, his revolutionary spirit refused to be intimidated by this disaster.

He was not one to mope over his losses and frustrations. He continued to go on demonstrations, even Aldermaston marches, and was active in all possible ways. He never hauled down his flag or departed from his principles. His lively mind and entertaining company, his courage, brought him many friends who themselves drew inspiration from him. He had everything, looks, charm, clarity of thought, breadth of vision – and a gift for leadership. This last was severely obstructed by his loss of mobility. The community's loss was the greater, because there was so much that by greater mobility he could have achieved.

When I met him or heard from him he would demand when the machine book was to be written. While I was writing it he constantly urged me on: why was it not there for him to read? At length a complete MS was in his hands. The last time that I saw him, on February 5 1983, he gave me his, as he said, carefully non-filial appraisal of my work. It did come up to his expectations. To someone he wrote that the book was an 'ideological thriller'.

A mining accident may be taken as one of the hazards of a working life. But idolatry of the machine, the wrongful and now evil use of its powers, is destroying human life and happiness and will make an end of all life on our earth.

Select bibliography

ADAMS, Henry, *The Education of Henry Adams*, 1906.

ARON, Raymond, *Dix-huit Lecons sur la société industrielle*, Gallimard, 1962.

BUDGE, Sir E. A. Wallis, *The Book of the Dead*, Routledge & Kegan Paul, 1956.

BRYCE, *The Holy Roman Empire*, Macmillan, 1907.

CHILDE, Gordon, *What Happened in History*, Pelican, 1942.

COWPER-POWYS, John, *The Brazen Head*, Picador, 1956.

CROMBIE, A. C., *Augustine to Galileo*, Falcon Books, 1952.

DANIEL, Glyn, *The First Civilisations*, Pelican, 1968.

DAVIES, John Langdon, *A Short History of Women*, Watts, 1928.

DYSON, Freeman, *Disturbing the Universe*, Harper & Row, 1979.

ELIADE, Mirvea, *Gods, Goddesses and Myths of Creation*, Harper & Row, 1967.

FREUD, Sigmund, *Totem and Taboo*, Routledge & Kegan Paul, 1950.

GIMPEL, Jean, *The Medieval Machine*, Futura, 1977.

GOLDING, William, *The Inheritors*, Pocket Books, 1962.

GELLNER, Ernest, *Thought and Change*, Weidenfeld & Nicolson, 1964.

HALLER, William, *Fox's Book of Martyrs*, Jonathan Cape, 1963.

HAZARD, Paul, *European Thought in the Eighteenth Century*, Pelican, 1946.

HEATH, Sir Thomas, *Aristarchus of Samos*, Oxford, 1913.

KOESTLER, Arthur, *Janus: A Summing Up*, Picador, 1978.

KNOWLES, L. C. A., *The Industrial and Commercial Revolutions in Great Britain during the 19th Century*, Routledge, 1921.

LASLETT, Paul, *The World We Have Lost*, Methuen, 1965.

de MAUSE, Lloyd, *The History of Childhood*, Souvenir Press, 1976.

MIDDLEMAS, Keith, *Politics in Industrial Society*, André Deutsch, 1979.

MIDGLEY, Mary, *Beast and Man*, Harvester Press, 1979.

MISHAN, E. J., *Pornography, Psychedelics & Technology*, Allen & Unwin, 1980.

MORGAN, Elaine, *Descent of Woman*, Souvenir Press, 1972.

MORRIS, Desmond, *The Human Zoo*, Panther, 1969.

MUMFORD, Lewis, *Technics and Civilisation*, Harcourt Brace, 1939.

MUMFORD, Lewis, *The Myth of the Machine*, Secker & Warburg, 1967.

PASSMORE, John, *Man's Responsibility for Nature*, Gerald Duckworth, 1974.

QUILLER-COUCH, Sir Arthur, *Oxford Book of English Verse*, Clarendon Press, 1939.

RUBINSTEIN, A. T., *From Shakespeare to Shaw*, Russell & Russell, 1953.

RUSSELL, Bertrand, *History of Western Philosophy*, Allen & Unwin, 1946.

SANDERS, N. K., *Poems of Heaven and Hell from Ancient Mesopotamia*, Penguin, 1971.

SHELDRAKE, Rupert, *New Science of Life*, Blond & Briggs, 1981.

SMITH's, *Dictionary of the Bible*, John Murray, 1907.

TURNER, Frederick, *Beyond Geography: The Western Spirit against the Wilderness*, Viking Press, 1980.

WELLS, H. G., *The Outline of History*, Cassell, 1920.

WELLS, H. G., *Mind at the End of its Tether*, Windmill Press, 1945.

WILSON, Edward, *Social Biology: The New Synthesis*, Belknap Press, 1975.

WOLLSTONECRAFT, Mary, *Vindication of the Rights of Women*, Pelican, 1975.

WHITEHEAD, A. N., *Science and the Modern World*, Mentor Books, 1948.

Index

Abelard, Peter, 95, 134
Adams, Henry, 90
Aeschylus, 43
Age of Enlightenment, 163
Albigenses, 105–6
Alcibiades, 54
Alexander the Great, 30, 45, 54–5
Alexandria, 54, 68
Allah, 81
alphabet, 20–1
Ambrose, bishop of Milan, 71, 72
Anacreon, 47
Anaximander, 45, 46
Anaximines, 45, 46
animal life, study of, 224–5, 229, 232
animals, 1–2
anthropology, 6, 9
Appleton, Sir Edward, 208
Arabs, 83, 95
architecture, 166
Archimedes, 129, 142
Aristarchus of Samos, 45
Aristophanes, 43, 52
Aristotle, 45, 51, 53, 54, 55, 95, 96, 101, 143, 150
Arius, 71
armies, 22
Aron, Professor Raymond, 214–15, 245
artistic creation, 4–5
ascetics, 87–8, 89

astronomy, 134–6, 147–8, 219
Athanasius, bishop, 71
Athens, 41, 45, 47, 48, 50, 62
Attenborough, David, 1
Augustine, St, bishop of Hippo, 71, 72–3, 75
Augustus, emperor, 58, 61
Averroes, 95, 96–7, 98, 100, 104, 124, 190
Avicenna, 95, 96–7, 98

Babylon, 17, 20, 36, 86; cities of, 21–3, 30; citizen armies of, 22; creation myths, 23–7; Cyrus the Persian and, 38; gods of, 21–7; Hanging Gardens, of, 20; Jews in, 31; literate class, 22; Tower of Babel, 20, 25, 31, 90; women in, 51
Bacon, Francis, 124–8, 129, 134–5, 138, 141, 168, 222; *Novum Organum*, 125; *State of Christendom*, 125; tribute to Elizabeth I, 130–2
Bacon, Roger, 96, 98–100, 103, 104, 110, 126, 129, 134
Bayle, Pierre, 146, 159
Benedict, Ruth, 9–10
Bentham, Jeremy, 183
Bergson, Henri Louis, 184, 225, 226–7
Besant, Annie, 183

biologists, 244
Black Death, 106, 107
Blake, William, 176
Bonaparte, Napoleon, 177, 178
books, 85, 87
Boyle, Robert, 154, 155
Brahe, Tycho, 134, 136
Britton, Lionel: *BRAIN: A Play of the Whole Earth*, 219
Bronowski, Jacob, 13, 244
Buddha, 38, 61
Budge, Wallis, 28, 29
Buffon, Georges-Louis Leclerc, Comte de, 184
Burke, Edmund, 175, 176
Burns, John, 189

Caesar, Julius, 58
Calvin, John, 135
capitalism, 202
Carson, Rachel: *Silent Spring*, 241
cathedrals, 90–2, 133
Charlemagne, Holy Roman Emperor, 83–4, 93
Charles I, king of England, 134, 137
Charles II, king of England, 145
Childe, Gordon, 12, 16
children, 51–2, 64, 237–8; early Christians and, 73, 74; Lucretius and, 62–3; in machine civilisation, 220–1; Philo and, 64
Children's Crusade, 86
China, x, 38, 92
Christianity, 57, 67, 68–70, 248; bishops, 71–2; building cathedrals, 90–2; Cartesian theories and, 155–6; changing ideas of God, 143–4, 166; Christian communities, 70–1; conversion to, 188; dark ages, 75–6; early controversy, 71; early leaders, 71–5, 76; early schisms, 72; evolution, 184; failings, 137; medieval schoolmen, 95–104; medieval

world and, 77, 85, 90; Renaissance and, 107–8; sectarian fanaticism, 119–21; state religion, 112
cities, 17–18, 34, 38; Babylonian, 21; Egyptian, 30; at end of Middle Ages, 112; Romans and, 58
classes, 19, 34, 37, 60, 89, 178
Clement of Alexandria, 73
clocks, 92–4
colonies, American, 173
Columbus, Christopher, 107
communication, 4–6, 78–9, 89–90, 112, 235–6
communism, xii–xv, 201–2
computers, 219–20, 221, 233, 245–6
Confucius, 38
consciousness, 61, 85, 102–3
conscious thought, 60, 78, 88, 105, 235
Constantine, emperor, 69–70, 71, 76
consumer goods, 209
Copernicus, Nicholas, 45, 129–30, 134, 135–6, 141, 142, 144, 147, 181, 191; *De Revolutionibus Orbium Celestium*, 136; universe of, 154, 158
Corneille, Pierre, 138
Cortes, Hernan, 107
Counter-reformation, 141
Cranmer, Thomas, archbishop of Canterbury, 120
creation, 8–9, 31–2, 40, 76
creative thought, 188–9
Crete, 38, 41
Crusades, 85–6, 88, 104
culture, 9–10, 178
Cyprian, 73–4

Dale, Sir Henry, 208
Dark Ages, 75–6
Darwin, Charles, 3, 184; *The Origin of Species*, 1, 190
dead, the, 16–17

death, 85

democracy, 133, 214, 240; in eighteenth century, 174; elementary d., 15; Greeks and, 48, 53; in medieval world, 104; origins of Switzerland, 117–18, 119; Renaissance and, 117–18; Romans and, 58

Democritus, 45

Descartes, René, 145, 146, 147, 151–2, 154, 157, 167, 168, 184; affinity with Romans, 199; *De Homine*, 146, 151; denial of purpose, 154; *Discourse of Method*, 146; opponents of, 154–6; *Principia Philosophiae*, 146; separation of mind and matter, 150, 190, 195, 225, 227

determinism, xii, xiv

Dialogue entre Messieurs Patru et D'Ablancourt sur les Plaisirs, 160–1

Diderot, Denis, 166–7, 168, 169, 170, 176

discovery, 107–8, 114, 133–4

Dondi, Giovanni di, 92–3

Duns Scotus, 100, 103

economic life, ix

economic system, 220

Edward VI, king of England, 119–20

Egypt, 17, 27, 29, 30, 35; obsession with death, 28; Pharaoh, 27, 30; pyramids, 27; society, 28, 30; *The Book of the Dead*, 28–30

eighteenth century, 158, 173–4; consciousness, 173; feelings of exhilaration, 159; French hedonists, 159–62, 174; new beliefs, 164–6; new ideals, 166; power in, 172–3; travel, 171–2

Einstein, Albert, 98, 201, 203, 206, 218, 225, 229

Electronic Age, 219

Elizabeth I, queen of England, 119, 120, 130–2, 133, 134, 138

emotions, 240

Encyclopedia, the, 164, 167, 168, 169

Engels, Friedrich, 190

England, 141; during Middle Ages, 117; Henry VII, 118; Henry VIII, 118, 119; Edward VI, 119–20; Elizabeth I, 119, 121, 122, 130–1, 133; absolute monarchy in, 119, 123–4; religious dissension, 119–21; martyrs, 120–1; national consciousness, 121, 123; democracy in, 124; James I, 124, 130; Puritans, 137; Charles I, 134, 137; science in, 142; Charles II, 145; tolerance in, 156; Augustan Age in, 163; Voltaire in, 163; industrial revolution, 169; wars with France, 172; religious dissent, 172, 175; enclosures, 172; political dissent, 175; enthusiasm for revolutionary France, 176; confusion of ideas, 177; landed classes, 178; class structure in, 178; government, 178; Established Church, 178; fears of French Revolution, 179; 'workshop of the world', 179, 187; industrialisation of, 179–80, 187; philanthropy in, 181–2; education in, 183, 185–6; at end of nineteenth century, 184–5; pre-1914, 188–9; Labour Party in, 196; General Strike, 197; between the wars, 204

Epicurianism, 154

Epicurus, 45, 62

eternal life, 65

eternal reality, 60–1

Euripides, 43, 52

Europe, x, 83; colonises Africa, 188; European soul, 107; feeling of superiority, 188; post-1918, 196; rise of

countries, 84; workers' risings, 189–90
Eve, 8
evolution, 3, 184, 195, 234

fear, 14, 17, 60, 85, 240
feminism, 173
fertility, 7
Foxe, John: *Foxe's Book of Martyres*, 120–1
France, 123, 137, 145, 156–7, 158, 159
Francis of Assisi, St, 96, 97, 104
French Revolution, 173, 175, 176, 177
Friars, Order of, 97

Galileo, 129, 134, 136, 138, 141, 143–4, 146, 147, 149–50, 152, 154, 157, 168, 181, 191, 225, 227; conception of science, 148; definition of matter, 149, 206; Inquisition and, 145
Gellner, Ernest, 214, 221; *Thought and Change*, 210–12
General Strike, 197, 204
Genesis, 7, 19
Germany, 187
ghosts, 17
gods: Athene, 41–2; Babylonian, 21–7; Egyptian, 27; Greek, 39–41, 42; Jehovah, 32, 35–7; personal god, 235
Golding, William: *The Inheritors*, 5
Goodall, Jane, 2, 232
government, 118
Graves, Robert, 239
Greek Orthodox church, 77, 84, 94
Greeks, 38–9, 42, 52, 57, 58; Academy, 45, 68; in Asia Minor, 45–7; Athene, 41–2; Athens, 41, 45, 47, 48, 50; Athens/Sparta war, 50, 53, 55; attitude to sex, 50–1; attitude to women, 50–1; city states, 41, 43; Crete and, 38, 41; defects

of character, 53–4; democracy and, 48, 53, 117; drama, 52; greatest achievement of, 42–3; heroism of, 42–3, 48; influence of, 114, 136–7; Ionian, 46; language of, 43–4; logic and, 44; Lyceum, 45; mathematics and, 44, 45; mythology of, 39–41, 42; Olympic Games, 43; Pericles, 48, 49–50; philosophy of, 42, 45, 48, 53, 55–7; science and, 45; sculpture of, 43; slavery, 48–9, 57; Sparta, 50; victory over Persians, 48; war and, 42–3, 48

happiness, 62, 79, 166; Louis de la Caze, 162; demand for, 168–9; Deslandes, 161, 162; Fontenelle: *Thoughts on Happiness*, 161; French hedonists, 159–62, 164, 197; Lamettrie, 162; Maupertuis, 162
Hardie, Kier, 189
Harvey, William, 141, 152
Hazard, Professor Paul: *European Thought in the Eighteenth Century*, 158, 159
Hegel, Georg, 190
Henry VII, king of England, 118
Henry VIII, king of England, 118, 119
heretics, 104, 105–6, 120
Herodotus, 43, 47, 48
heroism, 42–3
Hesiod: *Ages of Man*, 41; *Theogony*, 40–1
Hill, Professor Christopher: *God's Englishman*, 212
Hiroshima, 208, 215
history, theories of, 12–13
Hitler, Adolf, 207, 209
Hobbes, Thomas, 146
Holland, 146
Holy Roman Empire, 76, 83–5
Homer, 39–40
homosexuality, 241

Honnecourt, Villard de, 91, 92
human brotherhood, 174, 249
human consciousness, 2, 3, 14,
    95–104, 110, 121, 130, 173,
    183, 195, 239
human development, 3–4
human nature, 177
human relations, 4, 57, 243
human social condition, 37
Hume, David, 170
Huss, John, 106
Huxley, Julian, 191, 192, 244
Huxley, Thomas, 190–1, 192

imagination, 12, 60, 61, 85, 111,
    137, 141, 245
India, 17, 38
industrial civilisation, 197, 245
industrialisation, 179–81, 187,
    210, 214–15, 221; problems of,
    223–4
industrial man, 222–4
Inquisition, the, 105, 106, 145;
    Holy Office of, 144–5
instincts, 2–3, 4, 249–50;
intellect, 60, 61, 85, 96, 97, 100,
    109, 110–11, 124, 136, 141,
    183, 213–14, 231, 239, 240,
    244, 249; intellectuals, 138,
    183; isolation of, 230; Bertrand
    Russell on, 212–13
Italy, 38, 107, 123, 129, 141, 145

Jerome, St, 71, 72
Jerusalem, 86, 104
Jesus Christ, 57, 61, 70; followers
    of, 66–9, 70; importance of, 65;
    Mahomet's attitude to, 81;
    teaching of, 65–6, 77, 112–13
Jews, 30–6, 61–2, 247–8;
    Abraham, 32–3; Jehovah, 32,
    35–6; Jesus's disciples and, 66;
    Moses, 31–2, 35; Old
    Testament, 30–1, 76–7;
    priesthood, 33; Samuel, 33–4;
    Solomon, 34; Ten
    Commandments, 35–6
John of Salisbury, 96

Johnson, Joseph, 176

Kant, Immanuel, 190
Kepler, Johan, 134, 136, 147
knowledge, 184, 222; obsession
    for, 165
Koestler, Arthur, 234
Koran, 81

Labour Party, 196, 198
Langdon-Davies, John, 239
language, 19, 20, 236; birth of,
    4–5; English, 115; Greek,
    43–4, 114–15; Latin, 78–9, 85,
    114–15; rise of vernacular,
    84–5
Lansbury, George, 189
Lao Tse, 38
Laslett, Peter: *The World We
    Have Lost*, 185, 215
Latimer, Hugh, 120
Lenin, Vladimir, xi
Leo III, pope, 83
life impulse, 231–2
literature, 114, 159
living world, 165
Lloyd George, David, 189
Locke, John, 146, 163, 183
logic, 44
Lorenz, Konrad, 2, 229
Louis XIV, king of France, 137,
    163
Lucretius, 62–4; *On the Nature of
    Things*, 62–3
Luther, Martin, 135

MacDonald, Ramsay, 196
Machiavelli, Niccolo: *The Prince*,
    118
machine, the, xiv, 89, 111, 188,
    233, 241, 242, 244, 245;
    children in m. civilisation,
    220–1; civilisation of, 179;
    effects of m. production, 189;
    growing mastery of, 199–200,
    219–220; growing use of, 172;
    ms for perpetual motion, 142
machine worship, ix–x, 13–14,

196, 209, 214, 222; origins of, 157; H. G. Wells and, 194, 222
Magellan, Ferdinand, 134
magnetic attraction, 142, 243
Mahomet, 79–80
man: ambition of, 34; development of cities and, 18; differences between m. and woman, 250; dominance of, 7–9, 10, 34, 235, 236–7, 247; early groupings of, 15; love and, 237, 240–1; relations with woman, 7, 234, 240, 247
Marx, Karl, xi, 190
Marxism, 194–5, 198, 199, 200–1
Mary, queen of Scots, 119
mathematics, 44, 45, 56, 57, 61, 93, 95–6, 110, 111, 128, 135, 142, 143, 148, 157, 165, 218
Mead, Margaret, 9, 10
Medieval World, 72, 76, 78; attitudes in, 109–13; building of cathedrals, 90–2; Christian schoolmen, 95–104, 108, 109–10; church in disarray, 104; clocks in, 92; development in, 86–96; dissent in, 105; heretics in, 104; mechanical gadgetry in, 93–4; New World and, 107–8; plagues in, 106; 'realists' in, 101–2; society in, 78–9; 'tool-making man' in, 86; vision of God, 77
Michelangelo, 137, 138
Midgley, Mary, 229, 230: *Beast and Man: The Roots of Human Nature*, 227–8
Miletus, 46
Mill, John Stuart, 183
mills, 86–7, 88, 89
Milton, John, 137, 138–40; *Areopagitica*, 138–9, 140; *Defence of the English People*, 140; *Paradise Lost*, 139, 140–1; *Samson Agonistes*, 140
Mirabeau, Gabriel, Comte de, 140

modern life, 241–53; conflicting ideologies, 247; contempt for human life, 251; the future, 252–3; importance of women, 250, 251; purpose of, 241–3, 251
Molière, Jean-Baptiste, 138
monasteries, 79, 88–9, 93, 95, 111, 112, 119, 125
Montesquieu, Charles: *The Spirit of Laws*, 164
morality, 35, 60
More, Sir Thomas: *Utopia*, 117
Morgan, Elaine: *Descent of Woman*, 7, 239
Moslems, 80–2, 84, 111, 248
Mumford, Lewis, 12–13, 14, 16, 27–8, 93, 94, 224; *The Myth of the Machine*, 13, 215
myths, 6, 17, 247; Babylonian, 23–7; creation, 8–9, 31–2, 40; Persephone, 17; Prometheus, 6, 40

names, 19, 100–1
'natural laws', 137–8, 141, 159, 164
nature, 164, 165, 166, 224
Nazis, 207, 214
Nebuchadnezzar, 31, 46
Needham, Joseph, 244
neolithic period, 16–17
Newton, Sir Isaac, 145, 146–7, 152–4, 157, 158, 159, 184; *Principia*, 147; *Principia Mathematica*, 153
nominalism, 101, 102
nuclear power, 209
nuclear weapons, 208–9, 229

organic life, 224–5, 230
Origen, 71
over-population, 231, 241
Owen, Robert, 182
Oxford, university of, 96, 98, 100, 104, 134, 142, 168

Padua, university of, 142, 152

Paine, Thomas, 176
Pankhurst family, 189
papacy, 104, 137
Paris, 171–2
Paris, university of, 96, 97, 98, 100, 104, 134, 142, 168
Pascal, Blaise, 138, 156–7; attacked by Voltaire, 163–4; *Pensées*, 156–7
past, the, 247
patriarchy, 7, 238
Paul, St, 67, 68–9
peace, 249
Pericles, 48, 49–50, 55
perpetual motion, 142
Persians, 45, 46
Peter of Maricourt, 99–100, 110, 126, 134
Peter the Hermit, 85–6
Philip, king of Macedon, 54
Philo, 64
philosophers/philosophy, 11, 61, 62; Francis Bacon on, 126–7; Greek, 42, 48, 53, 55–7, 101; Moslem philosophers, 111; 'new' philosophy, 146, 147–8, 157; patrons of, 146; popular philosophy, 226; problems of universals, 101, 102; religious authorities and, 146; secular authorities and, 146; technical philosophy, 226; twentieth-century philosophy, 195, 206
physics, 143, 207, 243–4
Pizarro, Francisco, 108
Plato, 48, 53, 55–7, 60, 62, 82, 101, 110, 135
Plumb, Professor J. H.: *Death of the Past*, 210
poetry, 115–16
pollution, 241
power, 35, 88, 123–4, 137, 172, 184, 231, 234–5; artistic achievement, 18–19; of church and state, 172–3; environment and, 18, 60; Greeks and, 49; human, 19; knowledge equated with, 222; nature of,

173; personal and impersonal, 164; religious, 85; of scientific knowledge, 127; struggle for, 117, 234
prehistoric people, 4, 16–17
Price, Dr, 175–6
priests, 106
primitive peoples, 3–4, 11–12, 15, 232–3, 235; elementary democracy, 15; gods of, 6–7, 10
proletariat, 189, 194, 196
Prometheus, 6, 40
Protestantism, 137, 146
Puritans, 137
Pythagoras, 45, 47, 51, 61

Racine, Jean, 138
railways, 187
Ransome, Arthur, 201
Rashid, Haroun al, 80, 82, 84, 93
rationalism, 102
Ray, John, 154–6
reason, 96, 103, 109–11, 235
Reformation, 141
religion, 10, 79, 109–10, 157
Renaissance, 107, 114–17, 121, 123, 125–6, 133, 141
Ridley, Nicholas, bishop of London, 120
Ritchie-Calder, Lord, 244
Roman Catholic church, 77, 84, 104, 105, 110
Romans, 38, 48, 58, 70; Christianity and, 66, 67, 69–70; collapse of Roman Empire, 75–6; Roman citizens, 62
Rousseau, Jean-Jacques, 169–72, 207, 214; 'Social contract', 170
Royal Society, 125, 145, 208
Russell, Bertrand, xvi, 99, 128, 171, 192, 197–8, 212–13; Bergson and, 225, 226; *History of Western Philosophy*, 213, 239; importance of logic, 226; influence of Einstein upon, 218–19; *Practice and Theory of Bolshevism*, 200; *Principia*

Mathematica, 225; *The Prospects of Industrial Civilisation*, xvi, 204, 209–10; 'Remember your humanity and forget the rest', 229; theories of, 228–9; visits China, 200; visits Russia, 198

Russell, Dora, xvi–xvii, 197, 200, 204; on communism, 201–2, 204; on dogmatic belief, 202–3; education, 185–6; *In Defence of Children*, 236; on Marxism, 200–1, 203; on Newtonian cosmology, 200–1, 203; *The Prospects of Industrial Civilisation*, xvi, 204, 209–10; *The Right to be Happy*, 204–5, 225, 236; visits China, visits Russia, 198

Russia, x–xiv, 172, 173, 198–9, 204

Russian Revolution, 196, 198

Salk, Jonas, 244, 252
Salmasius, 140
salons, 159–60, 172
Samos, 47
Schiller, Friedrich von: *Maria Stuart*, 119
schoolmen, 95–104, 108, 109–10
science, 184, 206, 239; Francis Bacon and, 125–8; distaste for, 209; expansion of, 231; experimental, 142; Galileo's conception of, 148; provides for the consumer, 209; 'real world' and, 127–8
scientific enquiry, 105, 110, 124, 142–4
scientific knowledge, 133, 134, 208
scientific research, 183, 195, 245
scientists, 11, 142, 229–30; new cosmic vision of, 243; qualms of conscience, 208
Secular Society, the, 183
security, 14–15
sex, 235, 237, 240–1; Christianity and, 85; early Christians and, 73–5; Greeks and, 50–1; in Medieval World, 109
sex impulse, 235, 236
Shaftesbury, Anthony Ashley Cooper, seventh Earl of, 181–2
Shakespeare, William, 116–17, 119, 122–3, 124, 133, 137, 138, 248
Shaw, George Bernard, 189, 219
Sheldrake, Dr Rupert: *New Science of Life*, 226
sin, 77, 79, 81
slavery, 48–9, 57, 58, 164, 178
Snow, Sir Charles, 211–12
social association, 189
Socialism, 182, 194
social life, 34, 50–1
Socrates, 52–3, 54, 55
Song of Roland, 83
Sophocles, 43
Spain, 123
Spinoza, Benedict, 146
splitting the atom, 184, 206
state, the, 238
Stephen (first Christian martyr), 67
Stoics, 62
Sumerians, 5–6, 38
Swift, Jonathan: *Gulliver's Travels*, 159

Taylor, Henry Osborn, 99
technological society, 220, 241
technology, 86, 88
Tertullian, 74
Thales, 45, 46
Thomas of Aquinas, St, 96, 97, 100, 103, 109
Toledo, university of, 95
tool-making man, 86
totalitarian control, 209, 214
travel, 171–2
Turks, 85

unemployment, 223
United Nations, 208

United States of America, ix–x, 187–8

urban population, 19, 223, 249

Vinci, Leonardo da, 128–9, 134, 137, 138, 142

Virgin Mary, cult of, 112

Voltaire, François-Marie Arouet de, 146, 147, 163, 169, 170, 183; attacks Pascal, 163–4; *Lettres Anglaises*, 163

Wallingford, Richard of, 92–3

wars, 33, 245, 251; annihilation by, 231; Athenian/Spartan, 50, 53, 55; Boer War, 188; conduct of, 233; Greeks and, 42–3; Hundred Years War, 107; inevitability of, 238; Napoleonic, 177–8; nuclear weapons, 208–9; religious, 137; Romans and, 48; totalitarian, 207; Wars of the Roses, 107; weapons for, 114; World War I, 187, 206

Webb, Beatrice and Sydney, 189

Wells, H. G., 20, 170–1, 186, 190, 191–4, 207, 218, 239; *Mind at the End of Its Tether*, 215–17

Whitehead, Alfred North, 225

William of Occam, 96, 100, 103, 104, 106

William the Conqueror, king of England, 78

Wilson, Edward: *Social Biology: The New Synthesis*, 229, 234

witchcraft, 105

Wollstonecraft, Mary, 175, 176, 183; *Vindication of the Rights of Man*, 176; *Vindication of the Rights of Woman*, 173

woman, 189; agricultural labours and, 16; cult of the Virgin, 112; differences between man and woman, 250; education in the eighteenth century, 171; Elizabethan times and, 130; feminism, 173; 'femmes savantes', 159; Greeks and, 50–1; inequality of, 7–9, 14, 235, 237, 238, 239; influence of, 171; lesbianism and, 241; Medieval World and, 78, 109; Moslems and, 81; relationship with man, 7, 234, 240, 247; voice of, 251; H. G. Wells and, 193; witchcraft and, 105; women's rights, 183

working class, 182

writing, 5, 19, 22, 85

Wycliffe, John, 106